THROUGH *the* LANGUAGE GLASS

ALSO BY GUY DEUTSCHER

The Unfolding of Language:
The Evolution of Mankind's Greatest Invention

THROUGH
the
LANGUAGE
GLASS

How Words Colour Your World

GUY DEUTSCHER

WILLIAM HEINEMANN: LONDON

Published by William Heinemann 2010

2 4 6 8 10 9 7 5 3 1

Copyright © Guy Deutscher 2010

Guy Deutscher has asserted his right under the Copyright, Designs
and Patents Act 1988 to be identified as the author of this work

First published in Great Britain in 2010 by
William Heinemann
Random House, 20 Vauxhall Bridge Road,
London SW1V 2SA

www.rbooks.co.uk

Addresses for companies within The Random House Group Limited can be found at:
www.randomhouse.co.uk/offices.htm

The Random House Group Limited Reg. No. 954009

A CIP catalogue record for this book
is available from the British Library

ISBN 9780434016907

The Random House Group Limited supports The Forest Stewardship
Council (FSC), the leading international forest certification organisation.
All our titles that are printed on Greenpeace approved FSC certified paper
carry the FSC logo. Our paper procurement policy can be found at:
www.rbooks.co.uk/environment

Designed by Kelly Too

Printed and bound in Great Britain by
CPI Mackays, Chatham, ME5 8TD

To Alma

CONTENTS

Language, Culture, and Thought

'There are four tongues worthy of the world's use,' says the Talmud: 'Greek for song, Latin for war, Syriac for lamentation, and Hebrew for ordinary speech.' Other authorities have been no less decided in their judgement on what different languages are good for. The Holy Roman Emperor Charles V, king of Spain, archduke of Austria, and master of several European tongues, professed to speaking 'Spanish to God, Italian to women, French to men, and German to my horse'.

A nation's language, so we are often told, reflects its culture, psyche, and modes of thought. Peoples in tropical climes are so laid-back it's no wonder they let most of their consonants fall by the wayside. And one need only compare the mellow sounds of Portuguese with the harshness of Spanish to understand the quintessential difference between these two neighbouring cultures. The grammar of some languages is simply not logical enough to express complex ideas. German, on the other hand, is an ideal vehicle for formulating the most precise philosophical profundities, as it is a particularly orderly language, which is why the Germans have such orderly minds. (But can one not hear the goose-step in its gauche, humourless sounds?) Some languages don't even have a future tense, so their speakers naturally have no grasp of the future. The Babylonians would have been hard-pressed to understand *Crime and Punishment*, because their language used one and the same word to describe both of these concepts. The craggy fjords are audible in the precipitous intonation of Norwegian, and you can hear the dark *l*'s of Russian in Tchaikovsky's lugubrious tunes. French is not only a Romance language but the language of romance par excellence. English is an adaptable, even promiscuous language, and Italian – ah, Italian!

Many a dinner-table conversation is embellished by such vignettes, for few subjects lend themselves more readily to disquisition than the character of different languages and their speakers. And yet should these lofty observations be carried away from the conviviality of the dining room to the chill of the study, they would quickly collapse like a soufflé of airy anecdote – at best amusing and meaningless, at worst bigoted and absurd. Most foreigners cannot hear the difference between rugged Norwegian and the endless plains of Swedish. The industrious Protestant Danes have dropped more consonants onto their icy windswept soil than any indolent tropical tribe. And if Germans do have systematic minds, this is just as likely to be because their exceedingly erratic mother tongue has exhausted their brains' capacity to cope with any further irregularity. English speakers can hold lengthy conversations about forthcoming events wholly in the present tense (I'm flying to Vancouver next week . . .) without any detectable loosening in their grip on the concepts of futurity. No language – not even that of the most 'primitive' tribes – is inherently unsuitable for expressing the most complex ideas. Any shortcomings in a language's ability to philosophise simply boil down to the lack of some specialised abstract vocabulary and perhaps a few syntactic constructions, but these can easily be borrowed, just as all European languages pinched their verbal philosophical toolkit from Latin, which in turn lifted it wholesale from Greek. If speakers of any tribal tongue were so minded, they could easily do the same today, and it would be eminently possible to deliberate in Zulu about the respective merits of empiricism and rationalism or to hold forth about existentialist phenomenology in West Greenlandic.

If musings on nations and languages were merely aired over aperitifs, they could be indulged as harmless, if nonsensical, diversions. But as it happens, the subject has also exercised high and learned minds throughout the ages. Philosophers of all persuasions and nationalities have lined up to proclaim that each language reflects the qualities of the nation that speaks it. In the seventeenth century, the Englishman Francis Bacon explained that one can infer 'significant marks of the genius and manners of people and nations from their languages'. 'Everything confirms,' agreed the Frenchman Étienne de Condillac a century later, 'that each language expresses the character of the people who speak it.' His younger contemporary, the German Johann Gottfried Herder, concurred that 'the intellect and the character of every nation are stamped in its language'. Industrious nations, he said, 'have an abundance of moods in their verbs, while more refined nations have a large amount of nouns that have been exalted to abstract notions'. In short, 'the genius of a nation is nowhere better revealed than in the physiognomy of its speech'. The American Ralph Waldo Emerson summed it all up in 1844: 'We infer the spirit of the nation in great measure from the language, which is a sort of monument to which each forcible individual in a course of many hundred years has contributed a stone.'

The only problem with this impressive international unanimity is that it breaks down as soon as thinkers move on from the general principles to reflect on the particular qualities (or otherwise) of particular languages, and about what these linguistic qualities can tell about the qualities (or otherwise) of particular nations. In 1889, Emerson's words were assigned as an essay topic to the seventeen-year-old Bertrand Russell, when he was at a crammer in London preparing for the scholarship entrance exam to Trinity College, Cambridge. Russell responded with these pearls: 'We may study the character of a people by the ideas which its language best expresses. French, for instance, contains such words as "spirituel", or "l'esprit", which in English can scarcely be expressed at all; whence we naturally draw the inference, which may be confirmed by actual observation, that the French have more "esprit", and are more "spirituel" than the English.'

Cicero, on the other hand, drew exactly the opposite inference from the lack of a word in a language. In his *De oratore* of 55 BC, he embarked on a lengthy sermon about the lack of a Greek equivalent for the Latin word *ineptus* (meaning 'impertinent' or 'tactless'). Russell would have concluded that the Greeks had such impeccable manners that they simply did not need a word to describe a non-existent flaw. Not so Cicero: for him, the absence of the word was a proof that the fault was so widespread among the Greeks that they didn't even notice it.

The language of the Romans was itself not always immune to censure. Some twelve centuries after Cicero, Dante Alighieri surveyed the dialects of Italy in his *De vulgari eloquentia* and declared that 'what the Romans speak is not so much a vernacular as a vile jargon . . . and this should come as no surprise, for they also stand out among all Italians for the ugliness of their manners and their outward appearance'.

No one would dream of entertaining such sentiments about the French language, which is not only romantic and *spirituel* but also, of course, the paragon of logic and clarity. We have this on no lesser authority than the French themselves. In 1894, the distinguished critic Ferdinand Brunetière informed the members of the Académie française, on the occasion of his election to this illustrious institution, that French was 'the most logical, the clearest, and the most transparent language that has ever been spoken by man'. Brunetière, in turn, had this on the authority of a long line of savants, including Voltaire in the eighteenth century, who affirmed that the unique genius of the French language was its clearness and order. And Voltaire himself owed this insight to an astonishing discovery made a whole century earlier, in 1669, to be precise. The French grammarians of the seventeenth century had spent decades trying to understand why it was that French possessed clarity beyond all other languages in the world and why, as one member of the Académie put it, French was endowed with such clarity and precision that simply translating into it had the effect of a real commentary. In the end, after years of travail, it was Louis Le Laboureur who discovered in 1669 that the answer was simplicity itself. His painstaking grammatical researches revealed that, in contrast to speakers of other languages, 'we French follow in all our utterances exactly the order of thought, which is the order of Nature'. No wonder, then, that French can never be obscure. As the later thinker Antoine de Rivarol put it: 'What is not clear may be English, Italian, Greek or Latin,' but 'ce qui n'est pas clair n'est pas français.'

Not all intellectuals of the world unite, however, in concurring with this analysis. Equally distinguished thinkers – strangely enough, mostly from outside France – have expressed different opinions. The renowned Danish linguist Otto Jespersen, for example, believed that English was superior to French in a whole range of attributes, including logic, for, as opposed to French, English is a 'methodical, energetic, business-like and sober language, that does not care much for finery and elegance, but does care for logical consistency'. Jespersen concludes: 'As the language is, so also is the nation.'

Great minds have churned out even richer fare when advancing from the issue of how language *reflects* the character of its speakers to the grander question of how language *influences* the thought processes of its speakers. Benjamin Lee Whorf, to whom we shall return in a later chapter, captivated a whole generation when he taught that our habit of separating the world into objects (like 'stone') and actions (like 'fall') is not a true reflection of reality but merely a division thrust upon us by the grammar of European languages. According to Whorf, American Indian languages, which combine the verb and the object into one word, impose a 'monistic view' on the universe, so their speakers would simply not understand our distinction between objects and actions.

A generation later, George Steiner reasoned in his 1975 book, *After Babel*, that the 'conventions of forwardness in our syntax', our 'articulate futurity', or, in other words, the existence of the future tense, is what gives us hope for the future, saves us from nihilism, even from mass suicide. 'If our system of tenses was more fragile,' said Steiner, 'we might not endure.' (He was clearly touched by prophetic inspiration, for dozens of languages that do not possess a future tense are becoming extinct every year.)

More recently, one philosopher has revolutionised our understanding of Tudor history by uncovering the real cause for Henry's break with the Pope. The Anglican revolution, he established, was not a result of the king's desperate wish for an heir, as previously assumed, nor was it a cynical ploy to siphon off the Church's wealth and property. Rather, the birth of Anglican theology ensued inevitably from the exigencies of the English language: English grammar, being halfway between French and German, compelled English religious thought inexorably towards a position halfway between (French) Catholicism and (German) Protestantism.

⟡

In their pronouncements on language, culture, and thought, it seems that big thinkers in their *grandes œuvres* have not always risen much above little thinkers over their *hors d'œuvre*. Given such an unappetizing history of precedents, is there any hope of getting something savoury out of the discussion? Once one has sifted out the unfounded and the uninformed, the farcical and the fantastic, is there anything sensible left to say about the relation between language, culture, and thought? Does language reflect the culture of a society in any profound sense, beyond such trivia as the number of words it has for snow or for shearing camels? And even more contentiously, can different languages lead their speakers to different thoughts and perceptions?

For most serious scholars today, the answer to all these questions is a resounding no. The dominant view among contemporary linguists is that language is primarily an instinct, in other words, that the fundaments of language are coded in our genes and are the same across the human race. Noam Chomsky has famously argued that a Martian scientist would conclude that all earthlings speak dialects of the same language. Deep down, so runs the theory, all languages share the same universal grammar, the same underlying concepts, the same degree of systemic complexity. The only important aspects of language, therefore, or at least the only ones worth investigating, are those that reveal language as an expression of innate human nature. Finally, there is a broad consensus that if our mother tongue influences the way we think at all, any such influence is negligible, even trivial – and that fundamentally we all think in the same way.

In the pages to follow, however, I will try to convince you, probably against your initial intuition, and certainly against the fashionable academic view of today, that the answer to the questions above is – yes. In this plaidoyer for culture, I will argue that cultural differences are reflected in language in profound ways, and that a growing body of reliable scientific research provides solid evidence that our mother tongue can affect how we think and how we perceive the world. But before you relegate this book to the crackpot shelf, next to last year's fad-diet recipes and the *How to Bond with Your Goldfish* manual, I give you my solemn pledge that we will not indulge in groundless twaddle of any kind. We shall not be imposing monistic views on any universes, we shall not soar to such lofty questions as which languages have more 'esprit', nor shall we delve into the mysteries of which cultures are more 'profound'. The problems that will occupy us in this book are of a very different kind.

In fact, the areas of culture we shall be concerned with belong to the most down-to-earth level of everyday life, and the aspects of language we shall encounter are on the most down-to-earth level of everyday speech. For it turns out that the most significant connections between language, culture, and thought are to be found where they are least expected, in those places where healthy common sense would suggest that all cultures and all languages should be exactly the same.

The high-level cultural differences that we immediately spot – in musical taste, sexual mores, dress code, or table manners – are in some sense superficial, precisely because we are so keenly aware of them: we know that pornography is just a matter of geography, and we are under no illusion that peoples around the globe share the same preferences in music or hold their forks in the same way. But culture can leave deeper marks exactly where we do not recognise it as such, where its conventions have been imprinted so indelibly on impressionable young minds that we grow up to take them for something else entirely.

If all these statements are to begin to make some sense, however, we first need to extend the concept of culture way beyond its normal use in everyday language. What is your first reaction when you hear the word 'culture'? Shakespeare? String quartets? Curling the little finger on the teacup? Naturally, the way you understand 'culture' depends on which culture you come from, as a quick glance through three lexicographic lenses will reveal:

> Culture: cultivation, the state of being cultivated, refinement, the result of cultivation, a type of civilisation.
>
> Chambers English dictionary

> Kultur: Gesamtheit der geistigen und künstlerischen Errungenschaften einer Gesellschaft.
>
> (*The totality of intellectual and artistic achievements of a society.*)
>
> Störig German dictionary

> Culture: Ensemble des moyens mis en œuvre par l'homme pour augmenter ses connaissances, développer et améliorer les facultés de son esprit, notamment le jugement et le goût.
>
> (*The collection of means employed by man to increase his knowledge, develop and improve his mental faculties, notably judgement and taste.*)
>
> ATLIF French dictionary

There is little, some would no doubt argue, that better confirms entrenched stereotypes about three great European cultures than the way they understand the concept of 'culture' itself. Is the *Chambers* definition not the quintessence of Englishness? Rather amateurish in its non-committal list of synonyms, politely avoiding any awkward definitions. And what could be more German than the German? Mercilessly thorough, overly intellectual, knocking the concept on the head with charmless precision. And as for the French: grandiloquent, hopelessly idealistic, and obsessed with *le goût*.

When anthropologists talk of 'culture', however, they use the word in a rather different sense from all of the definitions above, and in a far broader meaning. The scientific concept of 'culture' emerged in Germany in the mid-nineteenth century but was first articulated explicitly by the English anthropologist Edward Tylor in 1871. Tylor started his seminal book, *Primitive Culture*, with the following definition, which is still quoted today in almost any introduction to the subject: 'Taken in its wide ethnographic sense, [culture] is that complex whole which includes knowledge, belief, art, morals, law, custom, and any other capabilities and habits acquired by man as a member of society.' Culture is understood here as all human traits that are not the result of instinct – in other words, as a synonym for nurture as opposed to nature. Culture thus encompasses all aspects of our behaviour that have evolved as social conventions and are transmitted through learning from generation to generation. Scientists sometimes even speak of 'chimpanzee culture', when certain groups of chimps use sticks and stones in a way that differs from that of neighbouring groups and when this knowledge can be shown to have been transmitted through imitation rather than through the genes.

Human culture usually amounts to rather more than sticks and stones, of course. But the type of culture that will concern us in this book has little to do with high art, towering intellectual accomplishments, or impeccable refinement in manners and taste. The focus here will be on those everyday cultural traits that are impressed so deeply in our mind that we do not recognise them as such. In short, the aspects of culture that will be explored here are those where culture masquerades as human nature.

LANGUAGE AS A MIRROR

Is language one of these aspects? Is it an artefact of culture or a bequest of nature? If we hold language up as a mirror to the mind, what do we see reflected there: human nature or the cultural conventions of our society? This is the central question of the first part of the book.

On one level, even posing the question seems rather strange, because language is a cultural convention that doesn't masquerade as anything but a cultural convention. Languages vary greatly across the globe, and everyone knows that the particular language a child happens to learn is just an accident of the particular culture she stumbled into. A Bostonian toddler will grow up speaking Bostonian English because she happened to be born in a Bostonian English environment, not because she has Bostonian genes. And a newborn resident of Beijing will eventually speak Mandarin Chinese because he grows up in a Mandarin environment, not because of any genetic predisposition. If you switch the babies, the Beijing boy will end up speaking perfect Bostonian English and the Bostonian girl will end up speaking perfect Mandarin. There are millions of walking proofs that attest to this fact.

What is more, the most obvious difference between languages is that they choose different names, or labels, for concepts. And as everyone knows, these labels lay no claims to being anything other than cultural conventions. Apart from some marginal cases of onomatopoeia, such as the cuckoo bird, where the label does try to reflect the nature of the bird it denotes, the vast majority of labels are arbitrary. A rose by any other name would smell as douce, γλυκό, édes, zoet, sladká, sød, hoş, makea, magus, dolce, ngọt, or even sweet. The labels are thus fairly and squarely within the remit of each culture and have almost nothing of nature in them.

But what happens when we try to peer further through the language glass, beyond the superficial level of the labels, at the concepts that lurk behind them? Are the concepts behind the English labels 'rose' or 'sweet' or 'bird' or 'cat' just as arbitrary as the labels themselves? Is the way our language carves up the world into concepts also merely a cultural convention? Or is it nature that has drawn for us the distinguishing boundary between 'cat' and 'dog' or 'rose' and 'bird'? If the question comes across as rather abstract, let's put it to a practical test.

Imagine you are browsing in a forgotten corner of an old library and by chance you come across a musty eighteenth-century manuscript that seems never to have been opened since it was deposited there. It is entitled *Adventures on the Remote Island of Zift*, and it appears to relate in much detail a mysterious desert island that the author claims to have discovered. You leaf through it with trembling hands and start reading a chapter called 'A Farther Account of the Ziftish Tongue Wherein Its Phantastick Phænomena Are Largely Describ'd':

> While we were at Dinner, I made bold to ask the Names of several things in their Language; and those noble Persons delighted to give me Answers. Although my principal Endeavour was to learn, yet the Dif-

ficulty was almost insuperable, the whole Compass of their Thoughts and Mind being shut up to such Distinctions as to us appear most natural. They have, for example, no Word in their Tongue by which our Idea of B i r d can be expressed, nor are there any Terms, wherein that Language can express the Notion of a R o s e. For in their stead, Ziftish employs one Word, B o s e, which signifies white Roses and all Birds save those with crimson Chests, and yet another Word, R i r d, which betokens Birds with crimson Chests and all Roses save white ones.

Waxing ever more loquacious after his third Glass of Liquor, my Host began to orate a Fable he recollected from his Childhood: how the Bose and the Rird met their woful End: 'A bright plumed Rird and a mellifluous yellow Bose alighted on a high branch and fell a-twittering. They presently began to debate which of the twain sang the sweeter. Having failed in reaching a firm Conclusion, the Rird proposed that they should seek the Judgement of those Emblems of Beauty among the Flowers in the Garden below. Without more ado, they fluttered down to a fragrant Bose and a budding red Rird, and humbly begged their Opinion. The yellow Bose carolled with slender voice, and the Rird piped his quavering Air. Alas, neither the Bose nor the Rird could distinguish the Bose's cascading Cadences from the tremulous Trills of the Rird. Great was the Indignation of the proud Warblers. The Rird, his Rage inflamed, fell upon the red Rird and plucked off her petals, and the yellow Bose, his Vanity sore wounded, attacked the Bose with equal vehemence. Forthwith both Arbitresses stood naked and stripp'd of their petals, the Bose no longer fragrant and the Rird no longer red.'

Apprehending my Confusion, my Host intoned the Moral with much wagging of his Finger: 'And thus remember: never fail to distinguish a Rird from a Bose!' I offered him my sincere Assurance that I would endeavour never to do so.

What do you take this precious document to be? An undiscovered diary of an early explorer or a lost sequel to *Gulliver's Travels*? If you opted for fiction, it is probably because your common sense tells you that the purported Ziftish manner of distinguishing concepts is fundamentally implausible, and that it is patently unnatural to combine red-chested birds and non-white roses into one concept, 'rird', and to lump other birds together with white roses into the concept 'bose'. And if the Ziftish distinction between rird and bose is unnatural, the English division between bird and rose must in some way be natural. Healthy common sense suggests, therefore, that while languages can bestow labels entirely at whim, they cannot apply quite the same whimsy to the concepts behind the labels. Languages cannot group together arbitrary sets of objects, since it is birds of a feather that flock together under one label. Any language has to categorise the world in a way that brings together things that are similar in reality – or at least in our perception of reality. So it is natural for different types of birds to be named as one concept, but it is unnatural for a random set of birds and a random set of roses to be gathered together under one label.

In fact, even a cursory observation of the way children acquire language will confirm that concepts such as 'bird' or 'cat' or 'dog' have something natural about them. Children ask almost all imaginable (and many unimaginable) questions. But have you ever heard a child saying, 'Mummy, is this a cat or dog?' Rack your brains and rummage through your memories as hard as you can, you are unlikely to recall a child asking, 'How can I tell if this is a bird or a rose?' While children always need to be taught the labels for such concepts in the particular language of their society, they don't need to be told how to distinguish between the concepts themselves. It is quite enough for a toddler to see a few pictures of a cat in a picture book, and the next time she sees a cat, even if it's ginger rather than tabby, even if it has longer hair, a shorter tail, only one eye, and a hind leg missing, she will still recognise it as a cat rather than a dog or bird or rose. Children's instinctive grasp of such concepts shows that human brains are innately equipped with powerful pattern-recognition algorithms, which sort similar objects into groups. So concepts such as 'cat' or 'bird' must somehow correspond to this inborn aptitude to categorise the world.

So far, then, we seem to have arrived at a simple answer to the question of whether language reflects culture or nature. We have drawn a neat map and divided language into two distinct territories: the domain of labels and the land of concepts. The labels reflect cultural conventions, but the concepts reflect nature. Each culture is free to bestow labels onto concepts as it pleases, but the concepts behind these labels have been formed by the dictates of nature. A great deal can be said for this partition. It is clear, simple, and elegant, it is intellectually and emotionally satisfying, and, last but not least, it has a respectable pedigree that extends all the way back to Aristotle, who wrote in the fourth century BC that, although the sounds of speech may differ across the races, the concepts themselves – or, as he called them, the 'impressions of the soul' – are the same for the whole of mankind.

Are there any possible objections to this map? Just one: it bears scant resemblance to reality. The neat border we have just marked may be a pretty work of wishful cartography, but unfortunately it does not represent the actual power relations on the ground with any accuracy. For in practise, culture not only controls the labels, but embarks on incessant raids across the border into what ought to be the birthright of nature. While the distinction between some concepts, such as 'cat' and 'dog, ,may be delineated so clearly by nature that it is largely immune to culture's onslaught, cultural conventions do manage to meddle in the internal affairs of many other concepts, in ways that sometimes upset plain common sense. Just how deeply culture penetrates the land of concepts, and how difficult it can be to come to terms with this state of affairs, is something that will become clearer in the following chapters. But for the moment, we can start with a quick reconnaissance tour of a few of culture's strongholds across the border.

Consider first the realm of abstraction. What happens when we move away from simple physical objects like cats or birds or roses to abstract concepts such as 'victory', 'fairness', or 'Schadenfreude'? Have such concepts also been decreed by nature? I once knew someone who enjoyed saying that the French and the Germans have no mind. What he meant was that neither of their languages had a word for the English 'mind', and he was right in one sense: neither French nor German has a single concept, with a single label, that covers exactly the range of meanings of the English concept 'mind'. If you ask a bilingual dictionary how to translate 'mind' into French, the dictionary will explain patiently that it depends on the context. You will be given a list of possibilities, such as:

esprit (peace of mind = *tranquillité d'esprit*)
tête (it's all in the mind = *c'est tout dans la tête*)
avis (to my mind = *à mon avis*)
raison (his mind is going = *il n'a plus toute sa raison*)
intelligence (with the mind of a two-year-old = *avec l'intelligence d'un enfant de deux ans*)

Conversely, English does not have a single concept that covers exactly the range of meanings of the French *esprit*, as Bertrand Russell so spiritedly observed. Again, a dictionary would give a long list of different English words as possible translations, for instance:

wit (*avoir de l'esprit* = to have wit)
mood (*je n'ai pas l'esprit à rire* = I'm in no mood for laughing)
mind (*avoir l'esprit vif* = to have a quick mind)
spirit (*esprit d'équipe* = team spirit)

So concepts like 'mind' or '*esprit*' cannot be natural in the way that 'rose' or 'bird' are; otherwise they would have been identical in all languages. As early as the seventeenth century, John Locke recognised that in the realm of abstract notions each language is allowed to carve up its own concepts – or 'specific ideas', as he called them – in its own way. In his 1690 *Essay concerning Human Understanding*, he proved the point through the 'great store of words in one language which have not any that answer them in another. Which plainly shows that those of one country, by their customs and manner of life, have found occasion to make several complex ideas, and given names to them, which others never collected into specific ideas.'

Nature's first concession to culture has not come as too much of a wrench, for even if the neat borderline between culture and nature has to be redrawn somewhat, the notion that cultural conventions are involved in determining the shape of abstract concepts is not seriously at odds with our basic intuition. After all, if instead of the story about the Ziftish concepts 'bose' and 'rird', the eighteenth-century travelogue reported that Ziftish didn't have a single word that corresponds to the English concept 'fair', and that in lieu of it Ziftish uses the concept 'just' in some contexts and 'kind' in other contexts, our common sense would hardly be mobilised to march in protest.

But things quickly become less cosy when it transpires that culture interferes not just in the realm of abstraction but also in the simplest concepts of everyday discourse. Take pronouns such as 'I', 'you,' or 'we'. Could anything be more elementary or more natural than these? Of course, no one who is aware of the existence of foreign languages would be under the illusion that the labels for such concepts are dictated by nature, but it seems unimaginable that any language would not have the actual concepts themselves. Suppose, for instance, you continue thumbing through the travelogue and come across the claim that Ziftish doesn't have a word that corresponds to English 'we'. Instead, the author alleges, Ziftish has three distinct pronouns: *kita*, which means 'just the two of us, me and you', *tayo*, which means 'me and you and someone else', and *kami*, which means 'me and someone else, but not you'. The author relates how tickled the Ziftians were to hear that for these three entirely different concepts English uses just one little word, a wee 'we'. You may dismiss the system our chimerical author has invented as a lame joke, but Tagalog speakers in the Philippines would disagree, because this is exactly how they speak.

The strain on plain common sense is only just beginning, though. One might naturally expect that at least the concepts that describe simple physical objects would all be the prerogative of nature. As long as we restrict ourselves to cats, dogs, and birds, this expectation is in fact largely borne out, because these animals are so distinctly shaped by nature. But the moment nature shows the slightest doubt in its incision, culture is quick to pounce. Consider the parts of the human body, for instance. Among the simple physical things that matter most to our lives, it hardly gets any simpler or more physical than hands and toes and fingers and necks. And yet many of these allegedly distinct body parts were not delineated by nature with much zeal. The arm and the hand, for example, are the body's equivalent to the continents Asia and Europe – are they really one thing or two? It turns out that the answer depends on the culture you grew up in. There are many languages, my mother tongue included, that treat the hand and the arm as one concept and use the same label for both. If a Hebrew speaker tells you that when she was a child she got an injection in her hand, this is not because her doctors were sadistic, but simply because she is thinking in a language that doesn't make the distinction as a matter of course, so she has for-gotten to use a different word for that particular part of the hand that English curiously insists on calling an 'arm'. On the other arm, there was a fairly long period when my daughter, who had learned that *yad* in Hebrew meant 'hand', objected loudly whenever I used *yad* to refer to the arm, even when we spoke in Hebrew. She would point at the arm and explain to me in indignant tones: *ze lo yad* (it's not *yad*), *ze arm* (it's 'arm')! The fact that 'hand' and 'arm' are different things in one lan-guage but the same thing in another is not so easy to grasp.

There are also languages that use the same word for 'hand' and 'fin-ger', and a few languages, such as Hawaiian, even manage with using just one concept for the three distinct English body parts 'arm', 'hand', and 'finger'. Conversely, English lumps together certain body parts that speakers of other languages treat as distinct concepts. Even after two decades of speaking English, I still sometimes get tied up in knots with the neck. Someone starts talking about his neck, and I naturally take him at his word and assume he really means his neck – the part of the body that in my mother tongue is called *tsavar*. But after a while it tran-spires that he hasn't been talking about the neck at all. Or rather, he was talking about the neck, but he didn't mean the *tsavar*. What he actually meant was *oref*, the 'back of the neck', that body part which English most carelessly and inconsiderately conjoins with the front of the neck into one concept. In Hebrew, the neck (*tsavar*) refers only to the front part of this tube, whereas the back part, *oref*, has an entirely unrelated name and is considered just as distinct as the English 'back' is from 'belly' or 'hand' is from 'arm'.

Nature's concessions to culture are now starting to feel a little more grudging. While it is hardly unsettling that abstract concepts such as 'mind', or 'esprit', are culturally dependent, we are getting to the edge of the comfort zone with the notion that pronouns like 'we' or body parts like 'hand' or 'neck' all depend on the particular cultural conventions of our society. But if the forays of culture into the realm of concepts are beginning to hurt a little, all this is but a pinprick compared with the pains caused by culture's interference in the area that will occupy us in the first part of the book. In this field of language, culture's incursion into the land of concepts so offended, even outraged, plain common sense that for decades the defenders of nature were mobilised to fight to their last drop of ink to uphold her cause. In consequence, this enclave has been at the centre of a 150-year war between the proponents of nature and of culture, a conflict that is showing no sign of abating. This battleground is the language of colour.

Why should colour, of all things, be at the centre of so much cross-fire? Perhaps because in meddling with such a deep and seemingly instinctive area of perception, culture camouflages itself as nature more successfully there than in any other area of language. There is nothing remotely abstract, theoretical, philosophical, hypothetical, or any other -cal, so it seems, about the difference between yellow and red or between green and blue. And since colours are on the ground level of perception, the concepts of colour would appear to be the prerogative of nature. And yet nature has been rather negligent in staking out her boundaries on the spectrum. The colours form a continuum: green does not become blue at any definite point, but blurs gradually into blue through millions of shades of teal, turquoise, and aquamarine (see figure 11 in insert). When we speak about colours, however, we impose distinct boundaries on this variegated swathe: 'yellow', 'green', 'blue', and so on. But is our particular way of dividing the colour space a dictate of nature? Are the concepts 'yellow' or 'green' universal constants of the human race that were decreed by the biological make-up of the eye and brain? Or are they arbitrary cultural conventions? Could the boundaries have been set differently? And why should anyone dream up such abstruse hypothetical questions anyway?

As it happens, the controversy over the concepts of colour was not conjured up by any abstract philosophical ruminations but arose in the wake of entirely practical observations. A series of discoveries made in the middle of the nineteenth century led to the startling revelation that mankind's relation to colour has not always been as clear as it seems to us now, and that what appears obvious to us caused no end of difficulty to the ancients. The ensuing mission to discover the source of the 'colour sense' is a gripping Victorian adventure story, an episode in the history of ideas that can rival the derring-do of any nineteenth-century explorer. The colour expedition reached the remotest corners of the earth, got tangled up with the fiercest controversies of the day – evolution, heredity, and race – and was driven by a motley cast of unlikely heroes: a celebrated statesman whose intellectual feats are now almost entirely unknown, an Orthodox Jew who was led by his philological discoveries to the most heterodox evolutionary thoughts, an eye doctor from a provincial German university who set a whole generation in pursuit of a bright red herring, and a Cambridge don, dubbed the 'Galileo of anthropology', who finally put the quest back on course, against his own better judgement.

The nineteenth-century struggle to understand what it is that separates us from the ancients, the eye or the tongue, turned in the twentieth century into an all-out battle over the concepts of language, in which opposing world views were pitted against one another – universalism against relativism, and nativism against empiricism. In this world war of isms, the spectrum assumed totemic importance, as proponents of both nature and culture came to view their hold over colour as decisive for the control over language in general. At different times, each side declared colour as the trump card in their wider argument, and received opinion thus swung from one extreme to the other, from nature to culture, and in recent decades back to nature again.

The vicissitudes of this controversy make colour an ideal test case for adjudicating over nature's and culture's conflicting claims on the concepts of language. Or put another way: the seemingly narrow strip of colour can serve as a litmus test for nothing less than the question of how deep the communalities are between the ways human beings express themselves, and how superficial the differences – or vice versa!

◦—

The discussion so far may have given the impression that there is nothing more to language than a collection of concepts and their corresponding labels. But in order to communicate subtle thoughts involving intricate relations between different concepts, language needs much more than a list of concepts – it needs a grammar, a sophisticated system of rules for organising concepts into coherent sentences. Able as as be coherent communicate concepts even example for for grammar in likes many not of one one ordering rules rules sentence the the the thoughts to with without without words would. (I mean: without the rules of grammar, for example without the rules for ordering words in the sentence, one would not be able to communicate coherent thoughts, even with as many concepts as one likes.) And as it happens, the debates between the advocates of nature and of nurture, between nativists and culturalists, universalists and relativists have raged just as fiercely over grammar as over the concepts of language. Are the rules of grammar – word order, syntactic structures, word structure, sound structure – encoded in our genes, or do they reflect cultural conventions?

The dominant view among linguists today – advanced by Noam Chomsky and the influential research programme that he has inspired – is that most of the grammar of language, that is to say, of all human languages, is innate. This school of thought, which is known as 'nativist', contends that the rules of universal grammar are coded in our DNA: humans are born with brains pre-equipped with a specific toolkit of complex grammatical structures, so that children do not need to learn these structures when they acquire their mother tongue. For the nativists, therefore, grammar reflects universal human nature, and any differences between the grammatical structures of different languages are superficial and of little consequence.

According to the dissenting minority view, there is scant evidence to show that any specific rules of grammar are prewired in the brain and there is no need to invoke genes in order to account for grammatical structures, because these can be explained more simply and more plausibly as the product of cultural evolution and as a response to the exigencies of efficient communication. In *The Unfolding of Language*, I argued for this latter view, by showing how a sophisticated system of specific grammatical rules could have evolved from very humble beginnings, driven by forces of change that are motivated by broad traits of human nature, such as laziness (effort saving in pronunciation) and a need to impose order on the world.

This book will not dwell on the grammatical side of the great nature – culture controversy, but there is one aspect of grammar that will need to come under the magnifying glass, because there the role of culture is especially and almost universally under-appreciated. This aspect is complexity. Does the complexity of a language reflect the culture and society of its speakers, or is it a universal constant determined by human nature? If the subject of colour was the most bitterly contested area in the debate over concepts, the question of complexity is undoubtedly the issue in the battle over grammar that has been least contested – but ought to be. For decades, linguists of all persuasions, both nativists and culturalists, have been trotting out the same party line: all languages are equally complex. But I will argue that this refrain is merely an empty slogan and that the evidence suggests that the complexity of some areas of grammar reflects the culture of the speakers, often in unexpected ways.

LANGUAGE AS A LENS

If the questions explored in the first part of the book have stirred up fierce debates and raging emotions, these are but storms in a teacup compared with the gales of discord that beset the subject of the second part, the question of the mother tongue's influence on our thoughts. Could language have more than a passive role as a reflection of cultural differences and be an active instrument of coercion through which culture imposes its conventions on our mind? Do different languages lead their speakers to different perceptions? Is our particular language a lens through which we view the world?

At first sight, there seems to be nothing unreasonable about posing this question. Since culture has a great deal of leeway in defining concepts, it is – in principle – entirely sensible to ask whether our culture could affect our thoughts through the linguistic concepts it imposes. But while the question seems perfectly kosher in theory, in practise the mere whiff of the subject today makes most linguists, psychologists, and anthropologists recoil. The reason why the topic causes such intense embarrassment is that it carries with it a baggage of intellectual history which is so disgraceful that the mere suspicion of association with it can immediately brand anyone a fraud. The problem is that any influence of language on thought is very difficult to prove or disprove empirically, so that the subject has traditionally afforded a perfect platform to those who enjoy flashing their fantasies without the least danger of being caught out by the fact police. Like flies to the honeypot or philosophers to the unknowable, the most inspired charlatans, the most virtuoso con artists, not to mention hordes of run-of-the-mill crackpots, have been drawn to expostulate on the influence of the mother tongue on its speakers' thoughts. The second part of the book starts with a short sample from this Decameron of excesses, and concentrates on the most notorious of the con men, Benjamin Lee Whorf, who seduced a whole generation into believing, without a shred of evidence, that American Indian languages lead their speakers to an entirely different conception of reality from ours.

Today, partly because of this outrageous legacy, most respectable linguists and psychologists either categorically deny that the mother tongue can have any influence on speakers' thoughts, or claim that any such influence is at best negligible, even trivial. Nevertheless, in recent years some intrepid researchers have attempted to apply sound scientific methods to this question, and the findings that have emerged from their research have already revealed surprising ways in which the idiosyncrasies of the mother tongue do after all affect the mind. The second part of the book presents three examples where such influence seems to me to have been demonstrated most plausibly. As the story unfolds, it will become evident that the credible influence of language on speakers' thinking is of a radically different kind from what was touted in the past. Whorf's muse floated in the loftiest levels of cognition, fantasising about how languages could determine speakers' capacity for logical reasoning and how speakers of such-and-such a language would not be able to understand such-and-such an idea because their language does not make such-and-such a distinction. The effects that have emerged from recent research, however, are far more down to earth. They are to do with the habits of mind that language can instil on the ground level of thought: on memory, attention, perception, and associations. And while these effects may be less wild than those flaunted in the past, we shall see that some of them are no less striking for all that.

But first – off to the fighting over the rainbow.

PART I

The
LANGUAGE
MIRROR

1

Naming the Rainbow

London, 1858. On the first of July, the Linnean Society, in its magnificent new quarters at Burlington House in Piccadilly, will hear two
papers by Charles Darwin and Alfred Russel Wallace announcing
jointly a theory of evolution by natural selection. Before long, the flame
will flare up and illuminate the intellectual firmament, leaving no
corner of human reason untouched. But although the wildfire of
Darwinism will catch up with us soon enough, we do not begin quite
there. Our story starts a few months earlier and a few streets away, in
Westminster, with a rather improbable hero. At forty-nine, he is already
an eminent politician, Member of Parliament for Oxford University,
and ex-Chancellor of the Exchequer. But he is still ten years away from
becoming prime minister, and even further from being celebrated as
one of Britain's greatest statesmen. In fact, the Right Honourable William Ewart Gladstone has been languishing on the opposition benches
for the last three years. But his time has not been idly spent.

While out of office, he has devoted his legendary energies to the
realm of the mind, and in particular to his burning intellectual passion:
that ancient bard who 'founded for the race the sublime office of the

poet, and who built upon his own foundations an edifice so lofty and so firm that it still towers unapproachably above the handiwork not only of common, but even of many uncommon men'. Homer's epics are for Gladstone nothing less than 'the most extraordinary phenomenon in the whole history of purely human culture'. The *Iliad* and the *Odyssey* have been his lifelong companions and his literary refuge ever since his Eton schooldays. But for Gladstone, a man of deep religious conviction, Homer's poems are more than merely literature. They are his second Bible, a perfect compendium of human character and experience that displays human nature in the most admirable form it could assume without the aid of Christian revelation.

Gladstone's monumental oeuvre, his *Studies on Homer and the Homeric Age*, has just been published this March. Its three stout, door-stopping tomes of well over seventeen hundred pages sweep across an encyclopedic range of topics, from the geography of the *Odyssey* to Homer's sense of beauty, from the position of women in Homeric society to the moral character of Helen. One unassuming chapter, tucked away at the end of the last volume, is devoted to a curious and seemingly marginal theme, 'Homer's perception and use of colour'. Gladstone's scrutiny of the *Iliad* and the *Odyssey* revealed that there is something awry about Homer's descriptions of colour, and the conclusions Gladstone draws from his discovery are so radical and so bewildering that his contemporaries are entirely unable to digest them and largely dismiss them out of hand. But before long, Gladstone's conundrum will launch a thousand ships of learning, have a profound effect on the development of at least three academic disciplines, and trigger a war over the control of language between nature and culture that after 150 years shows no sign of abating.

Even in a period far less unaccustomed than ours to the concurrence of political power and greatness of mind, Gladstone's Homeric scholarship was viewed as something out of the ordinary. He was, after all, an active politician, and yet his three-volume opus would have been no mean achievement as the lifetime's work of a dedicated don. To some, especially political colleagues, Gladstone's devotion to the classics was the cause of resentment. 'You are so absorbed in questions about Homer

William Ewart Gladstone, 1809–1898

and Greek words,' a party friend complained, 'that you are not reading newspapers or feeling the pulse of followers.' But for the general public, Gladstone's virtuoso Homerology was a subject of fascination and admiration. *The Times* ran a review of Gladstone's book that was so long it had to be printed in two instalments and would amount to more than thirty pages in this book's type. Nor did Gladstone's erudition fail to impress in intellectual circles. 'There are few public men in Europe,' was one professor's verdict, 'so pure-minded, so quick-sighted, and so highly cultivated as Mr Gladstone.' In the following years, books by distinguished academics in Britain and even on the Continent were dedicated to Gladstone, 'the statesman, orator, and scholar', 'the untiring promoter of Homeric Studies'.

Of course, there was a but. While Gladstone's prodigious learning, his mastery of the text, and his fertility of logical resources were universally praised, the reaction to many of his actual arguments was downright scathing. Alfred Lord Tennyson wrote that on the subject of Homer 'most people think [Gladstone] a little hobby-horsical'. A professor of Greek at Edinburgh University explained to his students that 'Mr Gladstone may be a learned, enthusiastic, most ingenious and subtle expositor of Homer – always eloquent, and sometimes brilliant; but he is not sound. His logic is feeble, almost puerile, his tactical movements, though full of graceful dash and brilliancy, are utterly destitute of sobriety, of caution, and even of common sense.' Karl Marx, himself an avid reader of Greek literature and not one to mince his words, wrote to Engels that Gladstone's book was 'characteristic of the inability of the English to produce anything valuable in Philology'. And the epic review in *The Times* (anonymous, as reviews were in those days) twists itself into the most convoluted of circumlocutions to avoid explicitly calling Gladstone a fool. It starts by declaring that 'Mr Gladstone is excessively clever. But, unfortunately for excessive cleverness, it affords one of the aptest illustrations of the truth of the proverb that extremes meet.' The review ends, nearly thirteen thousand words later, with the regret that 'so much power should be without effect, that so much genius should be without balance, that so much fertility should be fertility of weeds, and that so much eloquence should be as the tinkling cymbal and the sounding brass'.

What was so wrong with Gladstone's *Studies on Homer*? For a start, Gladstone had committed the cardinal sin of taking Homer far too seriously. He was treating Homer 'with an almost Rabbinical veneration', snorted *The Times*. In an age that prided itself on its newly discovered scepticism, when even Holy Scripture's authority and authorship were beginning to yield to the scalpel of German textual criticism, Gladstone was marching to the beat of a different drum. He dismissed out of hand the theories, much in vogue at the time, that there had never been a poet called Homer and that the *Iliad* and the *Odyssey* were instead a patchwork of a great number of popular ballads cobbled together from different poets over many different periods. For him, the *Iliad* and the *Odyssey* were composed by a single poet of transcendental genius: 'I find in the plot of the *Iliad* enough beauty, order, and structure to bear an independent testimony to the existence of a personal and individual Homer as its author.'

Even more distasteful to his critics was Gladstone's insistence that the story of the *Iliad* was based on at least a core of historical fact. To the enlightened academics of 1858, it seemed childishly credulous to assign any historical value to a story of a ten-year Greek siege of a town called Ilios or Troia, following the abduction of a Greek queen by the Trojan prince Paris, also known as Alexandros. As *The Times* put it, these tales were 'accepted by all mankind as fictions of very nearly the same order as the romances of Arthur'. Needless to say, all this was twelve years before Heinrich Schliemann actually found Troy on a mound overlooking the Dardanelles; before he excavated the palace of Mycenae, homeland of the Greek overlord Agamemnon; before it became clear that both Troy and Mycenae were rich and powerful cities at the same period in the late second millennium BC; before later excavations showed that Troy was destroyed in a great conflagration soon after 1200 BC; before sling stones and other weapons were found on the site, proving that the destruction was caused by an enemy siege; before a clay document was unearthed that turned out to be a treaty between a Hittite king and the land of Wilusa; before the same Wilusa was securely identified as none other than Homer's Ilios; before a ruler of Wilusa whom the treaty calls Alaksandu could thus be related to Homer's Alexandros, prince of Troy; before – in short – Gladstone's feeling that the *Iliad* was more than just a quilt of groundless myths turned out to have been rather less foolish than his contemporaries imagined.

There is one area, however, where it is difficult to be much kinder to Gladstone today than his contemporaries were at the time: his harping on about Homeric religion. Gladstone's was neither the first nor the last of great minds to be led astray by religious fervour, but in the case of his *Studies on Homer*, his convictions took the particularly unfortunate turn of trying to marry Homer's pagan pantheon with the Christian creed. Gladstone believed that at the beginning of mankind humanity had been granted a revelation of the true God, and while knowledge of this divine revelation later faded and was perverted by pagan heresies, traces of it could be detected in Greek mythology. He thus left no god unturned in his effort to detect Christian truth in the Homeric pantheon. As *The Times* put it, Gladstone 'strained all his faculties to detect, in the Olympian Courts, the God of Abraham who came from Ur of the Chaldees, and the God of Melchezedek who dwelt in Salem.' Gladstone argued, for instance, that the tradition of a Trinity in the Godhead left its traces on the Greek mythology and is manifested in the three-way division of the world between Zeus, Poseidon, and Hades. He claimed that Apollo displays many of the qualities of Christ himself and even went so far as to suggest that Apollo's mother, Leto, 'represents the

Blessed Virgin'. *The Times* was not amused: 'Perfectly honest in his intentions, he takes up a theory, and no matter how ridiculous it is in reality, he can make it appear respectable in argument. Too clever by half!'

Gladstone's determination to baptise the ancient Greeks did his *Studies on Homer* a sterling disservice, since his religious errings and strayings made it all too easy to discount his many other ideas. This was most unfortunate, because when Gladstone was not calculating how many angels could dance on the tip of Achilles' spear, it was exactly his other alleged great failing, that of taking Homer too seriously, that elevated him far above the intellectual horizon of most of his contemporaries. Gladstone did not believe that Homer's story was an accurate depiction of historical events, but unlike his critics he understood that the poems held up a mirror to the knowledge, beliefs, and traditions of the time and were thus a historical source of the highest value, a treasure house of data for the study of early Greek life and thought, an authority all the more trustworthy because an unconscious authority, addressing not posterity but Homer's own contemporaries. Gladstone's toothcombing analysis of what the poems said and – sometimes even more importantly – what they did not say thus led him to remarkable discoveries about the cultural world of the ancient Greeks. The most striking of these insights concerned Homer's language of colour.

For someone used to the doldrums and ditchwater of latter-day academic writing, reading Gladstone's chapter on colour comes as rather a shock – that of meeting an extraordinary mind. One is left in awe by the originality, the daring, the razor-sharp analysis, and that breathless feeling that however fast one is trying to run through the argument in one's own mind, Gladstone is always two steps ahead, and, whatever objection one tries to raise, he has pre-empted several pages before one has even thought of it. It is therefore all the more startling that Gladstone's tour de force comes to such a strange conclusion. To phrase it somewhat anachronistically, he argued that Homer and his contemporaries perceived the world in something closer to black and white than to full Technicolour.

In terms of its sheer implausibility, Gladstone's claim that the Greeks' sense of colour differed from ours seems at first sight to come a close second to his notions of a Christlike Apollo or a Marian Leto. For how could such a basic aspect of human experience have changed? No one would deny, of course, that there is a wide gulf between Homer's world and ours: in the millennia that separate us, empires have risen and fallen, religions and ideologies have come and gone, science and technology have transformed our intellectual horizons and almost every aspect of daily life beyond all recognition. But if in this great sea of change we could pick just one haven of stability, one aspect of life that must have remained exactly the same since Homer's day – even since time immemorial – then it would surely be the pleasure in the rich colours of nature: the blue of sky and sea, the glowing red of dawn, the green of fresh leaves. If there is one phrase that represents a rock of stability in the flux of human experience, then surely it would be that timeless question 'Daddy, why is the sky blue?'

Or would it? The mark of an exceptional mind is its ability to question the self-evident, and Gladstone's scrutiny of the *Iliad* and the *Odyssey* left no room for doubt that there was something seriously amiss with Homer's descriptions of colour. Perhaps the most conspicuous example is the way Homer talked about the colour of the sea. Probably the single most famous phrase from the whole *Iliad* and *Odyssey* that is still in common currency today is that immortal colour epithet, the 'wine-dark sea'. But let's consider this description with pernickety Gladstonian literal-mindedness for a moment. As it happens, 'wine-dark' is already an act of redemptive interpretation in the translation, for what Homer actually says is *oinops*, which literally means 'wine-looking' (*oinos* is 'wine' and *op-* is the root 'see'). But what does the colour of the sea have to do with wine? As an answer to Gladstone's simple question, scholars have suggested all manner of imaginable and unimaginable theories to wave away the difficulty. The most common answer was to suggest that Homer must have been referring to the deep purple-crimson shade, such as a troubled sea has at dawn or sunset. Alas, there is no indication that Homer used the epithet for the sea at dawn or sunset in particular. It has also been suggested, apparently in all earnestness, that the sea can sometimes look red because of certain types of algae. Another scholar, despairing of the possibility of painting the sea red, tried instead to turn wine blue and claimed that 'blue and violet reflects are visible in certain wines of southern regions, and especially in the vinegar from home-made wines'.

There is no need to dwell on why all these theories hold neither wine nor water. But there was one other method for circumventing the difficulty, which was applied by many a self-respecting commentator and which does deserve some comment. This was to call upon that foolproof catch all of literary criticism: poetic licence. One eminent classicist, for example, pooh-poohed Gladstone by claiming that 'if any man should say that the minstrel was deficient in the organ of colour because he designated the sea by this vague word, I would meet him by saying that the critic is deficient in the organ of poetry'. But when all is said and sung, the elegant conceit of the critics' animadversions does not bear up to Gladstone's sophisticated literal-mindedness, for his sure-footed analysis had all but eliminated the possibility that poetic licence could be the explanation for the oddities in Homer's colour descriptions. Gladstone was not poetically tone-deaf, and he was well attuned to the artful effect of what he called 'straining epithets of colour'. But he also understood that if the discrepancies were merely a bold exercise of the poet's art, then the straining should be the exception rather than the rule, for otherwise the result is not licence but confusion. And he showed, using methods which would today be considered exemplary applications of systematic textual analysis but which one of his contemporary critics derided as the bean-counting mentality of 'a born Chancellor of the Exchequer', that this vagueness in Homer's colour descriptions was the rule, not the exception. To prove it, Gladstone drew a circle of evidence consisting of five main points:

I. The use of the same word to denote colours which, according to us, are essentially different.

II. The description of the same object under epithets of colour fundamentally disagreeing one from the other.

III. The slight use of colour, and its absence in certain cases where we might confidently expect it.

IV. The vast predominance of the most crude and elemental forms of colour, black and white, over every other.

V. The small size of Homer's colour vocabulary.

He then proceeded to support these points with over thirty pages of examples, of which I will quote just a few. Consider first what other objects Homer describes as having the appearance of wine. Except for the sea, the only other thing that Homer calls 'wine-looking' is ... oxen. And none of the critics' philological somersaults could turn over Gladstone's simple conclusion: 'There is no small difficulty in combining these two uses by reference to the idea of a common colour. The sea is blue, grey, or green. Oxen are black, bay, or brown.'

Or what is one to make of the flower name 'violet' (*ioeis*), which Homer uses as a designation for the colour of ... the sea. (Homer's phrase *ioeidea ponton* is variously translated – according to the translator's muse – as the 'violet sea', the 'purple ocean', or the 'violet-coloured deep.') And is it also poetic licence that allows Homer to use the same flower to describe the sheep in the cave of the Cyclops as 'beautiful and large, with thick violet wool'? Presumably, what Homer was referring to were black sheep as opposed to white ones, and it may be granted that 'black sheep' are not really black but actually very dark brown. But violet? Or what about another place in the *Iliad*, where Homer applies the term 'violet' to describe iron? And if the violet seas, violet sheep, and violet iron are all to be written off as poetic licences, then what about a different passage, where Homer compares Odysseus's dark hair to the colour of the hyacinth?

Homer's use of the word *chlôros* is no less peculiar. In later stages of Greek, *chlôros* just means 'green' (and it is this meaning that has inspired familiar terms in the language of science, such as the pigment chlorophyll and the greenish gas chlorine). But Homer employs the word in a variety of senses that don't seem to suit greenness very comfortably. Most often, *chlôros* appears as a description of faces pale with fear. While this could merely be a metaphor, *chlôros* is also used for fresh twigs and for the olive-wood club of the Cyclops. Both twigs and olive wood would strike us today as brown or grey, but with a bit of goodwill we might still give Homer the benefit of the doubt here. This goodwill is stretched to the limit, however, when Homer uses the same word to describe honey. Hands up, anyone who has ever seen green honey.

But Gladstone's circle of evidence is only just beginning. His second point is that Homer often describes the same object with incompatible colour terms. Iron, for instance, is said to be 'violet' in one passage, 'grey' elsewhere, and in yet another place it is referred to as *aithôn*, a term otherwise used to refer to the colour of horses, lions, and oxen.

Gladstone's next point is how remarkably colourless Homer's vibrant verse is. Flick through anthologies of modern poetry, and colour stares you in the eye. Is there a self-respecting poet who has not drawn inspiration from 'the green fields and from yon azure sky'? Whose verse has not celebrated that time of year 'when daisies pied and violets blue and lady-smocks all silver white, and cuckoo-buds of yellow hue do paint the meadows with delight'? Goethe wrote that no one can be insensitive to the appeal of the colours that are spread out over the whole of visible nature. But Homer, it appears, was precisely that. Take his descriptions of horses. For us, Gladstone explains, 'colour is in horses a thing so prominent that it seems, whenever they are at all individualized, almost to force itself into the description. It is most singular that, though Homer so loved the horse that he is never weary of using him with his whole heart for the purposes of poetry, yet in all his animated and beautiful descriptions of this animal, colour should be so little prominent.' Homer's silence on the colour of the sky shouts even louder. Here, says Gladstone, 'Homer had before him the most perfect example of blue. Yet he never once so describes the sky. His sky is starry, or broad, or great, or iron, or copper; but it is never blue.'

It is not as if Homer was uninterested in nature: he is, after all, fabled as an acute observer of the world and admired for his vivid similes with elaborate descriptions of animals and natural phenomena. The marching of the warriors to the place of gathering, for example, is likened to 'the tribes of thronging bees that go forth from some hollow rock, ever coming on afresh, and in clusters over the flowers of spring fly in throngs, some here, some there'. The groups of soldiers pouring noisily onto the plain are said to be 'as the many tribes of winged fowl, wild geese or cranes or long-necked swans on the Asian mead by the streams of Caystrius, [which] fly this way and that, glorying in their strength of wing, and with loud cries settle ever onwards, and the mead resounds'. Homer had an especially keen eye for the play of light, for anything that shimmers, glints, and glitters: 'As obliterating fire lights up a vast forest, along the crests of a mountain, and the flare shows far off, so – as [the soldiers] marched – the gleam went dazzling from the magnificent bronze all about through the upper air to the heavens.' Since Homer's similes are so rich in the use of all sensible imagery, says Gladstone, we might have expected to find colour a frequent and prominent ingredient in them. And yet his poppies may have 'their head aslant, laden with seed and with the rain of spring', but there is never so much as a hint of scarlet. His spring flowers may be a multitude in the field, but their colour is not revealed. His fields may be 'well-grown of wheat' or 'new moistened with rain in summer-time', but their hue is not divulged. His hills may be 'woody' and his woods may be 'thick' or 'dark' or 'shady', but they are not green.

Gladstone's fourth point is the vast predominance of the 'most crude and elemental forms of colour' – black and white – over every other. He counts that Homer uses the adjective *melas* (black) about 170 times in the poems, and this does not even include instances of the corresponding verb 'to grow black', as when the sea is described as 'blackening beneath the ripple of the West Wind that is newly risen'. Words meaning 'white' appear around a hundred times. In contrast to this abundance, the word *eruthros* (red) appears thirteen times, *xanthos* (yellow) is hardly found ten times, *ioeis* (violet) six times, and other colours even less often.

Finally, Gladstone rummages through the Homeric poems in search of what is not there and discovers that even some of the elementary primary colours, which, as he puts it, 'have been determined for us by Nature', make no appearance at all. Most striking is the lack of any word that could be taken to mean 'blue'. The word *kuaneos*, which in later stages of Greek meant blue, does make an appearance in the poems, but it must have just meant 'dark' for Homer, because he uses it for neither the sky nor the sea, only to describe the eyebrows of Zeus, the hair of Hector, or a dark cloud. Green is hardly mentioned either, for the word *chlôros* is used mostly for non-green things, and yet there is no other word in the poems that can be supposed to represent this commonest of colours. And there doesn't seem to be anything equivalent to our orange or pink in Homer's entire colour palette.

When Gladstone finishes drawing his circle of evidence, any reader with at least half an open mind would have to accept that something far more serious is afoot here than merely a few indulgences in poetic licence. There is no escaping the conclusion that Homer's relation to colour is seriously askew: he may often talk about light and brightness, but seldom does he venture beyond grey scale into the splendour of the prism. In those instances when colours are mentioned, they are often vague and highly inconsistent: his sea is wine-coloured, and when not wine-coloured, it is violet, just like his sheep. His honey is green and his southern sky is anything but blue.

According to later legend, Homer, like any bard worth his salt, was supposed to have been blind. But Gladstone gives this story short shrift. Homer's descriptions – in everything except colour – are so vivid that they could never have been conceived by a man who couldn't see the world for himself. What is more, Gladstone proves that the oddities in the *Iliad* and the *Odyssey* could not have stemmed from any problems that were peculiar to Homer the individual. To start with, if Homer's condition was an exception among his contemporaries, surely his defective descriptions would have grated on their ears and would have been corrected. Not only is this not the case, but it seems that traces of the very same oddities still abounded among the ancient Greeks even centuries later. 'Violet-coloured hair', for example, was used as a description in Pindar's poems in the fifth century BC. Gladstone shows in fact that the colour descriptions of later Greek authors, even if not quite as deficient as Homer's, 'continued to be both faint and indefinite, in a degree which would now be deemed very surprising'. So whatever was wrong with Homer must have afflicted his contemporaries and even some later generations. How can all this be explained?

⌒

Gladstone's solution to this conundrum was an idea so radical and so strange that he himself seriously doubted whether he should dare to include it in his book. As he reminisced twenty years later, he eventually published it 'only after submitting the facts to some very competent judges. For the case appeared to open up questions of great interest, with respect to the general structure of the human organs, and to the laws of hereditary growth.' What makes his proposal even more astonishing is the fact that he had never heard of colour blindness. Although, as we shall see, this condition would become famous soon enough, in 1858 colour blindness was unknown among the general public, and even those few specialists who were aware of it hardly understood it. And yet, without using the term itself, what Gladstone was proposing was nothing less than universal colour blindness among the ancient Greeks.

The sensitivity to differences in colour, he suggested, is an ability that evolved fully only in more recent history. As he put it, 'the organ of colour and its impressions were but partially developed among the Greeks of the heroic age'. Homer's contemporaries, Gladstone said, saw the world primarily through the opposition between light and darkness, with the colours of the rainbow appearing to them merely as indeterminate modes between the two extremes of black and white. Or, to be more accurate, they saw the world in black and white with a dash of red, for Gladstone conceded that the colour sense was beginning to develop in Homer's time and had come to include red hues. This could be deduced from the fact that Homer's limited colour vocabulary is heavily slanted towards red and that his main 'red' word, *eruthros*, is rather untypically used *only* for red things, such as blood, wine, or copper.

The undeveloped state of colour perception, Gladstone argues, can immediately explain why Homer had such lively and poetic conceptions of light and darkness while being so tight-lipped on prismatic colours. What is more, Homer's seemingly erratic colour epithets will now 'fall into their places, and we shall find that the Poet used them, from his own standing-ground, with great vigour and effect'. For if Homer's 'violet' or 'wine-looking' are to be understood as describing not particular hues but only particular shades of darkness, then designations such as 'violet sheep' or 'wine-looking sea' no longer seem so strange. Likewise, Homer's 'green honey' becomes far more appetizing if we assume that what caught his eye was a particular kind of lightness rather than a particular prismatic colour. In terms of etymology, *chlôros* derives from a word meaning 'young herbage', which is typically fresh light green. But if the hue distinction between green, yellow, and light brown was of little consequence in Homer's time, then the prime association of *chlôros* would have been not the greenness of the young herbage but rather its paleness and freshness. And as such, Gladstone concludes, it makes perfect sense to use *chlôros* to describe (yellow) honey or (brown) freshly picked twigs.

Gladstone is well aware of the utter weirdness of the idea he is proposing, so he tries to make it more palatable by evoking an evolutionary explanation for how sensitivity to colours could have increased over the generations. The perception of colour, he says, seems natural to us only because mankind as a whole has undergone a progressive 'education of the eye' over the last millennia: 'the perceptions so easy and familiar to us are the results of a slow traditionary growth in knowledge and in the training of the human organ, which commenced long before we took our place in the succession of mankind'. The eye's ability to perceive and appreciate differences in colour, he suggests, can improve with practise, and these acquired improvements are then passed on to the offspring. The next generation is thus born with a heightened sensitivity to colour, which can be improved even further with continued practise. These subsequent improvements are bequeathed to the next generation, and so on.

But why, one may well ask, should this progressive refinement of colour vision not have started much earlier than the Homeric period? Why did this process have to wait so long to get going, given that from time immemorial all things bright and beautiful have been blazing us in the eye? Gladstone's answer is a masterstroke of ingenuity, but one that seems almost as bizarre as the state of affairs it purports to account for. His theory was that colour – in abstraction from the object that is coloured – may start mattering to people only once they become exposed to artificial paints and dyes. The appreciation of colour as a property independent of a particular material may thus have developed only hand in hand with the capacity to manipulate colours artificially. And that capacity, he notes, barely existed in Homer's day: the art of dyeing was only in its infancy, cultivation of flowers was not practised, and almost all the brightly coloured objects that we take for granted were entirely absent.

This dearth of artificial colours is particularly striking in the case of blue. Of course, the Mediterranean sky was just as sapphire in Homer's day, and the Côte just as azure. But whereas our eyes are saturated with all kinds of tangible objects that are blue, in all imaginable shades from the palest ice blue to the deepest navy, people in Homer's day may have gone through life without ever setting their eyes on a single blue object. Blue eyes, Gladstone explains, were in short supply, blue dyes, which are very difficult to manufacture, were practically unknown, natural flowers that are truly blue are also rare.

Merely to be exposed to the haphazard colours of nature, Gladstone concludes, may not be enough to set off the progressive training of colour vision. For this process to get going, the eye needs to be exposed to a methodically graded range of hues and shades. As he puts it, 'The eye may require a familiarity with an ordered system of colours, as the condition of its being able closely to appreciate anyone among them.' With so little experience in manipulating and controlling colours artificially and so little reason to dwell on the colour of materials as an independent property, the progressive improvement in the perception of colour would thus have barely started in Homer's time. 'The organ was given to Homer only in its infancy, which is now full-grown in us. So full-grown is it, that a child of three years in our nurseries knows, that is to say sees, more of colour than the man who founded for the race the sublime office of the poet.'

What are we to make of Gladstone's theory? The verdict of his contemporaries was unequivocal: his claims were almost universally scoffed at as the fantasies of overzealous literal-mindedness, and the oddities he had uncovered were unceremoniously brushed away as poetic licence, or as proof of the legend of Homer's blindness, or both. With the benefit of hindsight, however, the verdict is less black and white. On one level, Gladstone was so accurate and far-sighted that it would be inadequate to class him as merely ahead of his time. Fairer would be to say that his analysis was so brilliant that substantial parts of it can stand almost without emendation as a summary of the state of the art today, 150 years later. But on another level, Gladstone was completely off course. He made one cardinal error in his presuppositions about the relation between language and perception, but in this he was far from alone. Indeed, philologists, anthropologists, and even natural scientists would need decades to free themselves from this error: underestimating the power of culture.

2

A Long-Wave Herring

In the autumn of 1867, distinguished natural scientists from all over Germany convened in Frankfurt for the Assembly of German Naturalists and Physicians. The times they were exciting: the world in 1867 bore little resemblance to what it had been nine years earlier, when Gladstone published his *Studies on Homer*. For in the meantime, *The Origin of Species* had appeared and Darwinism had conquered the collective psyche. As George Bernard Shaw later wrote, 'Everyone who had a mind to change changed it'. In those heady early days of the Darwinian revolution, the convened scientists would have been used to the airing of all kinds of peculiar notions about matters evolutionary. But the topic announced for the plenary lecture at the closing session of their conference must have seemed unusual even by the exacting standards of the time: 'On the Colour Sense in Primitive Times and its Evolution'. Even more unusual than the title was the identity of the young man who stood at the lectern, for the honour of addressing the final session of the conference fell to someone who was neither a natural scientist nor a physician, who was only in his thirties, and who was an Orthodox Jew.

In fact, very little was usual about the philologist Lazarus Geiger. He was born in 1829 to a distinguished Frankfurt family of rabbis and scholars. His uncle Abraham Geiger was the leading light in the Reform movement that transformed German Jewry in the nineteenth century. Lazarus did not share his uncle's taste for religious modernisation, but while in all matters practical he insisted on obeying the laws of his ancestral religion to the letter, in matters of the intellect his mind soared entirely unfettered and he entertained ideas far more daring than those of even his most liberal Jewish or Christian contemporaries. Indeed, his linguistic investigations convinced him – long before Darwin's ideas became known – that he could trace in language evidence for the descent of man from a beast-like state.

Geiger possessed almost unparalleled erudition. As a seven-year-old boy, he declared to his mother that he would like to learn 'all languages' one day, and in the course of his short life – he succumbed to heart disease at the age of forty-two – he managed to come closer to this ideal than perhaps anyone else. But what made him stand out as a thinker was the combination of this phenomenal learning with a seemingly inexhaustible stream of bold original theories, particularly on the development of language and the evolution of human reason. And it was on such an evolutionary theme that he addressed the men of science who gathered in his home town in September 1867. His lecture started with a provocative question: 'Has human sensation, has perception by the senses, a history? Did everything in the human sense organs thousands of years ago function exactly as it does now, or can we perhaps show that at some remote period these organs must have been partly incapable of their present performance?'

Geiger's curiosity about the language of colour had been piqued by Gladstone's discoveries. While most contemporaries wrote off Gladstone's claims about the rawness of Homer's colours out of hand, Geiger was inspired by what he read to examine the colour descriptions of ancient texts from other cultures. And what he discovered there bore uncanny resemblances to the oddities in Homer. Here, for instance, is how Geiger described the ancient Indian Vedic poems, in particular their treatment of the sky: 'These hymns, of more than ten thousand lines, are brimming with descriptions of the heavens. Scarcely any subject is evoked more frequently. The sun and reddening dawn's play of colour, day and night, cloud and lightning, the air and the ether, all these are unfolded before us over and over again, in splendour and vivid fullness. But there is only one thing that no one would ever learn from those ancient songs who did not already know it, and that is that the sky is blue'. So it was not just Homer who seemed to be blue-blind, but the ancient Indian poets too. And so, it would appear, was Moses, or at least whoever wrote the Old Testament. It is no secret, says Geiger, that the heavens play a considerable role in the Bible, appearing as they do in the very first verse – 'In the beginning God created the heavens and the earth' – and in hundreds of places after that. And yet, like Homeric Greek, biblical Hebrew does not have a word for 'blue'. Other colour depictions in the Old Testament also show deficiencies remarkably similar to those in the Homeric poems. Homer's oxen are wine-coloured – the Bible mentions a 'red horse' and a 'red heifer without spot'. Homer tells of faces 'green with fear' – the prophet Jeremiah sees all faces 'turned green' with panic. Homer raves about 'green honey' – the Psalms rove not far away, on 'the wings of a dove covered with silver, and her feathers with green gold'.* So whatever condition caused the deficiencies in Homer's descriptions of colour, it seems that the authors of the Indian Vedas and of the Bible must have had it too. In fact, the whole of humanity must have languished in that condition over the course of millennia, says Geiger, for the Icelandic sagas and even the Koran all bear similar traits.

But Geiger is only just beginning to gather momentum. Widening Gladstone's circle of evidence, he now dives into the murky deep of etymology, an area that he had made entirely his own, navigating it with more confidence than perhaps anyone else at the time. He shows that the words for 'blue' in modern European languages derive from two sources: the minority from words that earlier meant 'green' and the majority from words that earlier meant 'black'. The same coalescing of blue and black, he adds, can be seen in the etymology of 'blue' in languages further afield, such as Chinese. This suggests that at an earlier period in the his-

---

* Most Bible translations smooth over oddities such as 'green gold' (Psalms 68:13) and render the adjective יְרַקְרַק as 'yellow'. But the etymology of the word derives from plants and leaves, just like Homer's *chlôros.*

tory of all these languages, 'blue' was not yet recognised as a concept in its own right and was subsumed under either black or green.

Geiger proceeds to plumb successively deeper into the etymological past, to layers that lie beneath the pre-blue stage. Words for the colour green, he argues, extend a little further back into antiquity than for blue, but then disappear as well. He posits an earlier period, before the pre-blue stage, when green was not yet recognised as a separate colour from yellow. At an even earlier time, he suggests, not even 'yellow' was what it seems to us, since words that later come to mean 'yellow' had originated from words for reddish colours. In the pre-yellow period, he concludes, a 'dualism of black and red clearly emerges as the most primitive stage of the colour sense'. But even the red stage is not where it all starts, for Geiger claims that with the aid of etymology one can reach further back, to a time when 'even black and red coalesced into the vague idea of something coloured'.*

On the basis of a few ancient texts and supported only by inspired inferences from some faint etymological traces, he thus reconstructs a complete chronological sequence for the emergence of sensitivity to different prismatic colours. Mankind's perception of colour, he says, increased 'according to the schema of the colour spectrum': first came the sensitivity to red, then to yellow, then to green, and only finally to blue and violet. The most remarkable thing about it all, he adds, is that this development seems to have occurred in exactly the same order in different cultures all over the world. Thus, in Geiger's hands, Gladstone's discoveries about colour deficiencies in one ancient culture are transformed into a systematic scenario for the evolution of the colour sense in the whole human race.

Geiger went further than Gladstone in one other crucial respect. He was the first to pose explicitly the fundamental question on which the whole debate between nature and culture would centre for decades to come: the relation between what the eye can see and what language can

---

* Geiger seems somewhat confused about whether black and white should be considered real colours and about how they relate to the more general concepts of dark and bright. In this one respect, his analysis is a step backwards from Gladstone's masterly account of the primacy of dark and bright in Homer's language.

describe. Gladstone had simply taken it as read that the colours on Homer's tongue matched exactly the distinctions his eye was able to perceive. The possibility never even crossed his mind that there could be any discrepancy between the two. Geiger, on the other hand, realised that the relation between the perception of colour and its expression in language was an issue in need of addressing. 'What could be the physiological state of a human generation,' he asked, 'which could describe the colour of the sky only as black? Can the difference between them and us be only in the naming, or in the perception itself?'

His own answer was that it is highly unlikely that people with the same eyesight as us could nevertheless have made do with such strikingly deficient colour concepts. And since it is so unlikely, he suggests that the only plausible explanation for the defects in the ancients' colour vocabulary must be an anatomical one. Geiger thus rounds off his lecture by throwing down the gauntlet to his audience and challenging them to find the explanation: 'The fact that colour words emerge according to a definite succession, and that they do so in the same order everywhere, must have a common cause.' Now you naturalists and physicians go figure out the evolution of colour vision.

As we shall see a little later, clues from an unexpected source started cropping up shortly after Geiger's lecture, which – if anyone had taken notice – should have pointed to an entirely different way of explaining Gladstone's and Geiger's discoveries. There are some tantalising hints in Geiger's own notes that suggest he had become aware of these trails and was beginning to realise their importance. But Geiger died *in media vita*, only three years after delivering his lecture, while still in the thick of his research into the language of colour. The clues went unheeded, and instead the following decades would be spent in pursuit of a bright red herring.

❧

The person who decided to take up Geiger's challenge was an ophthalmologist by the name of Hugo Magnus, a lecturer in eye medicine at the Prussian university of Breslau. A decade after Geiger's lecture, in 1877, he published a treatise, *On the Historical Evolution of the Colour Sense*, which claimed to explain exactly how the human retina developed its sensitivity to colour over the course of the last few millennia. Magnus may not have been a thinker of Gladstone's or Geiger's stature, but what he lacked in genius he made up for in ambition, and it is largely to his credit that the question of the ancients' colour sense came into the public eye. His campaign to promote his ideas was greatly helped by a train of events which had nothing to do with any philological preoccupations but which nevertheless brought the subject of defective colour vision into the public arena with a resounding great crash.

On the night of 14 November 1875, two Swedish express trains collided on the single-track main line between Malmö and Stockholm. The late-running northbound train was due to make an unscheduled stop at a small station to let the southbound train pass. The train slowed on approach to the station, but then, instead of obeying the red stop light and coming to a complete halt, it suddenly sped out of the station again, ignoring the lineman who ran after it frantically waving a red lamp. A few miles later, near the small village of Lagerlunda, it collided head-on with the southbound express, causing nine deaths and many injuries. Such disasters on the fledgling railway system were a matter of great horrified fascination, and the accident was widely reported in the press. After an inquiry and trial, the stationmaster was duly convicted of negligence in his signalling, dismissed, and sentenced to six months in prison.

But that was not the end of the affair, for a real-life Sherlock Holmes, a specialist in the anatomy of vision from Uppsala University, had an alternative hypothesis for what had led to the accident. Frithiof Holmgren suspected that the reason for the unexplained behaviour of the northbound train was that the driver or the engine-man, who had been overheard shouting something to the driver as they were speeding out of the station, mistook the red stop light for a white go light because he had some form of colour blindness. Both the driver and the engine-man died in the crash, so the suspicion could not be verified directly. And needless to say, the railway authorities flatly denied that any of their employees could have had a problem distinguishing the colours of the signs without it having been detected earlier. But Holmgren per-

Train crash in Lagerlunda, Sweden, 1875

sisted and finally managed to persuade the director of one Swedish railway line to take him along on an inspection tour and let him test a large number of personnel.

Holmgren had devised a simple and efficient test for colour blindness that used a set of some forty skeins of wool in different hues (see figure 1 in insert). He would show people one colour and ask them to pick up all the skeins of similar colour. Those who picked unusual colours, or even just unduly hesitated in their choice, would immediately stand out. Of the 266 railway workers Holmgren tested on just one railway line, he found thirteen cases of colour blindness, among them a stationmaster and a driver.

The practical dangers of colour blindness in an age of a rapidly expanding rail network thus became acutely apparent, catapulting colour vision to a status of high public priority. The subject was rarely out of the newspapers, and within a few years governmental committees were formed in many countries, leading to mandatory testing for colour blindness among all railway and marine personnel. The climate could not have been more favourable for a book which implied that latter-day colour blindness was a vestige of a condition that had been universal in ancient times. And this was exactly the theory proposed in Hugo Magnus's 1877 treatise on the evolution of the colour sense. What Gladstone's groundbreaking chapter never managed in 1858 (most people never got beyond the second volume, and the chapter on colour was hidden at the end of the third), what even Geiger's rousing lecture failed to accomplish in 1867, Magnus and the Lagerlunda train crash achieved ten years later: the evolution of the colour sense turned into one of the hottest topics of the age.

Magnus's treatise purported to provide the anatomical nuts and bolts, or rather nerves and cells, to Gladstone's and Geiger's philological discoveries. The perception of the ancients, Magnus wrote, was similar to what modern eyes can see at twilight: colours fade, and even brightly coloured objects appear in indefinite grey. The ancients would have perceived the world in this way even in full daylight. To account for the refinements in the colour sense over the last millennia, Magnus adopted the same evolutionary model that Gladstone had relied on two decades earlier, that of improvement through practise. 'The retina's performance', he argued, 'was gradually increased by the continuously and incessantly penetrating rays of light. The stimulus produced by the unremitting pounding of the ether particles continually refined the responsiveness of the sensitive elements of the retina, until they stirred the first signs of colour perception.' These acquired improvements were inherited by the next generation, whose own sensitivity was further increased through practise, and so on.

Magnus then combined Gladstone's insights about the primacy of the opposition between light and dark with Geiger's chronological sequence for the emerging sensitivity to the prismatic colours. He claimed to know why the sensitivity to colour started with red and progressed gradually along the spectrum. The reason was simply that the long-wave red light is 'the most intense colour', the one with the highest energy. The energy of light, he said, decreases as one progresses along the spectrum from red to violet, and so the 'less intense' cooler colours could come into view only once the retina's sensitivity considerably improved. By the Homeric period, the sensitivity had got only to around yellow: red, orange, and yellow were fairly clearly distinguished, green was only beginning to be perceived, whereas blue and violet, the least intense colours, were 'still just as closed and invisible to the human eye as the ultra-violet colour is today'. But the process continued in the last few millennia, so that gradually, green, blue, and violet came to be perceived just as clearly as red and yellow. Magnus hypothesised that the process may still be ongoing, so that in future centuries the retina will extend its sensitivity to ultraviolet light as well.

Magnus's theory became one of the most ardently discussed scientific questions of the day and received support from a range of prominent figures in different disciplines. Friedrich Nietzsche, for instance, integrated the colour blindness of the Greeks into his philosophical edifice and drew from it fundamental insights about their theology and world view. Gladstone, now an ex–prime minister and at the height of his fame, was gratified to find a scientific authority so enthusiastically championing his findings of twenty years earlier and wrote a favourable review in the popular journal *The Nineteenth Century*, which ensured that the debate spilled over to other popular magazines and even the daily press.

The claim that the colour sense evolved only in the last millennia also received a considerable amount of support from eminent scientists, including some of the brightest luminaries in the evolutionary movement. Alfred Russel Wallace, the co-discoverer with Darwin of the principle of evolution by natural selection, wrote in 1877 that 'if the capacity of distinguishing colours has increased in historic times, we may perhaps look upon colour-blindness as a survival of a condition once almost universal; while the fact that it is still so prevalent is in harmony with the view that our present high perception and appreciation of colour is a comparatively recent acquisition'. Another stellar convert was Ernst Haeckel, the biologist who had proposed the theory that an embryo recapitulates the evolutionary development of the species. In a lecture to the Scientific Club of Vienna in 1878, Haeckel explained that 'the more delicate cones of the retina, which impart the higher colour-sense, have probably developed gradually only during the last millennia'.

THE NECK OF THE GIRAFFE

Looking back at Magnus's theory from today's vantage point, we cannot but wonder how such eminent scientists could have failed to pick up on the various rather odd things about it. But we have to put ourselves in the mind-set of the late nineteenth century and remember that much of what we take for granted nowadays, for instance about the physics of light or the anatomy of the eye, was a complete mystery to scientists just over a century ago. The distance between us and Magnus's contemporaries is even greater in all that concerns knowledge of biological heredity, or, as we call it today, genetics. And, since heredity is the pivot of the whole debate over language's place between nature and culture, if we are to understand this debate, we need to pause for a moment and try first to jump over the gap of imagination that separates us from the 1870s. This task is far from easy, since the gap is about as long as the neck of the giraffe.

We are all acquainted with the logic of 'just so' stories: the giraffe got his long neck because his ancestors stretched and stretched to reach higher branches, Kipling's elephant got his long trunk because the crocodile pulled his nose until it stretched and stretched, and Ted Hughes's lovelorn hare got his long, long ears from listening and listening, all through the night, for what his beloved, the moon, was saying high in the sky. Today's children realise at a fairly early stage that all this is only fireside fable. The main reason why the logic of such stories is confined to the nursery is a truth so universally acknowledged that hardly anyone even bothers to state it explicitly nowadays. This is the understanding that physical changes you undergo during your lifetime will not be passed on to your offspring. Even if you do manage to stretch your neck, like the Padaung women of Burma with their neck rings, your daughters will not be born with longer necks as a result. If you spend hours on end lifting weights, this will not make your sons be born with bulging muscles. If you waste your life staring at computer screens, you may ruin your own eyes but the damage will not be passed on to your children. And training your eye to recognise the finest shades of colour may make you a great art connoisseur, but it will have no effect on the colour vision of your newborn offspring.

But what – to paraphrase Gladstone – every child in our nurseries knows today was not even remotely obvious in the nineteenth century. In fact, the inheritance of acquired characteristics wasn't classed as fairy tale until well into the twentieth. Today, under the bright neon light of the genetics lab, when the human genome has been mapped, when scientists can twiddle their pincers to clone sheep and engineer soybeans, and when children learn about DNA in primary school, it is difficult to imagine the complete darkness in which even the greatest minds were groping just over a century ago in all that concerned life's recipe. Nobody knew which properties could be inherited and which could not, and nobody had any idea about the biological mechanisms that are responsible for transmitting properties down the generations. Many conflicting theories about the workings of heredity were doing the rounds at the time, but in this great cloud of unknowing, there seemed to be just one thing that everyone agreed on: that properties acquired during the lifetime of an individual could be inherited by the progeny.

Indeed, before natural selection came along, the inheritance of acquired characteristics had been the only available model for explaining the origin of species. The French naturalist Jean-Baptiste Lamarck proposed this model in 1802 and argued that species evolve because certain animals start exerting themselves in a particular way, and in so doing improve the functioning of specific organs. These successive improvements are then passed down the generations and eventually lead to the formation of new species. The giraffe, Lamarck wrote, contracted a habit of stretching itself up to reach the high boughs, 'and the results of this habit in all the individuals of the race, and over many generations, was that its neck became so elongated that it could raise its head to the height of six metres [nearly twenty feet] above the ground'.

In 1858, Charles Darwin and Alfred Russel Wallace jointly published papers that outlined the idea of evolution by natural selection, and proposed an alternative mechanism to Lamarck's evolution-through-stretching: the combination of accidental variations and natural selection. The giraffe, they explained, did not get its long neck by attempting to reach the foliage of higher shrubs and constantly stretching its neck for the purpose but rather because some of its ancestors that were accidentally born with longer necks than usual secured some advantage in mating or survival over their shorter-necked peers, and so when the going got tough, the longer-necked giraffes could outlive the shorter-necked ones. Darwin and Wallace's joint papers were followed a year later by Darwin's *Origin of Species*, and – so most people would assume nowadays – Lamarckian evolution was immediately dispatched to the nursery.

Strangely enough, however, one of the only things that the Darwinian revolution did not change (not for half a century, that is) was the universal belief in the inheritance of acquired characteristics. Even Darwin himself was convinced that the result of exertions in particular organs can be passed on to the next generation. Although he insisted that natural selection was the main mechanism that drives evolution, he actually assigned the Lamarckian model a role in evolution as well, albeit an ancillary one. In fact, Darwin even believed until the end of his life that injuries and mutilations could be inherited. In 1881, he published a short article on 'inheritance' in which he recounted reports about a gentleman, who 'when a boy, had the skin of both thumbs badly cracked from exposure to cold, combined with some skin disease. His thumbs swelled greatly, and when they healed they were misshapen, and the nails ever afterwards were singularly narrow, short, and thick. This gentleman had four children, of whom the eldest had both her thumbs and nails like her father's.' From the perspective of modern science, the only explanation for the story is that the man in question had a genetic disposition to a certain disease, which remained latent until he was frostbitten. What his daughter inherited, then, was not his injury, but this pre-existing genetic trait. But as Darwin knew nothing of genetics, he thought that the most plausible explanation for such stories was that the injuries themselves were passed on to the offspring. According to Darwin's own theory of heredity, this assumption was perfectly sensible, because he believed that each organ in the body manufactures its own 'germinal material' with information about its own hereditary properties. So it was only natural to conclude that if a certain organ is injured during the lifetime of an individual, it may fail to send its germinal material to the reproductive system, and so the offspring may be born without the proper recipe for building the organ in question.

The belief in the inheritance of acquired characteristics was virtually universal until the mid-1880s. Only after Darwin's death in 1882 were doubts starting to be raised, at first by one lone voice in the wilderness, the German biologist August Weismann. In 1887, Weismann embarked on his most notorious – and most often ridiculed – research project, the one that George Bernard Shaw lampooned as the 'three blind mice' experiment. 'Weismann began to investigate the point by behaving like the butcher's wife in the old catch,' Shaw explained. 'He got a colony of mice, and cut off their tails. Then he waited to see whether their children would be born without tails. They were not. He then cut off the children's tails, and waited to see whether the grand-children would be born with at least rather short tails. They were not, as I could have told him beforehand. So with the patience and industry on which men of science pride themselves, he cut off the grandchil-dren's tails, too, and waited, full of hope, for the birth of curtailed great-grandchildren. But their tails were quite up to the mark, as any fool could have told him beforehand. Weismann then gravely drew the inference that acquired habits cannot be transmitted.'

As it happens, Shaw greatly underestimated Weismann's patience and industry. For Weismann went on far beyond the third generation: five years later, in 1892, he reported on the still ongoing experiment, now at the eighteenth generation of mice, and explained that not a single one of the eight hundred bred so far had been born with an even slightly shorter tail. And yet, *pace* Shaw, it wasn't Weismann who was the fool but the world around him. Weismann, perhaps the greatest evolutionary scientist after Darwin, never for a moment believed the mice's tails would get shorter. The whole point of his perverse experi-ment was to prove this obvious point to an incredulous scientific com-munity, which persisted in its conviction that acquired characteristics and even injuries are inherited. Weismann's inspiration for the mice experiment was not the wife in the nursery rhyme but rather a tailless cat that was paraded to great acclaim before the Assembly of German Naturalist Scientists and Physicians in 1877 (the very year in which Hugo Magnus's book was published). This tailless cat was flaunted as walking proof that injuries can be inherited, for its mother was said to have lost her tail in an accident and it was alleged to have been born tailless in consequence.

The received opinion at the time was that, even if mutilations do not affect the immediate offspring, they will crop up somewhere further down the line. This was why Weismann felt obliged not to limit his experiment to children and grandchildren but rather to curtail generation upon generation of hapless mice. Still, as bizarre as it may sound to us today, even Weismann's endless genealogies of full-length mice tails did not manage to disabuse the scientific community of the belief in the heredity of injuries and mutilations. Nor did Weismann's myriad other arguments find much favour, such as his invoking at least a hundred generations of circumcised Jewish males, who betrayed no disposition to be born without the offensive appurtenance and had to undergo the operation to remove it with each generation afresh. Weismann's remained the minority view for at least two more decades, well into the twentieth century.

THE EYE OF THE MIND

Throughout the second half of the nineteenth century, the debate on the evolution of the colour sense was thus conducted entirely in the shadow of the assumption that acquired characteristics are inheritable. When Gladstone published his *Studies on Homer*, a year before *The Origin of Species* appeared, the mechanism that he proposed for the refinement of the colour sense relied on the only model of evolution available at the time: Lamarck's evolution-through-stretching. Gladstone's assertion that 'the acquired aptitudes of one generation may become the inherited and inborn aptitudes of another' was simply spouting received wisdom. Twenty years later, by the time Hugo Magnus came out with his anatomical explanation for the emergence of the colour sense, the Darwinian revolution was already in full swing. But Magnus's evolutionary model in 1877 was still identical to that proposed by Gladstone two decades earlier: it assumed that the retina's ability to perceive colours increased through training and practise and that this progressive training was then passed on from generation to generation. While this reliance on the Lamarckian model seems to us like a great cavity right in the middle of Magnus's theory, the flaw was not visible at the time. Evolution-through-stretching was not perceived as a direct contradiction to Darwinism, so the Lamarckian nature of Magnus's theory did not raise any eyebrows and was not attacked even by his critics.

Nonetheless, a few eminent Darwinists, not least Darwin himself, felt that Magnus's scenario was problematic on other grounds, principally because of the very short time span it assumed for the development of colour vision. It seemed implausible to these scientists that such a complex anatomical mechanism could have evolved so radically in the span of just a few millennia. Critical reviews of Magnus's scenario were thus not long in coming.

But if – as the critics argued – vision itself had not changed in historical times, how could one explain the deficiencies in ancient languages that Gladstone and Geiger had uncovered? The only solution was to reconsider the question that Geiger had raised in the previous decade: is it possible that people who could perceive colours just as we do still failed to distinguish in their language even between the most elementary of colours? For the first time, the question was now being thrashed out in earnest. Are the concepts of colour directly determined by the nature of our anatomy – as Gladstone, Geiger, and Magnus believed – or are they merely cultural conventions? The debate over Magnus's book was thus the start of the open war between the claims of nature and of culture on the concepts of language.

The opinion of Magnus's critics was that since vision could not have changed, the only explanation must be that the deficiencies in ancient colour descriptions were due to 'imperfections' in the languages themselves. Their argument, in other words, was that one cannot infer from language which colours the ancients were able to perceive. The first person who made this point explicitly was Ernst Krause, one of Darwin's earliest German disciples. But it was a biblical scholar, Franz Delitzsch, who put it most memorably when he wrote in 1878 that 'we see in essence not with two eyes but with three: with the two eyes of the body and with the eye of the mind that is behind them. And it is in this eye of the mind in which the cultural-historical progressive development of the colour sense takes place.'

The problem for the critics – whom we can dub somewhat anachronistically as the 'culturalists' – was that their proposed explanation seemed just as implausible as Magnus's anatomical scenario, perhaps even more so. For how can one imagine that people who saw the difference between purple and black, or green and yellow, or green and blue, simply could not be bothered to differentiate these colours in their language? The culturalists tried to make the idea more appealing by pointing out that even in modern languages we use idioms that are rather imprecise about colour. Don't we speak of 'white wine', for instance, even if we can see perfectly well that it is really yellowish green? Don't we have 'black cherries' that are dark red and 'white cherries' that are yellowish red? Aren't red squirrels really brown? Don't the Italians call the yolk of an egg 'red' (*il rosso*)? Don't we call the colour of orange juice 'orange', although it is in fact perfectly yellow? (Check it next time.) And another example that would not occur to people in the nineteenth century: would race relations between the 'dark browns' and 'pinkish browns' have been as tortured as between 'blacks' and 'whites'?

But a few haphazard idioms are still a long way off from the consistent 'defects' of the ancient texts, so by itself this argument was not very convincing. The culturalists thus sought supporting evidence from a different direction: not from language itself but from material facts that would show that the ancients saw all colours. Indeed, one ancient culture seemed to offer such evidence in plentiful supply. As one of the culturalists explained, a short visit to the British Museum is enough to demonstrate that the ancient Egyptians used blue paint. As it happens, Lazarus Geiger had already admitted in his lecture of 1867 that the Egyptians were an exception to the near-universal blue blindness of the ancients. He acknowledged that the Egyptians had a much more refined vocabulary of colour than other ancient cultures and that their language had words for 'green' and 'blue'. But that only showed, he argued, that the progressive refinement of colour vision started much earlier in Egypt than elsewhere. For after all, 'who would want to take the architects of the temple in Karnak as representatives of the state of humanity in a primitive stage?'

A more precious piece of evidence was lapis lazuli, a gemstone from the mountains of Afghanistan that was highly prized throughout the ancient Near East. The Babylonians, for example, referred to it as 'the treasure of the mountains' and valued it so highly that they would petition their gods with the words 'may my life be as precious to you as lapis lazuli'. Archaeological excavations from the palace in Mycenae, from a period much earlier than Homer's, proved that the Greek royalty were also in possession of small quantities of this gemstone. And while many other precious stones are at least partly transparent and thus can show various reflection effects, lapis lazuli is entirely opaque. Its main claim to beauty is its magnificent deep blue colour. But if the dwellers of the Mycenaean palace could not see blue, why should they have bothered about a stone that would have appeared to them just like any other polished pebble?

All these arguments, however, hardly impressed Magnus and his followers. In his replies to the culturalists, Magnus seemed merely to be summing up the common-sense view when he asserted that 'it does not seem plausible to us that a language which, like Homer's, possessed such a rich vocabulary for the most varied and subtle effects of light should not have been able to create for itself words for the most important colours'.

The culturalists needed more, an argument clincher. They needed incontrovertible proof that someone who saw all colours could still call honey and gold 'green', horses and cows 'red', and sheep 'violet'. And so they finally hit upon the idea of turning to the 'savages'.

3

The Rude Populations Inhabiting
Foreign Lands

Passers-by in the elegant Kurfürstendamm in Berlin on the morning of 21 October 1878, would have come across rather a funny sight. There, in front of the entrance to the zoo, was a large group of eminently bearded scientists waiting for a private tour. These gentlemen were the distinguished members of the Berlin Society for Anthropology, Ethnology, and Prehistory, and they had a special appointment to watch the hottest show in town. On display that day were not the stars of the regular menagerie or Knut the cuddly polar bear cub, but even more exotic creatures, never before exhibited in Europe. They had been imported by the circus impresario and animal dealer Carl Hagenbeck and had been put on view in zoos across the country, causing a sensation wherever they went. In Berlin alone, some sixty-two thousand people had come to watch the show in a single day.

What the throngs of wildly excited spectators flocked to see was a group of about thirty dark-skinned savages and their strange costumes (or lack thereof). They were called the 'Nubians' and were in fact a group of men, women, and children from the Sudan. Naturally, the anthropological society did not wish to share its business with hoi polloi, so Herr Hagenbeck kindly offered them a private viewing. And so it was that on this autumnal Monday morning the bearded gentlemen, armed with measuring tapes, rulers, and coloured skeins of wool, arrived at the zoo to slake their scientific curiosity. As practitioners of what would now be known as physical anthropology, the scientists were primarily interested in measuring sizes of noses and earlobes, shapes of genitals, and other such vital statistics of the rare specimens on display. But the other thing they were all agog to examine was the Nubians' sense of colour. For the controversy over Magnus's book was now in full swing, and it had finally dawned on the scientific community that the 'rude populations inhabiting foreign lands', as one American ethnologist put it, could hold the key to the mystery.

As it so happens, there had been clues lying around for almost a decade that suggested that ethnic groups from around the world could resolve the question of the ancients' colour sense. In 1869, two years after Geiger had revealed the remarkable parallels between the colour vocabularies of different ancient cultures, the newly established German *Journal of Ethnology* published a short note by Adolf Bastian, an anthropologist and best-selling travel writer. Bastian argued that oddities in the description of colours were not confined to ancient epics, since there were nations around that still marked the border between green and blue differently from Europeans. His servant in Burma, he wrote, 'apologised once that he couldn't find a bottle that I called blue (*pya*), because it was in fact green (*zehn*). In order to punish him by making him the object of ridicule of his peers, I reproached him in the presence of the other servants, but quickly noticed that the object of ridicule wasn't he but myself.' Bastian also argued that Tagalog speakers in the Philippines had not even distinguished between green and blue until the arrival of the Spanish colonisers, because the Tagalog words for 'green' and 'blue' were clearly recent borrowings from Spanish *verde* and *azul*. And he claimed that the language of the Teda tribe in Chad still did not distinguish green from blue at all.

Back in 1869, no one took much heed of Bastian's stories. But once the debate over Magnus's theory had flared up, the relevance of this information became apparent to the culturalists, and so suggestions were made that more information should be collected from peoples in remote corners of the globe. And thus it was that Rudolf Virchow, the founder and chairman of the Berlin Society for Anthropology, Ethnology, and Prehistory, took up the challenge by leading his entire society on the arduous trek across the Tiergarten to the Berlin Zoo, in order to check the Nubians first-hand. More intrepid scholars were extending the research beyond the confines of the zoo to examine the sense of colour of primitive peoples in situ. The first such investigation was carried out in the same year, 1878, by Ernst Almquist, a doctor on board a Swedish expedition ship that was ice-locked in the Polar Sea. As the ship was forced to winter just off the Chukchi Peninsula in eastern Siberia, Almquist made the most of the opportunity by testing the colour sense of the Chukchis, the nomadic reindeer herdsmen and seal hunters who inhabited the area. The Americans had it easier, because they had so many savages living right under their noses. Army doctors were instructed to test the colour sense of the Indian tribes with whom they came in contact, and their evidence was compiled into a detailed report by Albert Gatschet, the ethnologist of the US Geological Survey. In Britain, the science writer Grant Allen devised questionnaires to be sent to missionaries and explorers requesting that they provide data on the colour sense of the natives they encountered. And finally, faced with this direct challenge to his claims, Magnus himself decided to conduct a survey of his own and sent questionnaires accompanied by colour charts to hundreds of consulates, missionaries, and doctors all over the world.

When the results started coming in, they constituted – in one sense – the most spectacular confirmation of Gladstone's and Geiger's perspicacity. No one could any longer just brush off their findings as the overreaction of overly literal philologists, and no one could dismiss the peculiarities in the colour descriptions of ancient texts as merely instances of poetic licence. For the deficiencies that Gladstone and Geiger had uncovered were replicated exactly in living languages from all over the world. The Nubians that Virchow and his colleagues probed in the Berlin Zoo had no word for 'blue' at all. When they were shown a blue skein of wool, some of them called it 'black' and others called it 'green'. Some of them didn't even distinguish between yellow, green, and grey, calling all three colours by the same word.

In America, Albert Gatschet wrote that the Klamath Indians in Oregon were happy to use the same term for 'the colour of any grass, weed or plant, and though the plant passes from the green of spring time and summer into the faded yellow of autumn, the colour-name is not changed'. The Sioux from Dakota used the same word, *toto*, for both blue and green. This 'curious and very frequent coincidence of green and yellow, and of blue and green' was common among other American Indian languages as well.

Similar stories emerged from the questionnaires sent back by missionaries and travellers from other parts of the world. When they spoke about colours, many of the savages – or 'nature peoples', as the Germans kindly called them – betrayed exactly the same confusions that Gladstone and Geiger found in ancient texts. Even Geiger's bold evolutionary sequence, which he had deduced from the faintest etymological scraps of evidence, received a dramatic corroboration. Just as Geiger had anticipated, red was always the first of the prismatic colours to receive a name. Indeed, it transpired that there were peoples around even in the nineteenth century who had not yet progressed beyond the red stage. Ernst Almquist, the doctor of the Swedish expedition to the Polar Sea, reported that the Chukchis in Siberia were quite content with using just three terms – black, white, and red – to describe any colour. *Nukin*, the word for 'black', was used also for blue and all dark colours, as long as they did not contain a trace of red; *nidlikin* was used for white and all bright colours; and *tschetlju* for red and anything with a trace of reddish tint.

Further languages were discovered that corresponded exactly to the subsequent stages of development that Geiger had predicted: the inhabitants of the island of Nias in Sumatra, for example, were reported to use only four basic colour words: black, white, red, and yellow. Green, blue, and violet were all called 'black'. And some languages had black, white, red, yellow, and green, but no blue, just as Geiger had assumed.

Geiger, who had died in 1870, was not allowed to bask in posthumous glory, however. And no one was queuing up to pat the septuagenarian Gladstone on the back either. In fact, Geiger, Gladstone, and especially Magnus came under heavy fire, for it turned out they were as short-sighted as they were perspicacious. Their philological insights may have been vindicated, for languages across the world were behaving exactly as predicted. But the reports about the *eyesight* of the natives directly contradicted the assumption that defective vocabulary reflected defective colour vision, for no tribe was found that failed to *see* the differences between the colours. Virchow and the gentlemen of the Berlin anthropological society administered a Holmgren colour test to the Nubians and asked them to pick from a pile of wools those matching in colour to a master wool. None of the Nubians failed to pick the right colours. The same picture emerged with other ethnic groups. Admittedly, some reports about various tribes mentioned much greater hesitation in differentiating the cooler colours compared with reds and yellows. But no population, be they ever so rude, was found to be blind to these distinctions. The missionary who lived among the Ovaherero in Namibia, for instance, wrote that they could see the difference between green and blue but simply thought it was ridiculous that there should be different names for these two shades of the same colour.

What had seemed almost impossible to contemplate a few years before turned out to be a plain fact: people can spot the difference between different colours but can still fail to give them separate names. And surely, if that was the case with primitive tribes in the nineteenth century, it must have been the same with Homer and all the other ancients. The only possible conclusion was that, had Homer been administered a Holmgren test, he would have been able to spot the difference between green and yellow, just as he would have been able to tell apart purple wools from brown ones, had he been asked to do so by a German anthropologist.

But why then did he call his honey 'green' and his sheep 'purple'? The culturalists may have had their proof that the ancients could distinguish all colours, but they were less successful in formulating a convincing alternative explanation, for culture's assault on the concepts of colour still crashed against a solid wall of disbelief. Magnus now modified his counter-argument and declared that it was implausible that those primitive peoples perceived all colours *just as vividly* as Europeans. Instead of conceding colours to culture, therefore, Magnus offered a revised anatomical explanation. He admitted that the ancients and the natives of his own day could spot the difference between all colours, but he argued that the cooler colours still appeared to them duller than to modern Europeans (see figure 3 in the insert for an illustration of his revised theory). This lack of vividness, he said, would account for their lack of interest in finding separate names for such colours, and it would also explain the reports from the respondents to his questionnaires, which frequently mentioned the greater hesitation among the natives in distinguishing the cooler colours for which they had no names.

At the time, it was impossible to confirm or to disprove such claims empirically, for while it is easy to test whether someone can spot the difference between two colours or not, it is far more difficult to devise experiments that can tell exactly how vividly this distinction appears to different people. Certainly it was impossible to decide the question on the basis of the available evidence, which was mostly gathered from questionnaires. As no decisive new evidence was forthcoming, the heated discussion gradually subsided over the following years and the question of the colour sense remained in limbo for almost two decades, until the first attempt to conduct sophisticated experiments on the mental traits of natives in situ. Substantial progress had to wait for the 1898 Cambridge anthropological expedition to the Torres Straits, and for a remarkable man who finally swung established consensus in favour of culture – much against his better judgement.

RIVERS IN THE STRAITS

To most people who have heard of him, W. H. R. Rivers is the compassionate psychiatrist who treated Siegfried Sassoon during World War I.

Rivers worked at Craiglockhart Hospital near Edinburgh, where he was a pioneer in applying psychoanalytic techniques to help officers suffering from shell shock. Sassoon was sent to him in 1917 after being declared insane for publicly questioning the sanity of the war, throwing his Military Cross into the River Mersey, and refusing to return to his regiment. Rivers treated him with sympathy and understanding, and eventually Sassoon voluntarily returned to France. The affection, even devotion, that Rivers inspired in many of his patients seems to have lost none of its intensity years after the war. Sassoon, a man so fearless in battle that he was nicknamed Mad Jack, collapsed with grief at Rivers's funeral in 1922. And some forty years later, in July 1963, a frail old man called in at the library of St John's, Rivers's old Cambridge college, and asked to see his portrait, explaining that he had been treated by Rivers at Craiglockhart Hospital in 1917. According to the librarian's account, the man stood before the picture at the salute and thanked Rivers for all he had done for him. The visitor returned on at least two other occasions, and every time he asked to see the portrait. On his last visit he was obviously in poor health and finished with the words 'goodbye my friend – I don't suppose we shall ever meet again'.

But Rivers's vocation as the salve of shell-shocked souls came only later in life, after a distinguished career in two other fields: experimental psychology and then anthropology. It was the experimental psychologist Rivers who was invited in 1898 to join the Cambridge University anthropological expedition to the islands of the Torres Straits, between Australia and New Guinea. But while on the islands, he developed his interest in human institutions, and it was there that he began his seminal studies on kinship relations and social organisation, which are widely regarded as laying the foundations for the discipline of social anthropology and are what led Claude Lévi-Strauss to dub him the 'Galileo of anthropology'.

The aim of the Cambridge Torres Straits expedition was to shed light on the mental characteristics of primitive peoples. The fledgling discipline of anthropology was struggling to define its subject matter, 'culture', and to determine the boundaries between acquired and innate

W. H. R. Rivers with friends

aspects of human behaviour. In order to shed light on this question, it was essential to determine to what extent the cognitive traits of primitive people differed from those of civilised people, and the role of the expedition was to advance beyond the mostly anecdotal evidence that had been available before. As the leader of the expedition explained, 'For the first time trained experimental psychologists investigated by means of adequate laboratory equipment a people in a low stage of culture under their ordinary conditions of life.' The multi-volume meticulous reports that were published by Rivers and the other members in subsequent years helped to make the distinction between natural and cultural traits clearer, and the Torres Straits expedition is thus widely credited as the event that turned anthropology into a serious science.

Rivers's own reason for joining the expedition in 1898 was the opportunity to conduct detailed experiments on the eyesight of the natives. During the 1890s, he had been immersed in the study of vision, and so was keen to resolve the controversy over the colour sense, which had not progressed much in the previous two decades. He wanted to see for himself how the colour vision of the natives related to their colour vocabulary and whether the capacity for appreciating differences correlated with the power of expressing those differences in language.

Rivers spent four months on the remote Murray Island, at the eastern edge of the Torres Straits, right at the northern tip of the Great Barrier Reef. With a population of about 450, the island offered a manageably small community of friendly natives who were 'sufficiently civilised' to enable him to make all his observations and yet, as he put it, 'were sufficiently near their primitive condition to be thoroughly interesting. There is no doubt that thirty years ago they were in a completely savage stage, absolutely untouched by civilisation.'

What Rivers found in the colour vocabulary of the islanders fitted well with the reports from the previous twenty years. Descriptions of colour were generally vague and indefinite, and sometimes a cause of much uncertainty. The most definite names were for black, white, and red. The word for 'black', *golegole*, derived from *gole*, 'cuttlefish' (Rivers suggested that this referred to the dark ink secreted by the animal), 'white' was *kakekakek* (with no obvious etymology), and the word for 'red', *mamamamam*, was clearly derived from *mam*, 'blood'. Most people used *mamamamam* also for pink and brown. Other colours had progressively less definite and conventional names. Yellow and orange were called by many people *bambam* (from *bam*, 'turmeric'), but by others *siusiu* (from *siu*, 'yellow ochre'). Green was called *soskepusoskep* by many (from *soskep*, 'bile,' 'gallbladder'), but others used 'leaf colour' or 'pus colour'. The vocabulary for blue and violet shades was even vaguer. Some younger speakers used the word *bulu-bulu*, obviously a recent borrowing from English 'blue'. But Rivers reports that 'the old men agreed that their own proper word for blue was *golegole* (black)'. Violet was also mostly called *golegole*.

Rivers noted that often 'lively discussions were started among the natives as to the correct name of a colour'. When asked to indicate the names of certain colours, many islanders said they would need to consult wiser men. And when pressed to give an answer nevertheless, they simply tended to think of a name of particular objects. For example, when shown a yellowish green shade, one man called it 'sea green' and pointed to the position of one particular large reef in view.

The vocabulary of the Murray Islanders was clearly 'defective', but what about their eyesight? Rivers examined more than two hundred of them for their ability to distinguish colours, subjecting them to rigorous tests. He used an improved and extended version of the Holmgren wool test and devised a series of experiments of his own to detect any sign of inability to perceive differences. But he did not find a single case of colour blindness. Not only were the islanders able to distinguish between all primary colours, but they could also tell apart different shades of blue and of any other colour. Rivers's meticulous experiments thus demonstrated beyond any possible doubt that people can see the differences between all imaginable shades of colours and yet have no standard names in their language even for basic colours such as green or blue.

Surely, there could have been only one possible conclusion for such an acutely intelligent researcher to draw from his own findings: the differences in colour vocabulary have nothing to do with biological factors. And yet there was one experience which struck Rivers so forcefully that it managed to throw him entirely off track. This was the encounter with that weirdest of all weirdnesses, a phenomenon which philologists could infer only from ancient texts but which he met face to face: people who call the sky 'black'. As Rivers points out with amazement in his expedition reports, he simply could not grasp how the old men of Murray Island regarded it as quite natural to apply the term 'black' (*golegole*) to the brilliant blue of the sky and sea. He mentions with equal disbelief that one of the islanders, 'an intelligent native', was happy to compare the colour of the sky to that of dark dirty water. This behaviour, Rivers writes, 'seemed almost inexplicable, if blue were not to these natives a duller and a darker colour than it is to us'.

Rivers thus concluded that Magnus was right in assuming that the natives must still suffer from a 'certain degree of insensitiveness to blue (and probably green) as compared with that of Europeans'. Being such a scrupulous scientist, Rivers was not only aware of the weaknesses of his own argument but careful to air them himself. He explains that his own results proved that one cannot deduce from language what the speakers can see. He even mentions that the younger generation of speakers, who have borrowed the word *bulu-bulu* for 'blue', use it without any apparent confusion. And still, after acknowledging all such objections, he parries them with one fact, as if it were sufficient to undermine everything else: 'One cannot, however, wholly ignore the fact that intelligent natives would regard it as perfectly natural to apply the same name to the brilliant blue of the sky and sea which they give to the deepest black.'

LEGACY FRUIT AND OTHER THOUGHT EXPERIMENTS

At the last hurdle, then, Rivers's imagination simply lost its nerve and baulked at the idea that 'blue' is ultimately a cultural convention. He could not bring himself to concede that people who saw blue just as vividly as he did would still find it natural to regard it as a shade of black. And in all fairness, it is difficult to blame him, for even with the wealth of incontrovertible evidence at our disposal today, it is still very hard for us to muster the imagination needed to accept that blue and black seem separate colours just because of the cultural conventions we were reared on. Our deepest instincts and guttest of feelings yell at us that blue and black are *really* separate colours, as are green and blue, whereas navy blue and sky blue, for instance, are *really* just different shades of the same colour. So before we continue with the final episode of the quest for the origin of the colour sense, we can take a short break from the historical narrative and embark on three thought experiments that might help to make the power of cultural conventions sink in.

The first experiment is an exercise in counterfactual history. Let's imagine how the colour-sense debate might have unfolded had it been conducted not in England and Germany but in Russia. Imagine that a nineteenth-century Russian anthropologist, Yuri Magnovievitch Gladonov, goes on an expedition to the remote British Isles off the northern coast of Europe, where he spends a few months with the reclusive natives and conducts detailed psychological tests on their physical and mental skills. On his return, he surprises the Royal Academy of Sciences in St Petersburg with a sensational report. It turns out that the

natives of Britain show the most curious confusions in their colour terminology in the *siniy* and *goluboy* area of spectrum. In fact, the aboriginal population of those cloud-swept isles does not distinguish between
siniy and *goluboy* at all and calls them by the same name! At first,
Gladonov says, he assumed the natives had a defect in their vision, perhaps because of lack of sufficient sunlight during most of the year. But
when he tested their eyesight, he found that they could distinguish perfectly well between *siniy* and *goluboy*. It was just that they insisted on
calling both these colours 'blue'. If pressed to explain the difference
between these two colours, they would say that one was 'dark blue' and
the other 'light blue.' But they insisted it was 'ridiculous' to call these
two shades different colours.

Now, when the mirror is turned on our own linguistic vagueness,
the idea that our 'defective' colour vocabulary has anything to do with
defective eyesight immediately appears ludicrous. Of course English
speakers can see the difference between navy blue and sky blue. It's simply that their cultural conventions regard these as shades of the same
colour (even though the two colours actually differ by wavelength just
as much as sky blue does from green, as can be seen in the picture of the
spectrum in figure 11 in the insert). But if we can bring ourselves to
view the spectrum through Russian eyes and look at *siniy* and *goluboy*
as two separate colours, it might also become a little easier to empathise
with those clueless primitives who do not separate 'blue' from 'green', for
instance. Just as English lumps *goluboy* and *siniy* under one 'blue' concept, other languages extend this lumping principle to the whole green–
blue range. And if you happened to grow up in a culture where this
chunk of the spectrum has just one label, let's say 'grue', wouldn't it
seem silly that some languages treat leaf grue and sea grue as two separate colours rather than as two shades of the same colour?

⌒

The second thought experiment may require less imagination than the
first, but it needs some precious equipment. Rivers did not have children of his own, but it is tempting to think that if he had examined

Western children's struggles with colour, he might not have been so flummoxed by the Torres Strait islanders. Scientists have long been aware that children's acquisition of colour vocabulary is remarkably slow and laborious. And yet the acuteness of the difficulties never fails to amaze. Charles Darwin wrote that he had 'attended carefully to the mental development of my young children, and with two, or as I believe three of them, soon after they had come to the age when they knew the names of all common objects, I was startled by observing that they seemed quite incapable of affixing the right names to the colours in coloured engravings, although I tried repeatedly to teach them. I distinctly remember declaring that they were colour-blind, but this afterwards proved a groundless fear.' Estimates of the age at which children can reliably name the major colours have dropped considerably since the earliest studies a century ago, which reported the incredibly high figures of seven to eight years of age. According to modern surveys, children learn to use the main colour words reliably a lot earlier, in their third year. Nevertheless, what seems so strange is that by an age when children's linguistic ability is already fairly developed, they are still entirely thrown by colours. It is surprising to see how children who would effortlessly find a circle or square or triangle when asked to point at it, still react with complete bemusement when asked to pick out the 'yellow one' from a group of objects, and reach completely at random for whatever is closest at hand. With intense training, children in their second year can produce and use colour words accurately, but the dozens of repetitions required for learning the concept of colour as an attribute independent of particular objects contrast dramatically with the effortless ease with which children learn the names for the objects themselves – usually after hearing the names for them just once.

So what happens to children who grow up not in a culture that shoves brightly coloured plastic toys before their eyes and stuffs colour names down their ears, but rather in a culture where artificially manufactured colours are scarce and colour is of very limited communicative importance? Two Danish anthropologists who had once immersed themselves in the society of a Polynesian atoll called Bellona described their surprise at how rarely the Bellonese talked about colour with their children. When explaining the differences between objects such as fruits or fish, which to our mind would be most easily classified by their colour, the Bellonese hardly ever seemed to mention colour at all. The anthropologists could not resist asking why, but the only answer they got was 'we don't talk much about colour here'. Without such coaching in colours, it is perhaps not so surprising that Bellonese children end up being quite content with a very 'defective' inventory of colour names.

As it so happened, I started researching this book just as my elder daughter was learning to speak, and my obsession with colour meant she was trained intensely and so learned to recognise colour names relatively early on. Since there was one particular 'failure' that struck Gladstone, Geiger, and above all Rivers so forcefully, I decided to conduct a harmless experiment. Gladstone could not conceive how Homer failed to notice that 'most perfect example of blue', the southern sky. Geiger spent pages marveling at the absence of the sky's blueness in ancient texts, and Rivers could not get over the natives' designation of the sky as black. So I wanted to test how obvious the colour of the sky really was to someone who had not yet been culturally indoctrinated. I decided never to mention the colour of the sky to my daughter, although I talked about the colour of all imaginable objects until she was blue in the face. When would she hit upon it herself?

Alma recognised blue objects correctly from the age of eighteen months, and started using the word 'boo' herself at around nineteen months. She was used to games that involved pointing at objects and asking what colour they were, so I started occasionally to point upwards and ask what colour the sky was. She knew what the sky was, and I made sure the question was always posed when the sky was well and truly blue. But although she had no problems naming the colour of blue objects, she would just stare upwards in bafflement whenever I asked her about sky, and her only answer was a 'What are you talking about?' look. Only at twenty-three months of age did she finally deign to answer the question, but the answer was . . . 'white' (admittedly, it was a bright day). It took another month until she first called the sky 'blue', and even then it had not yet become canonically blue: one day she said 'blue', another day 'white', and on another occasion she couldn't make up her mind: 'blue', then 'white', then 'blue' again. In short, more than six months had passed from when she was first able to recognise blue objects confidently until she named the blueness of the sky. And it seems that her confusions were not entirely over even by the age of four, because at this age she once pointed at the pitch-black sky late at night and declared that it was blue.

Now consider how much easier her task was compared with Homer's or the Murray Islanders'. After all, Alma had been actively trained to recognise blueness in objects and had been explicitly taught that blue was a different colour from white or black or green. The only things she was required to do, therefore, were first to recognise that the sky had a colour at all, and then to work out that this colour was similar to the numerous blue objects she was surrounded with, rather than to black or white or green objects. Nevertheless, it still took her six months to work it out.

It is hard to say for certain where exactly the difficulty lay. Was it primarily the unfamiliar notion that a vast empty space, rather than a tangible object, can have a colour at all? Or was it that the pale unsaturated blue of the sky is actually very different from the highly saturated blues of artificial objects? Perhaps my anecdotal evidence will inspire others to examine this question more systematically. But even without the benefit of such research, the mere fact that Alma found this particular blueness so challenging makes it easier to imagine why people who may never have clapped eyes on blue objects do not lose much sleep over the colour of the sky. If that quintessence of azurity, that 'most perfect example of blue', is actually far from obvious even under conducive circumstances, then it seems far less surprising that people who have never seen an object with a colour similar to the sky fail to find a special name for this great expanse of nothingness. And if they are nevertheless pressed to give some answer by a nagging anthropologist, is it not natural that they would choose the closest colour label in their limited palette and say 'black' or 'green'?

The final exercise that can help to demonstrate the power of cultural conventions is a bit of science fiction fantasising. Imagine we are sometime in the distant future when every home is equipped with a machine that looks a bit like a microwave but in fact does far more than merely warm food up. It creates food out of thin air – or rather out of frozen stock cubes it teleports directly from the supermarket. Put a cube of fruit stock in the machine, for example, and at the touch of a few buttons you can conjure up any imaginable fruit: one button gives you a perfectly ripe avocado, another button a juicy grapefruit.

But this is an entirely inadequate way to describe what this wonderful machine can do, because it is by no means limited to the few 'legacy fruits' that were available in the early twenty-first century. The machine can create thousands of different fruits by manipulating the taste and the consistency on many different axes, such as firmness, juiciness, creaminess, airiness, sliminess, sweetness, tanginess, and many others that we don't have precise words to describe. Press a button, and you'll get a fruit that's a bit like an avocado in its oily consistency, but with a taste halfway between a carrot and a mango. Twiddle a knob, and you'll get a slimy lychee-like fruit with a taste somewhere between peach and watermelon.

In fact, even coarse approximations like 'a bit like X' or 'halfway between Y and Z' do not do justice to the wealth of different flavours that will be available. Instead, our successors will have developed a rich and refined vocabulary to cover the whole space of possible tastes and consistencies. They will have specific names for hundreds of distinct areas in this space and will not be bound by the few particular tastes of the fruit we happen to be familiar with today.

Now imagine that an anthropologist specialising in primitive cultures beams herself down to the natives in Silicon Valley, whose way of life has not advanced a kilobyte beyond the Google age and whose tools have remained just as primitive as they were in the twenty-first century. She brings along with her a tray of taste samples called the Munsell Taste System. On it are representative samples of the whole taste space, 1,024 little fruit cubes that automatically reconstitute themselves on the tray the moment one picks them up. She asks the natives to try each of these and tell her the name of the taste in their language, and she is astonished at the abject poverty of their fructiferous vocabulary. She cannot comprehend why they are struggling to describe the taste samples, why their only abstract taste concepts are limited to the crudest oppositions such as 'sweet' and 'sour', and why the only other descriptions they manage to come up with are 'it's a bit like an X', where X is the name of a certain legacy fruit. She begins to suspect that their taste buds have not yet fully evolved. But when she tests the natives, she establishes that they are fully capable of telling the difference between any two cubes in her sample. There is obviously nothing wrong with their tongue, but why then is their langue so defective?

Let's try to help her. Suppose you are one of those natives and she has just given you a cube that tastes like nothing you've ever tried before. Still, it vaguely reminds you of something. For a while you struggle to remember, then it dawns on you that this taste is slightly similar to those wild strawberries you had in a Parisian restaurant once, only this taste seems ten times more pronounced and is blended with a few other things that you can't identify. So finally you say, very hesitantly, that 'it's a bit like wild strawberries'. Since you look like a particularly intelligent and articulate native, the anthropologist cannot resist posing a meta-question: doesn't it feel odd and limiting, she asks, not to have precise vocabulary to describe tastes in the region of wild strawberries? You tell her that the only things 'in the region of wild strawberry' that you've ever tasted before were wild strawberries, and that it has never crossed your mind that the taste of wild strawberries should need any more general or abstract description than 'the taste of wild strawberries'. She smiles with baffled incomprehension.

If all this sounds absurd, then just replace 'taste' with 'colour' and you'll see that the parallel is quite close. We do not have the occasion to manipulate the taste and consistency of fruit, and we are not exposed to a systematic array of highly 'saturated' (that is, pure) tastes, only to a few random tastes that occur in the fruit we happen to know. So we have not developed a refined vocabulary to describe different ranges of fruity flavour in abstraction from a particular fruit. Likewise, people in primitive cultures – as Gladstone had observed at the very beginning of the colour debate – have no occasion to manipulate colours artificially and are not exposed to a systematic array of highly saturated colours, only to the haphazard and often unsaturated colours presented by nature. So they have not developed a refined vocabulary to describe fine shades of hue. We don't see the need to talk about the taste of a peach in abstraction from the particular object, namely a peach. They don't see the need to talk about the colour of a particular fish or bird or leaf in abstraction from the particular fish or bird or leaf. When we do talk about taste in abstraction from a particular fruit, we rely on the vaguest of opposites, such as 'sweet' and 'sour'. When they talk about colour in abstraction from an object, they rely on the vague opposites 'white/ light' and 'black/dark'. We find nothing strange in using 'sweet' for a wide range of different tastes, and we are happy to say 'sweet a bit like a mango', or 'sweet like a banana', or 'sweet like a watermelon'. They find nothing strange in using 'black' for a wide range of colours and are happy to say 'black like a leaf' or 'black like the sea beyond the reef area'.

In short, we have a refined vocabulary of colour but a vague vocabulary of taste. We find the refinement of the former and vagueness of the latter equally natural, but this is only because of the cultural conventions we happen to have been born into. One day, others, who have been reared in different circumstances, may judge our vocabulary of taste to be just as unnatural and just as perplexingly deficient as the colour system of Homer seems to us.

CULTURE'S TRIUMPH

If it now feels a little easier to appreciate the power of culture over the concepts of language, then we can return to our story just in time to witness the outright triumph of culture in the early twentieth century. For it is an irony of history that while Rivers himself was unable to grasp the full force of culture, it was his work that was largely responsible for securing culture's victory. In the end, what made the real impression was not Rivers's agonised interpretation of the facts he was reporting but the force of the facts themselves. His expedition reports were so honest and so meticulously thorough that others could look through his argumentation and reach exactly the opposite conclusion from the facts: that the islanders could see blue and all other colours just as clearly and vividly as we do and that their indistinct vocabulary of colour had nothing to do with their vision. In the following years, some influential reviews of Rivers's work appeared in America, where the vanguard of anthropological research was now forming. These reviews finally established a consensus about the universality of colour vision among different races and, by implication, about the stability of colour vision in the previous millennia.

This developing consensus was also corroborated by advances in physics and biology, which had exposed the critical flaws in Magnus's scenario of recent refinements in colour vision. The Lamarckian nature of Magnus's model now emerged as just one of the gaping holes in his Emmental of a theory. Magnus's physics of light, for example, turned out to be entirely upside down (or, rather, violet-side red). He had assumed that red light was the easiest colour to perceive because it had the highest energy. But by 1900, it had become clear through the work of Wilhelm Wien and Max Planck that the long-wave red light actually has the *lowest* energy. Red is in fact the coolest light: a rod of iron glows red only because it is not yet *very* hot. Older and cooler stars glow red (red dwarves), whereas really hot stars glow blue (blue giants). It is actually the violet end of the spectrum that has high energy, and ultraviolet light has even higher energy, enough in fact to damage the skin, as we are constantly reminded nowadays. Magnus's belief that the retina's sensitivity to colours increased *continuously* along the spectrum also proved to be misguided, since, as explained in the appendix, our perception of colour is based on only three distinct types of cells in the retina, called cones, and everything suggests that the development of these cones proceeded not continuously but in discrete leaps.

In short, by the first decades of the twentieth century it had become clear that the tall story about recent physiological changes in vision had been a red herring. The ancients could see colours just as well as we do, and the differences in colour vocabulary reflect purely cultural developments, not biological ones. Just as one Great War was beginning in the political arena, another great war seemed to have ended in the realm of ideas. And culture was the outright winner.

But culture's triumph did not solve all mysteries. In particular, it left one riddle dangling: Geiger's sequence. Or rather, it should have done.

til-la ša-du₁₁-ba-ta ud-da an-ga-me-a.

The life of yesterday was repeated today.

(Sumerian proverb, early second millennium BC)

ḥr ntt rf wḥmw ḏddwt, i̓w ḏddwt ḏd(w).

What is said is just repetition, what has been said has been said.

('The Complaints of Khakheperre-seneb',
Egyptian poem, early second millennium BC)

מַה שֶׁהָיָה הוּא שֶׁיִּהְיֶה וּמַה שֶׁנַּעֲשָׂה הוּא שֶׁיֵּעָשֶׂה וְאֵין כָּל חָדָשׁ
תַּחַת הַשָּׁמֶשׁ. יֵשׁ דָּבָר שֶׁיֹּאמַר רְאֵה זֶה חָדָשׁ הוּא כְּבָר הָיָה
לְעֹלָמִים אֲשֶׁר הָיָה מִלְּפָנֵנוּ. אֵין זִכְרוֹן לָרִאשֹׁנִים וְגַם לָאַחֲרֹנִים
שֶׁיִּהְיוּ לֹא יִהְיֶה לָהֶם זִכָּרוֹן עִם שֶׁיִּהְיוּ לָאַחֲרֹנָה

What has been is what will be, and what has been done is what will be done; there is nothing new under the sun. Even if there is anything of which one might say, 'See this, it is new,' it has already existed in ages that have gone before us. There is no memory of those in the past; of those in the future there will be no memory among those who will come afterwards.

(Ecclesiastes 1:9, *c.* third century BC)

Nullum est iam dictum, quod non dictum sit prius.

Nothing is now said that has not been said before.

(Terence, *The Eunuch*, 161 BC)

Pereant qui ante nos nostra dixerunt.

Perish those who said our things before us.

(Aelius Donatus, commentary on Terence, fourth century AD)

4

Those Who Said Our Things Before Us

The year 1969 was particularly blessed with momentous historical events: man landed on the moon, I was born, and a little book called *Basic Color Terms: Their Universality and Evolution* was published in Berkeley and became an instant sensation in linguistics and anthropology. Such was its revolutionary impact that forty years later, most linguists believe that the study of colour started in the summer of '69. And even those who are vaguely aware that anyone had given any thought to the subject before *Basic Color Terms* would still consider the pre-1969 period as distant prehistory, a Dark Age of no relevance or consequence except perhaps for ancient historians. To appreciate why one book had such an explosive effect, we have to step back to where our story left off and witness the curious fate that befell Geiger's sequence in the early decades of the twentieth century. Or, to be more precise, we have to diagnose one of the severest cases of collective amnesia in the history of science.

It would be natural to expect that once culture had asserted its authority over the concepts of colour, an obvious question would land at the top of everyone's to-do list: why do the colour names of so many unrelated languages nevertheless evolve in such a predictable order? If each culture can refine its colour vocabulary according to its whim and special circumstances, then why do peoples from the polar regions to the tropics, from Africa to America, always have a word for red, for instance, even if they have names for no other prismatic colour? Why are there no desert languages with a name just for yellow but not for anything else? Why are there no jungle languages with names only for green, brown, and blue? The old explanation for Geiger's sequence, which blamed it on the evolution of the retina during the last millennia, was now off the table. But if it was not the gradual refinement of vision that determined the order in which colour names emerge, an alternative explanation for Geiger's evolutionary progression was needed. Surely, then, the search for this explanation would now become the most pressing task on the agenda.

But linguists and anthropologists had other agendas. Instead of trying to solve the question, they chose to ignore it. It was as if the whole research community had fallen under an enchantment of forgetfulness, for within a few years Geiger's sequence simply faded from consciousness and was never heard of again. This turn of events may seem barely comprehensible at first, but it must be viewed in the context of the seismic shifts in world view that the human sciences were undergoing at the time: the profound changes in attitudes towards so-called savages and the growing abhorrence of any hierarchies that graded ethnic groups according to their alleged degree of evolution, a term that among anthropologists was rapidly becoming a dirty word.

The received opinion in the nineteenth century had been that the 'savages' were anatomically inferior to civilised people, and that they were not fully evolved humans. It was widely assumed that various ethnic groups around the globe simply represented earlier way stations in the biological evolution of European man. The attitudes of the outgoing century were nowhere better summed up than in the huge exhibition that took place in the first years of the new century – the Louisiana Purchase Exposition of 1904. This grand event, the greatest world fair to date, was held in St Louis, Missouri, to commemorate the centenary of the Louisiana Purchase (Thomas Jefferson's acquisition from Napoleon of a huge chunk of the North American continent). One of the main highlights of the Louisiana Purchase Exposition was an unprecedentedly large anthropological display. Exotic ethnic groups from all over the world were brought to St Louis and exhibited in separate 'villages' arranged according to their alleged degree of evolution. The official report of the exposition explained its choice of the range of races on display in the following words (take a big breath!): 'The physical types chosen for representation were those least removed from the sub-human or quadrumane [ape] form, beginning with the pygmy aborigines of Africa, and including the negrito folk of interior Mindanao [Philippines]; the Ainu of the northern island of the Japanese Archipelago . . . and varying physical types among North American natives.'

As hard as such sentiments are to comprehend in retrospect, they were not at odds with the scientific assumptions of the time. Given the general belief in the inheritance of acquired characteristics, it was only natural to conclude that primitiveness was a state one is born *with*, not merely born *into*. For if the mental attitudes of one generation affect the offspring's heredity, then it follows fairly logically that primitiveness is a biologically inherited condition, not just a state of education. It was widely accepted, for example, even among the most enlightened of scientists, that mental traits such as tendency towards superstition, lack of inhibition, and lack of powers of abstraction were all *hereditary* traits that characterised the 'low savages'.

All this began to change, however, in the early years of the new century. As doubts about the inheritance of acquired characteristics increased, the belief in biological primitiveness was gradually laid to rest and made way for a new understanding of culture's sovereignty over mental traits. In America, it was now being explicitly proclaimed as a tenet of anthropological science that culture was the only admissible factor in explaining mental differences between ethnic groups. The gulf between the old and new attitudes is nowhere more apparent than in the differences between the official report of the Louisiana Purchase Exposition and an alternative account by the psychologist Robert Woodworth from Columbia University, the centre of the new American anthropology. Woodworth had been inspired by Rivers's experimental methods with the Torres Strait islanders (though not impressed by Rivers's interpretation of his results) and decided to use the gathering of so many different ethnic groups in St Louis to conduct his own examinations. He tested hundreds of people from different races and ethnic types, not just for vision but also for many other mental processes. His findings about those whom the official report characterised as 'least removed from the sub-human' were published in the magazine *Science* in 1910 and may now appear as the most banal statement of the obvious, but at the time they seemed so radical that they had to be hedged with a profusion of 'maybe's', 'possibly's', and 'probably's'. The underlying message was crystal clear nonetheless: 'We are probably justified in inferring that the sensory and motor processes, and the elementary brain activities, though differing in degree from one individual to another, are about the same from one race to another.'

While this new understanding may not have immediately sunk into the public consciousness, in the scientific community the changes in attitude were fairly rapid. The new anthropology required each culture to be understood on its own terms, as a product of its own evolution rather than as merely an earlier stage in the ascent towards Western civilisation. Gradations of different cultures were decidedly out, and anything that smacked of the old evolutionary hierarchy from ape to European man was now being treated with suspicion and distaste.

⌒

Unfortunately, Geiger's evolutionary progression was felt to be exactly such an unwanted hangover. The hypothesis of a common order in the development of colour vocabulary (black and white > red > yellow > green > blue) seemed to be committing the worst sins of the past: it placed different languages on a straight hierarchy in which the simplest cultures, with the fewest colour names, were at the bottom, and European languages, with their refined and sophisticated colour vocabulary, were at the top. What is worse, Geiger's sequence inevitably made the colour systems of primitive peoples appear like mere way stations on the road towards European civilisation. In the new intellectual climate, such an evolutionary hierarchy was an embarrassment. And the thought that in this particular case the hierarchy might actually be true must have made the embarrassment all the more painful. The temptation to forget about it was hard to resist, and as it turned out, an excuse for doing just that was not too difficult to come by. A suggestion was made that Geiger's sequence may have been just a coincidence: the precedence of red over yellow, for instance, may just have been an accident of the sample of languages for which information happened to be available. Perhaps when a larger number of languages were examined, so the new argument ran, some would be found to have acquired a name for yellow before red. Not that anyone did find such languages, then or later (although one aspect of Geiger's sequence did eventually require modification, as we shall see in a moment). But merely the hope that counterexamples might crop up one day was considered a good enough reason not to bother with explaining the inconvenient parallels in the development of colour vocabulary among so many unrelated languages. Geiger was thus thrown out with the dirty bathwater of nineteenth-century bigotry.

In the decades following the First World War, Geiger's sequence was simply erased from memory, as was the whole protracted debate of the nineteenth century. All that now remained was one mantra: colour vocabularies vary greatly between cultures. The deep similarities that underlie those differences no longer seemed to be worth a mention, and each culture was now claimed to carve up the spectrum entirely according to its whim. In 1933, the leading American linguist of the generation, Leonard Bloomfield, stated the now established creed with confidence: 'Physicists view the colour-spectrum as a continuous scale, but languages mark off different parts of this scale quite arbitrarily.' The equally eminent Danish linguist Louis Hjelmslev echoed Bloomfield a decade later, asserting that each language 'arbitrarily sets its boundaries' on the spectrum. By the 1950s, the formulations became even more extreme. The American anthropologist Verne Ray declared in 1953 that 'there is no such thing as a "natural" division of the spectrum. The colour systems of man are not based upon psychological, physiological, or anatomical factors. Each culture has taken the spectral continuum and has divided it upon a basis which is quite arbitrary.'

How could such piffle be spouted by sober scientists? Just imagine what these statements would actually mean if they were true. Suppose the colour concepts of each language were really arbitrary and there was nothing natural about them at all. We could then expect that any random way of carving up the spectrum would have the same likelihood of being adopted by languages around the world. But is this the case? Let's take a simple example. English has three colour concepts, 'yellow', 'green', 'blue', that divide the relevant part of the colour space roughly as shown in figure 4a in the insert.

Now, if that division were merely arbitrary, we would expect it to be no more common among the world's languages than, say, the division into: 'grellow' (green + yellow), 'turquoise', and 'sapphire', roughly as in figure 4b in the insert.

So are there dozens of languages that do things roughly like English, and none reported with the alternative division?

If this example sounds too Anglocentric, consider a more exotic one. We have already seen that there are languages that divide the whole colour space into just three concepts. If colours really were arbitrary, then one would expect that any three-way partition of the colour space would be just as likely to be adopted by languages around the globe. In particular, we would expect the following two options to be found with roughly equal frequency. The first option (figure 5a) is represented by the language of Bellona, the Polynesian atoll that I mentioned earlier. The three concepts of Bellonese divide the colour space as follows: 'white', which includes also all very bright colours; 'black', which also includes purple, blue, brown, and green; and 'red', which also includes orange, pink, and dark yellow. The second option (figure 5b) is said to be found in another island language with which we are also familiar. In Ziftish, the division differs from Bellonese in one important detail: green belongs with 'red' rather than with 'black'. In other words, the 'red' concept in Ziftish includes red, orange, pink, dark yellow, and green, whereas the 'black' concept includes just black, purple, blue, and brown. Now, if each culture really set the boundaries between colours 'quite arbitrarily', then we would expect the Ziftish way to be just as common as the Bellonese. So why is it that there are dozens of languages that behave like Bellonese but not a single one is known to behave like the proverbial Ziftish?

For decades such facts were considered beneath the notice of serious scholars, and the claims about the arbitrary concepts of colour were promulgated unchallenged in textbooks and lecture halls. The theory of arbitrariness may have had no legs to stand on, nor bottom, nor back. But as with the chair in the ditty, the theory just sat, ignoring little things like that.

⌒

All that changed in 1969, when a little book by two researchers from Berkeley, Brent Berlin and Paul Kay, rudely interrupted half a century of blissful oblivion and reinvented the spectrum. Having sensed the absurdity of the claims about arbitrariness in colour vocabulary, Berlin and Kay set out to do some systematic comparisons: they collected judgements about colour names from informants in twenty different languages, using an array of coloured chips as in figure 6 in the insert.

Their analysis led them to two startling discoveries, and as the news of these discoveries began to spread, their book was heralded as a new dawn in the study of language, a revolutionary breakthrough, a watershed that would transform both linguistics and anthropology. One reviewer wrote: 'It seems no exaggeration to claim for Berlin and Kay's *Basic Color Terms* a place among the most remarkable discoveries of anthropological science.' And another added: 'Only very occasionally is a discovery as ostensibly significant and important as that reported in *Basic Color Terms*. . . . Either of [Berlin and Kay's two main] findings would be startling, but attending both in a single small book is truly amazing.'

What were those two amazing findings? First, Berlin and Kay discovered that colour terms were not so arbitrary after all. Although there are considerable variations between the colour systems of different languages, some ways of dividing the spectrum are still far more natural than others: some are adopted by many unrelated languages while others are not adopted by any.

It was their second discovery, however, that left the academic community reeling. This was the revelation, which Berlin and Kay themselves termed a 'totally unexpected finding', that languages acquire the names for colours in a predictable order. To be more precise, Berlin and Kay discovered the sequence that Lazarus Geiger had postulated 101 years before and that in Magnus's hands turned into the subject of intense and protracted debate in the last decades of the nineteenth century.

Admittedly, Berlin and Kay's evolutionary sequence differed from their predecessors' in a few details. First, they refined Geiger's prediction about yellow and green. Geiger thought that yellow always receives a name before green, but Berlin and Kay's data revealed that some languages actually develop a name for green before yellow. So they added an alternative sequence and allowed for two different paths of evolution:

black and white > red > yellow > green > blue
black and white > red > green > yellow > blue

On the other hand, Berlin and Kay also attempted to make a few additions to Geiger's sequence that eventually turned out not to have been improvements. They believed, for instance, that the universal sequence can be extended to other colours and claimed that brown is the colour that always receives a separate name after blue and that either pink, purple, orange, or grey is always the colour that comes after brown.

Notwithstanding such cosmetic differences, Berlin and Kay rediscovered Geiger's 101-year-old sleeping beauty essentially unchanged and woke it up with a smacking great kiss. Of course, no one dreamed of calling it Geiger's sequence anymore, as Geiger's claims on it had been erased from the collective consciousness. Instead, the progression is now universally known as 'Berlin and Kay, 1969'. But matters of copyright aside, the sequence that had dogged the debate in the nineteenth century suddenly trotted back on stage and demanded explanation: why do so many languages acquire colour words in the same

order, and why – underlying the variation – is there still so much similarity between the colour concepts of different languages?

Berlin and Kay's response to these questions swung the pendulum
all the way back to nature. After half a century in which culture not
only enjoyed the fruits of its rightful victory but was hailed as an absolute monarch with unlimited powers, Berlin and Kay went almost all the
way back to Gladstone's original belief that 'our own primary colours
have been given to us by Nature'. They did not deny, of course, that cultures can vary in how they set the boundaries between colours. But they
argued that underlying the superficial divergence in boundaries, there
is a far deeper communality, indeed universality, that was revealed in
what they called the 'foci' of the different colours.

Their notion of 'focus' was based on an intuition that we all share,
namely that some shades are better or 'more typical' examples of a given
colour than others. There may be millions of different shades of red, for
instance, but we still feel that some of these are redder than others. If you
were asked to choose the best example of red from the chart in figure 6,
it is unlikely that you would choose a bordeaux colour like H5 or a pale
pinkish red like D1. While both of these are undoubtedly red, you would
probably point at some shade in the area of G1 as a better example. Similarly, we feel that a grassy green in the region of F17 is greener than some
other greens. Berlin and Kay thus defined the focus of each colour as the
particular shade that people feel is the best example of this colour.

When they asked speakers of different languages to point at the best
examples of various colours, there was surprising cross-cultural
similarity in the choice of foci. The case of blue and green was
particularly striking. There are many languages that don't make a
distinction between green and blue and treat these as shades of one
colour. One of them is Tzeltal, a Mayan language from Mexico that uses
one term, *yaš*, for the whole 'grue' area. One might expect that when
Tzeltal speakers are asked to choose the best example of *yaš*, they would
point at something right in the middle of this range, a perfect turquoise
halfway between green and blue, say around F24. But of the forty Tzeltal
speakers who were tested, not a single one chose a turquoise focus.
Instead, the majority pointed at clear green shades (mostly in the area

of G18–20, which is a darker focus than what English speakers tend to choose for green, but is nevertheless a pure green rather than a bluish green), and a minority of Tzeltal speakers pointed to clear blue shades as the best example of *yaš* (mostly in the area of G–H/28–30). Berlin and Kay concluded from this behaviour that there was something natural and universal about our 'green' and 'blue' after all, since even speakers of languages that treat them as just one colour still choose either clear green or clear blue as prototypical examples, whereas no one feels there is anything special about turquoise.

Since Berlin and Kay also found strong agreement about the foci of other colours among the informants from the twenty languages that they tested, they concluded that these foci were universal constants of the human race that are biologically determined and independent of culture. There is an inventory of exactly eleven natural foci, they claimed, that correspond exactly to the eleven basic colours of English: white, black, red, green, yellow, blue, brown, purple, pink, orange, and grey.

Berlin and Kay did not provide an actual explanation for the particular order in which the foci receive names. This, they said, was a matter for future research. But they did claim they knew where the explanation must be sought: in the nature of human vision. The only thing that culture was free to choose, they said, was how many of these foci receive separate names (and what labels to give them, of course). Once a culture has decided on a number, nature takes care of all the rest: it dictates which foci will receive names, it dictates in which order, and it draws the rough boundaries around these foci according to a predetermined design.

⌒

Like any pendulum worth its weight, received opinion finds it difficult to swing from one extreme position and settle directly in the middle, without first hurtling all the way to the opposite extreme. In the years following the 1969 revolution, lecture halls resounded with the new creed, and textbooks proclaimed – just as ardently as they had preached the diametrically opposed position in previous years – that colour terms were natural and universal after all. Colour was now hailed as the most striking example for the conceptual unity of mankind, and the language of colour was declared as the trump argument in the wider nature versus culture debate, which was now being settled squarely in favour of nature.

Berlin and Kay's book inspired many researchers to re-examine the concepts of colour in many more languages, and in far greater detail and with greater accuracy than anything attempted before 1969. In the following decades, speakers' intuitions about borders and foci in dozens of languages were systematically collected and compared. But as the number of languages grew from the twenty in Berlin and Kay's original sample, and as the methods of elicitation became more sophisticated, it gradually emerged that the situation was less straightforward than Berlin and Kay had initially proposed. In fact, most of the categorical claims from 1969 about absolute universals in colour naming had to be watered down in subsequent years.

To start with, it turned out that many languages contradict Berlin and Kay's extensions to Geiger's sequence, for they show that brown is not always the first colour to receive a name after blue. What is more, later revisions had to abandon the claim that there are exactly eleven universal foci that correspond neatly to the English colours white, black, red, green, yellow, blue, brown, purple, pink, orange, and grey. In light of the new data, the alleged universal status of five of the foci – brown, purple, pink, orange, and grey – could no longer be defended, and the revised theory concentrated only on the six 'major' foci: white, black, red, green, yellow, and blue. But even with these major colours, the foci turned out to be less uniform across languages than Berlin and Kay had initially assumed, as speakers' choices in some languages strayed significantly from what were meant to be the universal foci. And finally, the larger database revealed languages that lump together under one concept combinations of foci that were deemed impossible in Berlin and Kay's original model. There are languages, for instance, that have one colour term that covers the light colours yellow, light green, and light blue. All in all, while some of the original rules formulated by Berlin and Kay still hold as strong tendencies among languages, hardly any of their claims remained intact as a universal law without exceptions.

FREEDOM WITHIN CONSTRAINTS

After so much to-ing and fro-ing, from nature to culture, and back, and again, where has the debate ended up? The belief that colour naming follows absolute natural laws has turned out to be wishful thinking, as there are exceptions to almost all the rules. And yet the similarities among languages in the choice of foci are still far too striking to be dismissed as haphazard: the great majority of languages still behave in a highly predictable way that would be hard to explain if cultures were free to divide the colour concepts entirely at whim. This uneasy balance between conformity and divergence is particularly evident in the order in which colour names evolve in different languages. On the one hand, the larger sample of languages reveals exceptions to almost all the predictions: the only rule that has remained truly without exceptions is that red is always the first colour (after black and white) to receive a name. On the other hand, the great majority of languages conform to Geiger's sequence or to the alternative of green before yellow, and this cannot be a mere coincidence.

So the data that have emerged over the past decades leave neither side in the debate – neither culture vultures nor nativist nerds – entirely satisfied. Or, rather, both sides are happy and in business, since they can continue arguing to their hearts' content about whether colour concepts are determined *primarily* by culture or *primarily* by nature. (Academics don't make careers by agreeing with one another.) But anyone who reviews the evidence with a modicum of impartiality will realise that each side simply lays claim to a part of the truth: both culture and nature have legitimate claims on the concepts of colour, and neither side enjoys complete hegemony.

In light of all the evidence, it seems to me that the balance of power between culture and nature can be characterised most aptly by a simple maxim: culture enjoys freedom within constraints. Culture has a considerable degree of freedom in dissecting the spectrum, but still within loose constraints laid down by nature. While the precise anatomical basis of these constraints is still far from understood, it is clear that nature hardly lays down inviolable laws for how the colour space *must* be divided.* Rather, nature suggests optimal prototypes: partitions that are sensible given the idiosyncrasies of the eye's anatomy. The colour systems that are common among the world's languages orbit within reasonable distance of these optimal partitions, but languages do not have to follow the prototypes to the letter, so nature's guidelines can be supplemented or perhaps even overridden by cultural choices.

The explanation for Geiger's sequence should also be sought in a balance between natural constraints and cultural factors. There is undoubtedly something biologically special about our relation to red: like other Old World monkeys, humans seem to be designed to get excited by it. I once saw a sign in a zoo that warned people dressed in red not to venture too close to the cage of a gorilla. And experiments with humans have shown that exposure to red induces physiological effects such as increasing the electrical resistance of the skin, which is a measure of emotional arousal. There are sound evolutionary reasons for this, since red is a signal for many vital things, most importantly danger (blood) and sex (the female baboon's big red bottom, for example, signals she is ready for breeding).

But cultural reasons also contribute to the special status of red, and these ultimately boil down to the fact that people find names for things they feel the need to talk about. The cultural importance of red

---

* In 2007, three researchers, Terry Regier, Naveen Khetarpal, and Paul Kay (same one), made a tentative suggestion for explaining the nature of these anatomical constraints. They started from the idea that a concept is 'natural' if it groups together things that appear similar to us, and they argued that a natural division of the colour space is one in which the shades within each colour category are as similar to one another as they can be and as dissimilar as possible from shades in other categories. Or put more accurately, a natural division maximises the perceived similarity between shades inside each concept and minimises the similarity between shades that belong to different concepts. One might have imagined that any division of the spectrum into continuous segments would be equally natural in this respect, because neighbouring shades always appear similar. But in practise, the accidents of our anatomy make our colour space asymmetric, because our sensitivity to light is greater in certain wavelengths than in others. (More details can be found in the appendix.) Because of such non-uniformities, some divisions of the colour space are better than others in increasing the similarity within concepts and decreasing it across concepts.

is paramount in simple societies, above all as the colour of blood.* Moreover, as Gladstone suggested in 1858, the interest in colour as an abstract property is likely to develop hand in hand with the artificial manipulation of colours, when colour comes to be seen as detachable from a particular object. Red dyes are the most common and least difficult to manufacture, and there are many cultures that use only black, white, and red as artificial colours. In short, both nature and culture give red prominence over other colours, and this agreement must be the reason why red is always the first prismatic colour to receive a name.

After red, yellow and green are next in line, whereas blue comes only later. Both yellow and green appear brighter to us than blue, with yellow by far the brightest. (As explained in the appendix, the mutation in the primate line that brought about the special sensitivity to yellow increased our ancestors' ability to spot ripe yellowish fruit against a background of green foliage.) But if it was simply brightness that determined the interest in naming colours, then surely yellow, rather than red, would have been the first colour to be given a separate name. As this is not the case, we should seek the explanation for the precedence of yellow and green over blue in the cultural significance of these two colours. Yellow and green are the colours of vegetation, and the difference between them (for example with ripe and unripe fruit) has practical consequences that one might want to talk about. Yellow dyes also happen to be relatively easy to make. The cultural significance of blue, on the other hand, is very limited. As noted earlier, blue is extremely rare as a colour of materials in nature, and blue dyes are exceedingly difficult to produce. People in simple cultures might spend a lifetime without seeing objects that are truly blue. Of course, blue is the colour of the sky (and, for some of us, the sea). But in the absence of blue materials with any practical significance, the need to find a special name for this great stretch of nothingness is particularly non-pressing.

---

* In many languages the name of the colour red actually derives from the word 'blood'. And as it happens, this linguistic connection has exercised the minds of generations of biblical exegetes, because it bears on the name of none other than the father of mankind. According to the biblical etymology, Adam owes his name to the red tilled soil, *adamah*, from which he was made. But *adamah* derives from the Semitic word for 'red', *adam*, which itself comes from the word *dam*, 'blood'.

A lot of water has flowed down the Scamander since a great Homericist, who occasionally dabbled in prime ministry, set off on an odyssey across the wine-dark sea in pursuit of mankind's sense of colour. The expedition that he launched in 1858 has since circled the globe several times over, been swept hither and thither by powerful ideological currents, and got sucked into the most tempestuous scientific controversies of the day. But how much real progress has actually been made?

It is a sobering thought that, on one level, we are hardly further advanced today than Gladstone's original analysis of 1858. So sobering, in fact, that you would be hard-pressed to find contemporary accounts owning up to it. If you look up the subject in linguistic discussions, you will be lucky to find Gladstone mentioned at all. If he does make an entrance, he will be relegated to a perfunctory 'pioneering efforts' footnote, reserved for those whom one feels one ought to mention but whom one cannot be bothered to read. And yet Gladstone's account of Homer's 'crude conceptions of colour derived from the elements' was so sharp and far-sighted that much of what he wrote a century and a half ago can hardly be bettered today, not just as an analysis of Homeric Greek but also as a description of the situation in many contemporary societies: 'Colours were for Homer not facts but images: his words describing them are figurative words, borrowed from natural objects. There was no fixed terminology of colour; and it lay with the genius of each true poet to choose a vocabulary for himself.' In one oft-quoted passage, for example, the anthropologist Harold Conklin explained why the Hanunoo in the Philippines call a shiny, brown-coloured section of newly cut bamboo 'green' – essentially, because it is 'fresh', which is the main meaning of the 'green' word. Conklin probably never set eyes on Gladstone's explanation for why Homer used *chlôros* for brownish fresh twigs. But anyone comparing their analyses might be forgiven for thinking that Conklin simply lifted his passage wholesale from *Studies on Homer and the Homeric Age*.

What is more, Gladstone's fundamental insight that the opposition between bright and dark was the primary basis for the Homeric colour system could also stand virtually unimproved at the cutting edge of current thinking on the development of colour vocabulary. Not that anyone would admit nowadays that the insight is Gladstone's, mind you. In modern accounts, the idea that languages shift the emphasis from a brightness-based system towards hue is presented as a shiny new and ultra-modern theory. But while this modern theory is far more impressive than the old one in the complexity of its terminology, in actual content it offers little that cannot be found in Gladstone's original analysis.

But perhaps the greatest irony in the whole story is that even the seemingly infantile evolutionary model that Gladstone invoked at the very beginning of the colour debate was actually spot on. The Lamarckian evolution-through-stretching mechanism is a perfect way to explain the changes between Homer's time and ours – if only we overlook one little detail, namely that Gladstone thought he was describing *biological* developments. For while the Lamarckian model, whereby the acquired aptitudes of one generation may become the inherited and inborn aptitudes of another, is a ridiculous way to explain anatomical changes, it is a perfectly sensible way to understand cultural evolution. In biology, characteristics acquired within the lifetime of an individual are not passed on to the offspring, so even if exercising the eye could improve one's own sensitivity to colours, the improvement would not be genetically transmitted to the next generation. But the Lamarckian model does fit perfectly with the reality of cultural developments. If one generation exerts its *tongue* and 'stretches' the language to create a new conventional name for a colour, then the children will indeed 'inherit' this feature when they learn the language of their parents.

So Gladstone's assertion that the developments in the vocabulary of colour involved the 'progressive education' of mankind is in actual fact entirely correct, and so is his belief that 'Homer's organ' still needed to be trained in the discrimination of colours. It is only that Gladstone did not realise which human faculty underwent this progressive education and which organ it was that needed to be trained. And it is exactly in clarifying this troublesome question, in telling apart the eye from the tongue, education from anatomy, culture from nature, that substantial headway has been made in the century-and-a-half–long debate. It is here that our view has sharpened since the culture blindness of Gladstone in 1858, of Geiger in 1869, of Magnus in 1878, and of Rivers in 1903, but also since the nature blindness of Leonard Bloomfield in 1933 (languages mark off colour boundaries 'quite arbitrarily') and of Verne Ray in 1953 ('there is no such thing as a "natural" division of the spectrum'), and even since the culture myopia of Berlin and Kay in 1969.

BEYOND COLOUR

The fighting over the rainbow may have been fiercer and more prolonged than over any other concepts, but the insights that have emerged from the debate can be applied with equal benefit elsewhere in language. The framework of freedom within constraints, which I suggested above, provides the best way to grasp culture's role in shaping the concepts of language more generally, and even its grammatical system.

Different cultures certainly are not at liberty to carve up the world entirely at whim, as they are bound by the constraints set by nature – both the nature of the human brain and the nature of the world outside. The more decisive nature has been in staking out its boundaries, the less leeway there is for culture. With cats and dogs and birds and roses, for instance, culture hardly has any freedom of expression at all. We can be quite certain that in any society where there are birds and roses, there will be words that correspond to our 'bird' and 'rose', and there will not be words that correspond to the Ziftish 'rird' and 'bose'. Even if one tried to construct an artificial language brimful of unnatural Ziftish concepts, it is not clear that children would be able learn these. For obvious humanitarian reasons, the experiment has not been conducted, but if ever anyone is cruel enough to raise young children on a monolingual diet of rirds and boses, dats and cogs, steaves and lones, the result will probably be that the hapless children will fail to learn these concepts 'correctly' and instead impose an 'incorrect' interpretation with more sensible and more natural meanings, which will correspond to our birds and roses, cats and dogs, leaves and stones.

On the other hand, when nature has shown even the slightest dithering or fuzziness in marking its boundaries, different cultures have far more sway over the division of concepts than anyone exposed only to the conventions of one society would imagine. Of course, concepts must be based on some sensible logic and internal coherence if they are to be both useful and learnable. But within these limits, there are still many ways of dissecting the world that are perfectly sensible, perfectly learnable by children, perfectly suitable for the communicative needs of the speakers – and yet totally different from what we are used to.

The field of colour made it glaringly obvious that the unfamiliar may not always be unnatural. A language in which yellow, light green, and light blue are treated as shades of one colour, for instance, may seem to us almost incomprehensibly alien, but this division makes perfect sense within a system whose primary emphasis is on brightness rather than hue and where the main prismatic colour to be set apart is red, so that all bright hues that have no tinge of redness naturally belong to the same concept.

But there are many other examples of the discrepancy between what is unnatural and what is merely unfamiliar. We will encounter one striking but little-known case in a later chapter: the concepts used to describe space and spatial relations. A more famous example is kinship terms. The language of the Yanomamö Indians in Brazil, for instance, appears to us incomprehensibly hazy, because it lumps together relatives of entirely different kinds under one concept. Using one and the same term, *šoriwə*, for both cousins and brothers-in-law may already seem rather peculiar. But this is nothing compared with the unification of brothers and certain cousins: the Yanomamö term *εiwə* makes no distinctions between one's own brothers and the sons of a paternal uncle or of a maternal aunt! On the other hand, the Yanomamö would consider English unbearably vague in having just one term, 'cousin', which lumps together no less than four distinct type of relatives: *amiwə* (daughter of a paternal uncle or of a maternal aunt), *εiwə* (son of paternal uncle or of maternal aunt), *suwəbiyə* (daughter of maternal uncle or of paternal aunt), and *šoriwə* (son of maternal uncle or of paternal aunt). There are even weirder systems of kinship terms, such as the one that anthropologists call the Crow system, in which the same concept is used for one's own father and for some of one's cousins (the sons of a paternal aunt). All these ways of dividing up one's relatives have their own internal logic and coherence, but they nevertheless diverge radically from the categories that we find natural.

The freedom of culture is even more pronounced in the realm of grammar, since grammatical structures are by nature more abstract and, as we have seen, nature's hold loosens considerably in the realms of abstraction. One striking aspect of the grammatical system that varies even among mainstream languages is the order of words. Japanese and Turkish, for instance, arrange words and grammatical elements in a way that seems to us perversely back to front. In *The Unfolding of Language*, I discussed examples such as the Turkish sentence *Padişah vezirini ordular-ı-nın baş-ı-na getirdi*, where a literal translation of each element – 'Sultan vizier his troops his of head their to brought' – is almost as unenlightening to an English speaker as the Turkish itself. But for a Turkish speaker encountering English for the first time, the English arrangement – 'the Sultan brought his vizier to the head of the troops' – would appear just as peculiar.

While the extent of variation among different grammars is not contested, there have been vociferous arguments about how to interpret it. The divergence between grammatical systems poses a particular challenge to the nativist idea of an innate universal grammar, because if the rules of grammar are meant to be coded in the genes, then one could expect the grammar of all languages to be the same, and it is then difficult to explain why grammars should ever vary in any fundamental aspects. One influential nativist response to this challenge has been the theory of 'parametric variations' within universal grammar. According to this idea, the genetically coded grammar contains a few 'parametres', that is, a small set of preprogrammemed options that can be thought of as 'on–off' switches. Children who acquire their mother tongue, so the argument runs, do not need to *learn* its grammatical rules – their brains simply set the preprogrammemed parametres according to the language they happen to be exposed to. Nativists have claimed that different settings of these few switches must account for the whole variation in grammatical structures across the world's languages. The only freedom that different cultures are accorded is thus to decide on how to set each of the parametres: press a few switches one way and you'll get the grammar of English, set a few switches the other way and you'll get the grammar of Italian, and flip a few more and you'll get the grammar of Japanese.

The theory of parametres has met with much criticism and some ridicule among non-nativists, who maintain that the scope of variation among the world's languages is far too wide to be covered by a few parametres, and that from an evolutionary perspective it is exceedingly unlikely that a genetically determined grammar would emerge with such a set of switches (whatever for?). But the main argument against the theory of parametres is that it is merely a convoluted way to account for grammatical variation that can be explained far more simply and far more easily if one does not insist on believing that specific grammatical rules are innate.

In short, the adamant claims of nativists about the innateness of grammar have met with equally resolute opposition from culturalists. The controversy over grammar has thus produced a most impressive pile of paper over the last decades, and many a library shelf across the globe quietly groans under its burden. This book will not add much weight to the debate, because it concentrates on the concepts of language rather than on grammar. But there is one aspect of the grammatical system that nonetheless cries out for attention, precisely because it has – wholly unjustifiably – escaped the controversy almost entirely: the complexity of the grammatical system. On this subject, an eerie consensus prevails among linguists of all creeds and persuasions, who unite in severely underestimating the influence of culture.

5

Plato and the Macedonian Swineherd

Ask Joe the Plumber, Piers the Ploughman, or Tom the Piper's Son what sort of languages the half-naked tribes in the Amazonian rainforest speak, and they will undoubtedly tell you that 'primitive people speak primitive languages', Ask professional linguists the same question, and they'll say something quite different. Actually, you don't even need to ask – they will tell you anyway: 'All languages are equally complex.' This battle cry is one of the most oft-avowed doctrines of the modern discipline of linguistics. For decades, it has been professed from lecterns across the globe, proclaimed in introductory textbooks, and preached at any opportunity to the general public.

So who is right: the man in the street or the congregation of linguists? Is the complexity of language a universal constant that reflects the nature of the human race, as linguists assert, or is it a variable that reflects the speakers' culture and society, as Joe, Piers, and Tom assume? In the following pages, I'll try to convince you that neither side has got it quite right, but that linguists have fallen into the more serious error.

PRIMITIVE LANGUAGES?

The linguist R. M. W. Dixon, who pioneered the serious study of Australian aboriginal languages, reports in his memoirs about the attitudes he encountered in the 1960s on his first field trips to North Queensland. Not far from Cairns, a white farmer asked him what exactly he was working on. Dixon explained he was trying to write a grammar of the local aboriginal language. 'Oh, that should be pretty easy,' said the farmer. 'Everyone knows that they haven't got any grammar.' In Cairns itself, Dixon was interviewed about his activities on a local radio station. The astonished presenter could not believe his ears: 'You really mean the Aborigines have a language? I thought it was just a few grunts and groans.' When Dixon protested that they had much more than grunts and groans, the presenter exclaimed, 'But they don't have more than about two hundred words, surely?' Dixon replied that on that very morning, he had collected from two informants over five hundred names just for animals and plants, so the overall vocabulary must be much larger. But the greatest shock for the presenter was reserved to the end, when he asked which well-known language the local lingo was most similar to. Dixon replied that some grammatical structures in the aboriginal language he was studying were more similar to Latin than to English.

Today, the attitudes that Dixon encountered in the sixties may no longer be so common, at least not in such a crass form. And yet there still seems to be a widespread belief on the street – even on very good streets – that the languages of the Aborigines in Australia, Indians in South America, Bushmen in Africa, and other simple peoples around the world are just as simple as their societies. As folk wisdom would have it, an undeveloped way of life is reflected in an undeveloped way of speaking, primitive Stone Age tools are indicative of primitive grammatical structures, nakedness and naïveté are mirrored in infantile and inarticulate speech.

There is a fairly simple reason why this misconception is so common. Our perception of a language is based largely on our exposure to its speakers, and for most of us the exposure to aboriginal languages of all kinds comes mainly from popular literature, movies, and television. And what we get to hear in such depictions, from *Tintin* to Westerns, is invariably Indians, Africans, and sundry other 'natives' speaking in that rudimentary 'me no come, Sahib' way. So is the problem simply that we have been duped by popular literature? Is the broken speech we associate with the aborigines of diverse continents merely a prejudice, a figment of the twisted imagination of chauvinistic-imperialistic minds? If one took the trouble of travelling to North Queensland to check for oneself, would one discover that all the natives actually orate in torrents of Shakespearean eloquence?

Not quite. Although the popular accounts may not always conform to the highest standard of academic accuracy, their depictions are ultimately based on reality. As it happens, the aborigines do very often use a rough and ungrammatical type of language: 'no money no come,' 'no can do', 'too much me been sleep', 'before longtime me no got trouble' (I've never got into any trouble in the past), 'mifela go go go toodark' (we kept going until it became very dark). All these are authentic examples of 'native speak'.

But have you noticed the little snag here? The primitive language that we hear these people speak is always . . . English. And while it is true that when they avail themselves of the English tongue, they use a pared down, ungrammatical, rudimentary, inarticulate – in short, 'primitive' – version of the language, this is simply because English is not *their* language. Just imagine yourself for a moment, eloquent, subtle, grammatically sophisticated creature that you are, trying to make yourself understood in a language you have never been taught. You arrive in a godforsaken village somewhere where no one speaks English and are desperate to find somewhere to sleep. All you have is a pocket dictionary. Suddenly all the layers of sophistication and refinement of your speech are unceremoniously shed. No more 'would you be so kind as to tell me whether there might be anywhere in this village where I could find a room for the night?' Nothing of the sort: you stand there linguistically naked and stutter 'yo dormir aquí?' 'ana alnoom hoona?' or the equivalent of 'me sleep here?' in whatever language you are attempting to make yourself understood in.

When one is trying to speak a foreign language without years of schooling in its grammatical nuances, there is one survival strategy that one always falls back on: strip down to the bare essentials, do away with everything but the most critical content, ignore anything that's not crucial for getting the basic meaning across. The aborigines who try to speak English do exactly that, not because their own language has no grammar but because the sophistication of their own mother tongue is of little use when struggling with a foreign language that they have not learned properly. North American Indians, for example, whose own languages formed breathtakingly long words with a dazzling architecture of endings and prefixes, could not even cope with the one rudimentary -s ending on English verbs and would say 'he come', 'she work', and so on. And South American Indians, whose own languages often use several different past tenses to mark different degrees of anteriority, are not even able to handle the one elementary past tense of English or Spanish and say things like 'he go yesterday'. Or take the Amazonian tribe whose language requires them to specify the epistemological status of events with a degree of nicety that would leave even the most quick-witted lawyer stuttering in stupefaction (more on them in the next chapter). The same people, if they tried to speak Spanish or English, would be able to use only the most rudimentary language and so would come across as gabbling inarticulates.

If we define a 'primitive language' as something that resembles the rudimentary 'me sleep here' type of English – a language with only a few hundred words and without the grammatical means of expressing any finer nuances – then it is a simple empirical fact that no natural language is primitive. Hundreds of languages of simple tribes have now been studied in depth, but not one of them, be it spoken by the most technologically and sartorially challenged people, is on the 'me sleep here' level. So there is no question that Joe and Piers and Tom have got it wrong about 'primitive people speak primitive languages'. Linguistic 'technology' in the form of sophisticated grammatical structures is not a prerogative of advanced civilisations, but is found even in the languages of the most primitive hunter-gatherers. As the linguist Edward Sapir memorably put it in 1921, when it comes to the complexity of grammatical structures 'Plato walks with the Macedonian swineherd, Confucius with the head-hunting savage of Assam'.

But does all this necessarily mean that linguists are right in asserting that 'all languages are *equally* complex'? There is no need for an advanced course in logic to realise that the two statements 'there are no primitive languages' and 'all languages are equally complex' are not equivalent, and that the former does not imply the latter. Two languages can both be way above the 'me sleep here' level, but one of them could still be far more complex than the other. As an analogy, think of the young pianists who are admitted to the Juilliard School. None of them will be a 'primitive pianist' who can only play 'Mary Had a Little Lamb' with one finger. But that does not mean they are all *equally* proficient. In just the same way, no language that has served for generations as the means of communication in a society can lack a certain minimum of complexity, but that does not imply that all languages are *equally* complex. What precludes the possibility, for instance, that languages of sophisticated civilisations might be *more* complex than those of simple societies? Or for that matter, how do we know that languages of advanced cultures are not perhaps *less* complex?

We know because linguists tell us so. And we must surely be on terra firma if the combined forces of an entire academic discipline pronounce from every available platform that something is the case. Indeed, equal complexity is often among the very first articles of faith that students read in their introductory course book. A typical example is the most popular Introduction to Language ever, the staple textbook by Victoria Fromkin and Robert Rodman on whose numerous editions generations of students in America and in other countries have been raised, ever since it first appeared in 1974. Under the auspicious title 'What We Know about Language', the first chapter explains: 'Investigations of linguists date back at least to 1600 B.C.E. in Mesopotamia. We have learned a great deal since that time. A number of facts pertaining to all languages can be stated.' It then goes on to profess those twelve facts that any student should know at the outset. The first asserts that 'wherever humans exist, language exists' and the second that 'all languages are equally complex'.

A student with an enquiring mind might quietly wonder when and where exactly it was – during this long history of investigations since 1600 BCE – that 'we have learned' that all languages are equally complex. Who was it that made this spectacular discovery? Of course, it would be unreasonable to expect an introductory textbook to go into such detail in the very first chapter, and our student is not impatient. So she reads on, fully confident that a later chapter will make good the promise – or if not a later chapter, at least a more advanced textbook. She goes through chapter after chapter, course after course, textbook after textbook, but the craved information is never supplied. The 'equal complexity' tenet is repeated time and again, but nowhere is the source of this precious information divulged. Our student now begins to suspect that she must have missed something obvious along the way. Too embarrassed to expose her ignorance and admit she doesn't know something so elementary, she continues in her frantic search.

On a few occasions, she seems to be coming within a hair's breadth of the answer. In one book by an eminent linguist she finds that equal complexity is explicitly reported as a *finding*: 'It is a finding of modern linguistics that all languages are roughly equal in terms of overall complexity.' Our student is thrilled. By now she is au fait with the conventions of academic writing and knows that whenever a finding, rather than just a claim or an opinion, is reported, it is an iron rule that a reference must be supplied to tell the reader where this finding was found. After all, as she has been told by her tutors countless times, the ability to back up factual claims by solid evidence is the most important principle that distinguishes academic texts from journalese or popular writing. She leaps towards the endnotes. But how strange, something must have gone wrong with the typesetting, because this particular endnote is missing.

Some months later, our student experiences another moment of elation when she finds a book that elevates the equality principle to an even higher status: 'A *central* finding of linguistics has been that all languages, both ancient and modern, spoken by both "primitive" and "advanced" societies, are equally complex in their structure.' Once again she rushes towards the endnotes, but curiouser and curiouser: how could the typesetters have made the same omission yet again?

Shall we put our poor student out of her misery? She may go on searching for years without finding the reference. I for one have been looking for fifteen years and still haven't encountered it. When it comes to the 'central finding' about the equal complexity of all languages, linguists never bother to reveal where, when, or how the discovery was made. They are saying: 'Just trust us, we know.' Well, don't trust us. We have no idea!

As it happens, the dogma of equal complexity is based on no evidence whatsoever. No one has ever measured the overall complexity of even one single language, not to mention all of them. No one even has an idea *how* to measure the overall complexity of a language. (We will return to this problem shortly, but for the moment let's just pretend we know roughly what the complexity of language is.) The equal complexity slogan is just a myth, an urban legend that linguists repeat because they have heard other linguists repeat it before them, having in turn heard others repeat it earlier.

If, unlike our shy student, you do press linguists to reveal what their authority for this tenet is, the source that is most likely to be mentioned is a passage from a book called *A Course in Modern Linguistics*, which was written in 1958 by Charles Hockett, one of the fathers of American structural linguistics. The funny thing is that in this passage Hockett himself went out of his way to explain that the equal complexity was not a finding, merely his impression:

> Objective measurement is difficult, but impressionistically it would seem that the total grammatical complexity of any language, counting both morphology [word structure] and syntax [sentence structure], is about the same as that of any other. This is not surprising, since all languages have about equally complex jobs to do, and what is not done morphologically [that is, inside the word] has to be done syntactically [in the sentence]. Fox [an American Indian language of Iowa], with a more complex morphology than English, thus ought to have a somewhat simpler syntax; and this is the case.

Since Hockett takes pains to stress that he is speaking 'impressionistically', it may seem unfair to subject his passage to too much scrutiny. But given its impact on the course of modern linguistics, and given that, in the process of retelling, Hockett's 'impression' somehow metamorphosed into a 'central finding' of the discipline, a quick reality check is due nonetheless. Does Hockett's impression, or for this matter the logic behind it, come up to scratch? Hockett assumes, quite correctly, that all languages need to satisfy a minimum degree of complexity in order to fulfil their complex jobs. From this fact he infers that if one language is less complex than another in one area, it has to compensate by increasing complexity in another area. But a moment's reflection will reveal that this inference is invalid, because much of language's complexity is not *necessary* for effective communication, and so there is no need to compensate for its absence. Anyone who has tried to learn a foreign language knows only too dearly that languages can be full of pointless irregularities that increase complexity considerably without contributing much to the ability to express ideas. English, for instance, would have lost none of its expressive power if some of its verbs left their irregular past tense behind and becomed regular. And the same applies, to a much greater degree, to other European languages, which have many more irregularities in their word structures.

In fact, if we replace Fox, Hockett's American Indian example, with one of the major languages of Europe, say German, it will quickly become apparent how spurious his argument is. German word structure is far more complex than that of English. English nouns, for instance, generally form their plurals simply by adding an *s* or *z* sound (books, tables), and there are only a handful of exceptions to this rule. In German, on the other hand, there are at least seven different ways of forming plurals: some nouns, like *Auto*, add an *-s* just like in English; others, such as 'horse', add an *-e* (*Pferd, Pferde*); nouns like 'hero' add an *-en* (*Held, Helden*); nouns like 'egg' add *-er* (*Ei, Eier*); nouns like 'bird' do not add a suffix at all but rather change a vowel inside the word (*Vogel, Vögel*); some nouns, like 'grass', change the vowel *and* add a suffix (*Gras, Gräser*); and finally some nouns, like 'window', don't change anything at all (*Fenster, Fenster*). One could imagine that German would make up for this enormous complexity in nouns by the exemplary simplicity of its verbs, but in fact German verbs have far more forms than English ones, so the morphology of German is incomparably more complex than that of English. Paraphrasing Hockett, then, we would conclude that 'German, with a more complex morphology than English, thus ought to have a somewhat simpler syntax'. But does it? If anything, it's the other way round: German word-order rules, for instance, are far more complex than those of English.

More generally, the reason why Hockett's logic fails is that a lot of complexity is merely excess baggage that languages accumulate over the centuries. So when some of it goes missing for whatever reason (more about that later) there is no particular need to compensate by increasing complexity elsewhere in the language. Contrariwise, there is no pressing need to compensate for a rise in complexity in one area by reducing it in another, because the brain of a child learning a language can cope with a mind-boggling amount of linguistic complexity. The fact that millions of children grow up with at least two languages and master each of them perfectly shows that a single language does not even come close to exhausting the linguistic capacity of a child's brain. So all in all there is no a priori reason why different languages should all mysteriously converge on even roughly the same degree of complexity.

～

But why, you might well ask, should we waste time on such a priori speculations in the first place? What's the point of discussing the question of complexity in the abstract, when the obvious way to tell whether all languages are equal is simply to go out to the field with measuring instruments, compare languages' vital statistics, and determine the exact overall complexity of each one?

There is a joke from the days of plenty in the former Soviet Union about a woman who goes to the butcher's and asks, 'Could you measure me out two hundred grams of salami, please?' 'No problem, madam,' replies the butcher. 'Just bring me the salami.' In our case, the salami may be there, but the measuring instrument is missing. I would be happy to measure for you the overall complexity of any language, but I have no idea where to find a scale, and neither does anyone else. As it happens, none of the linguists who profess the equal complexity dogma has ever tried to define what the overall complexity of a language might be.

'But wait,' I can hear you thinking. 'Even if no one has bothered to define complexity so far, surely it can't be too difficult to do it ourselves. Couldn't we decide, for instance, that the complexity of a language is defined as the difficulty it poses for foreign learners?' But which learners exactly? The problem is that the difficulty of learning a foreign language crucially depends on the learner's mother tongue. Swedish is a doddle – if you happen to be Norwegian, and so is Spanish if you are Italian. But neither Swedish nor Spanish is easy if your native language is English. Still, both are incomparably easier for an English speaker than Arabic or Chinese. So does that mean that Chinese and Arabic are objectively more difficult? No, because if your mother tongue is Hebrew, then Arabic isn't difficult at all, and if your mother tongue is Thai, then Chinese is less challenging than Swedish or Spanish. In short, there is no obvious way to generalise a measure of overall complexity based on the difficulty of learning, because – just like the effort required for travelling somewhere – it all depends on where you are starting from. (A proverbial Englishman learned this the hard way when he got desperately lost in the wilds of Ireland one day. After hours of driving around in circles through deserted country lanes, he finally spotted an elderly man walking by the side of the road, and asked him how to get back to Dublin. 'If I were to go to Dublin,' came the reply, 'I wouldn't be starting from here.')

I can sense that you are not ready to give up so easily. If the notion of difficulty will not do, you may now suggest, then what about basing the definition of complexity on a more objective measure, such as the number of parts in the language system? Just as a puzzle is more complex the more pieces it has, couldn't we simply say that the complexity of language is determined by the number of distinct forms it has, or the number of distinctions it makes, or the number of rules in its grammar, or something along these lines? The problem here is that we will be comparing apples and oranges. Language has parts of very different kinds: sounds, words, grammatical elements such as endings, types of clauses, rules for word order. How do you compare such entities? Suppose language X has one more vowel than language Y, but Y has one more tense than X. Does this make X and Y equal in overall complexity? Or, if not, what is the exchange rate? How many vowels are worth one tense? Two? Seven? Thirteen for the price of twelve? It is even worse than apples and oranges, it is more like comparing apples and orangutans.

To make a long story short, there is no way to devise an objective and non-arbitrary measure for comparing the overall complexity of any two given languages. It's not simply that no one has bothered to do it – it's inherently impossible even if one tried. So where does all this leave the dogma of equal complexity? When Joe, Piers, and Tom claim that 'primitive people speak primitive languages', they are making a simple and eminently meaningful statement, which just happens to be factually incorrect. But the article of faith that linguists swear by is even worse than wrong – it is meaningless. The alleged central finding of the discipline is nothing more than a hollow mouthful of air, since in the absence of a definition for the overall complexity of a language, the statement that 'all languages are equally complex' makes about as much sense as the assertion that 'all languages are equally cornflakes'.

The campaign to convince the general public of the equality of all languages may be paved with best intentions, for it is undoubtedly a noble enterprise to disabuse people of the belief that primitive tribes speak primitive languages. But surely the road to enlightenment is not through countering factual errors with empty slogans.

⌒

While the pursuit of the *overall* complexity of language is a wild-goose chase, there is no need to give up on the notion of complexity altogether. In fact, we can considerably improve our chances of catching something meaty if we turn away from the phantom of overall complexity and instead aim for the complexity of *particular* areas of language. Suppose we decide to define complexity as the number of parts in a system. If we delineate specific areas of language carefully enough, it becomes eminently possible to measure the complexity of each of these areas individually. For example, we can measure the size of the sound system simply by counting the number of phonemes (distinct sounds) in a language's inventory. Or we can look at the verbal system and measure how many tense distinctions are marked on the verb. When languages are compared in this way, it soon emerges that they vary greatly in the complexity of specific areas in their grammar. And whereas the existence of such variations is hardly stop-press news in itself, the more challenging question is whether the differences in the complexity of particular areas might reflect the culture of the speakers and the structure of their society.

There is one area of language whose complexity is generally acknowledged to depend on culture – this is the size of the vocabulary. The obvious dividing line here is between languages of illiterate societies and those with a written tradition. The aboriginal languages of Australia, for example, may have many more words than the two hundred that the Cairns radio presenter was granting them, but they still cannot begin to compete with the word hoard of European languages. Linguists who have described languages of small illiterate societies estimate that the average size of their lexicons is between three thousand and five thousand words. In contrast, small-size bilingual dictionaries of major European languages typically contain at least fifty thousand entries. Larger ones would contain seventy to eighty thousand. Decent-size monolingual dictionaries of English contain about a hundred thousand entries. And the full printed edition of the *Oxford English Dictionary* has around three times that many entries. Of course, the *OED* contains many obsolete words, and an average English speaker would recognise only a fraction of the entries. Some researchers have estimated the passive vocabulary of an average English-speaking university student at about forty thousand words – this is the number of words whose meaning is recognised, even if they are not actively used. Another source estimates the passive vocabulary of a university lecturer at seventy-three thousand words.

The reason for the great difference between languages with and without a written tradition is fairly obvious. In illiterate societies, the size of the vocabulary is severely restricted precisely because there is no such thing as 'passive vocabulary' – or at least the passive vocabulary of one generation does not live to see the next: a word that is not actively used by one generation will not be heard by the next generation and will then be lost forever.

MORPHOLOGY

While the cultural dependence of the vocabulary is neither surprising nor controversial, we are entering more troubled waters when we try to ascertain whether the structure of society might affect the complexity of areas in the *grammar* of a language, for instance its morphology. Languages vary considerably in the amount of information they convey within words (rather than with a combination of independent words). In English, for example, verbs like 'walked' or 'wrote' express the pastness of the action within the verb itself, but they do not reveal the 'person', which is instead indicated with an independent word like 'you' or 'we'. In Arabic, both tense and person are contained within the verb itself, so that a form like *katabnā* means 'we wrote'. But in Chinese, neither the pastness of the action nor the person is conveyed on the verb itself.

There are also differences in the amount of information encapsulated within nouns. Hawaiian does not indicate the distinction between singular and plural on the noun itself and uses independent words for the purpose. Similarly, in spoken French, most nouns sound the same in the singular and plural (*jour* and *jours* are pronounced in the same way, and one needs independent words, such as the definite article *le* or *les*, to make the difference heard). In English, on the other hand, the distinction between singular and plural is audible on the noun itself (dog–dogs, man–men). Some languages make even finer distinctions of number and have special forms also for the dual. Sorbian, a Slavic language spoken in a little enclave in eastern Germany, distinguishes between *hród*, 'a castle', *hródaj*, 'two castles', and *hródy* '[three or more] castles'.

The information specified on pronouns also varies between languages. Japanese, for instance, makes finer distinctions of distance on demonstrative pronouns than modern English. It differentiates not just between 'this' (for close objects) and 'that' (for objects further away) but has a three-way division between *koko* (for an object near the speaker), *soko* (near the hearer), *asoko* (far from both). Hebrew, on the other hand, makes no such distance distinctions at all and can use just one demonstrative pronoun regardless of distance.

Is the amount of information expressed within the word related to the complexity of a society? Are hunter-gatherer tribes, for example, more likely to speak in short and simple words? And are words likely to encapsulate more elaborate information in languages of advanced civilisations? In 1992, the linguist Revere Perkins set out to test exactly this question, by conducting a statistical survey of fifty languages. He assigned the societies in his sample to five broad categories of complexity, based on a combination of criteria that have been established by anthropologists, including population size, social stratification, type of subsistence economy, and specialisation in crafts. On the simplest level, there are 'bands' that consist of only a few families, don't have permanent settlements, depend exclusively on hunting and gathering, and have no authority structure outside the family. The second category includes slightly larger groups, with incipient use of agriculture, semi-permanent settlement, and some minimal social organisation. The third category is for 'tribes' that produce most of their food by agriculture, have permanent settlements, a few craft specialists, and some form of authority figure. The fourth category refers to what is sometimes called 'peasant societies', with intensive agricultural production, small towns, craft specialisation, and regional authorities. The fifth category of complexity refers to urban societies with large populations and complex social, political, and religious organisations.

In order to compare the complexity of words in the languages of the sample, Perkins chose a list of semantic features like the ones I mentioned above: the indication of plurality on nouns, tense on verbs, and other such bits of information that identify the participants, the time, and the place of events. He then checked how many of these features are expressed within the word, rather than through independent words, in each language. His analysis showed that there was a significant correlation between the level of complexity of a society and the number of distinctions that are expressed inside the word. But contrary to what Joe, Piers, and Tom might expect, it was not the case that sophisticated societies tend to have sophisticated word structures. Quite the opposite: there is an *inverse* correlation between the complexity of society and of word structure! The simpler the society, the more information it is likely to mark within the word; the more complex the society, the fewer semantic distinctions it is likely to express word-internally.

Perkins's study did not really make waves at the time, perhaps because linguists were too busy preaching equality to pay much heed. But more recently, the increased availability of information, especially in electronic databases of grammatical phenomena from hundreds of languages, has made it easier to test a much larger set of languages, so in the last few years a few more surveys of a similar nature have been conducted. Unlike Perkins's study, however, the recent surveys do not assign societies to a few broad categories of cultural complexity but instead opt to use just one measure, which is both more easily determined and more conducive to statistical analysis: the number of speakers of each language. Of course, the number of speakers is only a crude indication for the complexity of social structures, but the fit is nevertheless fairly tight: at the one extreme the languages of the simplest societies are spoken by fewer than a hundred people, and at the other the languages of complex urban societies are typically spoken by millions. The recent surveys strongly support Perkins's conclusions and show that languages of large societies are more likely to have simpler word structure, whereas languages of smaller societies are more likely to have many semantic distinctions coded within the word.

How can such correlations be explained? One thing is fairly clear. The degree of morphological complexity in a language is not usually a matter of conscious choice or deliberate planning by the speakers. After all, the question of how many endings there should be on verbs or nouns hardly features in party political debates. So if words tend to be more elaborate in simple societies, the reasons must be sought in the natural and unplanned paths of change that languages tread over time. In *The Unfolding of Language*, I showed that words are constantly buffeted by opposing forces of destruction and creation. The forces of destruction draw their energy from a rather unenergetic human trait: laziness. The tendency to save effort leads speakers to take shortcuts in pronunciation, and with time the accumulated effects of such shortcuts can weaken and even flatten whole arrays of endings and thus make the structure of words much simpler. Ironically, the very same laziness is also behind the creation of new complex word structures. Through the grind of repetition, two words that often appear together can be worn down and, in the process, fuse into a single word – just think of 'I'm', 'he's', 'o'clock', 'don't', 'gonna'. In this way, more complex words can arise.

In the long run, the level of morphological complexity will be determined by the balance of power between the forces of destruction and creation. If the forces of creation hold sway, and at least as many endings and prefixes are created as are lost, then the language will maintain or increase the complexity of its word structure. But if more endings are eroded than created, words will become simpler over time.

The history of the Indo-European languages over the last millennia is a striking example of the latter case. The nineteenth-century German linguist August Schleicher memorably compared the sesquipedalian Gothic verb *habaidedeima* (first-person plural past subjunctive of 'have') with its cousin in modern English, the monosyllabic 'had', and likened the modern form to a statue that has been rolling around on a riverbed and whose limbs have been worn away, so that hardly anything remains but a polished stone cylinder. A similar pattern of simplification is evident also with nouns. Some six thousand years ago, the ancient ancestor, Proto-Indo-European, had a highly complex array of case endings that expressed the precise role of the noun in the sentence. There were eight different cases, and most of them had distinct forms for singular, plural, and dual, creating a mesh of almost twenty endings for each noun. But in the last millennia this elaborate mesh of endings largely eroded in the daughter languages, and the information that had previously been conveyed through endings is now mostly expressed with independent words (such as the prepositions 'of', 'to', 'by', 'with'). For some reason, then, the balance tipped towards destruction of complex morphology: old endings eroded, while relatively new fusions materialised.

Can the balance between creation and destruction have anything to do with the structure of a society? Is there something about the way people in small societies communicate that favours new fusions? And when societies become larger and more complex, can there be something in the communication patterns that tilts the balance towards simplification of word structures? All the plausible answers suggested so far go back to one basic factor: the difference between communication among intimates and among strangers.

To appreciate just how often we who live in larger societies communicate with strangers, just try to do a quick count of how many unfamiliar people you talked to over the last week. If you live a normally active life in a big city, there would be far too many to remember: from shop assistants to taxi drivers, from phone salespeople to waiters, from librarians to policemen, from the repairman who came to fix the boiler to the random person who asked you how to get to such-and-such street. Now add up a second circle of people who may not be complete strangers but whom you still hardly know: those you only occasionally meet at work, at school, or at the gym. Finally, if you add to these the number of people you have heard without actively speaking to, on the street or on the train or on television, it will be obvious that you have been exposed to the speech of a vast crowd of strangers – all in just one week.

In small societies the situation is radically different. If you are a member of an isolated tribe that numbers a few dozen people, you hardly ever come across any strangers, and if you do you will probably spear them or they will spear you before you get a chance to chat. You know every single person you talk to extremely well, and all the people you speak to know you extremely well. They also know all your friends and relatives, they know all the places you frequent and the things you do.

But why should all that matter? One relevant factor is that communication among intimates more often allows compact ways of expression than communication among strangers. Imagine that you are speaking to a member of the family or to an intimate friend and are reporting a story about people you both know extremely well. There will be an enormous amount of shared information that you will not need to provide explicitly, because it will be understood from the context. When you say 'the two of them went back there', your hearer will know perfectly well who the two of them are, where 'there' is, and so on. But now imagine you have to tell the same story to a complete stranger who doesn't know you from Adam, who knows nothing about where you live, and so on. Instead of merely 'the two of them went back there' you'll now have to say 'so my sister Margaret's fiancé and his ex-girlfriend's husband went back to the house in the posh neighbourhood near the river where they used to meet Margaret's tennis coach before she . . .'

More generally, when communicating with intimates about things that are close at hand, you can be more concise. The more common ground you share with your hearer, the more often you will be able merely to 'point' with your words at the participants and at the place and time of events. And the more frequently such pointing expressions are used, the more likely they are to fuse and turn to endings and other morphological elements. So in societies of intimates, it is likely that more 'pointing' information will end up being marked within the word. On the other hand, in larger societies, where a lot of communication takes place between strangers, more information needs to be elaborated explicitly rather than just pointed at. For instance, a relative clause like 'the house [where they used to meet . . .]' would have to replace a mere 'there'. And if compact pointing expressions are used less frequently, they are less likely to fuse and end up as part of the word.

Another factor that may explain the differences in morphological complexity between small and large societies is the degree of exposure to different languages or even to different varieties of the same language. In a small society of intimates everyone speaks the language in a very similar way, but in a large society we are exposed to a plethora of different Englishes. Among the throng of strangers you heard over the last week, many spoke a completely different type of English from yours – a different regional dialect, an English of a different social background, or an English flavoured with a foreign accent. Contact with different varieties is known to encourage simplification in word structure, because adult language learners find endings, prefixes, and other alterations within the word particularly difficult to cope with. So situations that involve widespread adult learning usually result in considerable simplification in the structure of words. The English language after the Norman Conquest is a case in point: until the eleventh century, English had an elaborate word structure similar to that of modern-day German, but much of this complexity was wiped out in the period after 1066, no doubt because of the contact between speakers of the different languages.

Pressures for simplification can also arise from contact between different varieties of the same language, since even minor differences in the make-up of words can cause problems for comprehension. In large societies, therefore, where there is frequent communication between people of different dialects and speech varieties, the pressures towards simplification of morphology are likely to be higher, whereas in small and homogeneous societies, where there is little contact with speakers of other varieties, the pressures to simplify are likely to be lower.

Finally, one factor that may slow down the creation of new morphology is that ultimate hallmark of a complex society – literacy. In fluent speech, there are no real spaces between words, so when two words frequently appear together they can easily fuse into one. In the written language, however, the word takes on a visible independent existence, reinforcing speakers' perception of the border between words. This doesn't mean that new fusions ain't never gonna happen in literate societies. But the rate at which new fusions occur may be substantially reduced. In short, writing may be a counterforce that retards the emergence of more complex word structures.

No one knows whether the three factors above are the whole truth about the inverse correlation between the complexity of society and of morphology. But at least there are plausible explanations that make the relation between the structure of words and the structure of a society less than a complete mystery. Unfortunately, the same cannot be said of another statistical correlation, which has recently been demonstrated in a different area of language.

SOUND SYSTEM

Languages vary considerably in the size of their sound inventories. Rotokas from Papua New Guinea has only six distinct consonants (*p, t, k, b, d, g*), Hawaiian has eight, but the !Xóõ language from Botswana has forty-seven non-click consonants and seventy-eight different clicks that appear at the beginning of words. The number of vowels also varies considerably: many Australian languages have just three (*u, a, i*), Rotokas and Hawaiian have five each (*a, e, i, o, u*), whereas English has around twelve or thirteen vowels (depending on variety) and eight diphthongs. The overall number of sounds in Rotokas is thus only eleven (six consonants and five vowels), whereas in !Xóõ it amounts to more than 140.

In 2007, the linguists Jennifer Hay and Laurie Bauer published the results of a statistical analysis of the sound inventories of over two hundred languages. They discovered that there is a significant correlation between the number of speakers and the size of the sound inventory: the smaller the society, the fewer distinct vowels and consonants the language tends to have; the larger the number of speakers, the larger the number of sounds. Of course, this is only a statistical correlation: it does not mean that every single language of small societies must have a small inventory of sounds and vice versa. Malay, spoken by more than seventeen million people, has only six vowels and sixteen consonants, so twenty-two sounds in total. Faroese, on the other hand, has fewer than fifty thousand speakers but sports around fifty sounds (thirty-nine consonants and more than ten vowels), more than twice the number in Malay.

Still, as far as statistical correlations go, this one seems pretty robust, so the only plausible conclusion is that there is something about the modes of communication in small societies that favours smaller sound inventories, whereas something about large societies tends to make new phonemes more likely to emerge. The problem is that no one has yet come up with any compelling explanation for why this should be so.

One factor that could be relevant, perhaps, is contact with other languages or dialects. As opposed to word structure, which tends to be simplified as a result of contact, a language's sound inventory not uncommonly increases due to contact with other languages. For instance, when sufficiently many words with a 'foreign' sound are borrowed, the sound can eventually be integrated into the native system. If such contact-induced changes are less likely in smaller and more isolated societies, that fact might go some way towards explaining their smaller sound inventories. But this clearly cannot be the whole story.

SUBORDINATION

Finally, there is one area of language whose relation to the complexity of society may after all correspond to the considered opinion of the man in the street: this is the complexity of sentences and, in particular, the reliance on subordinate clauses. Subordination is a syntactic process that is often touted (by syntacticians, at least) as the jewel in the crown of language, and the best example for the ingenuity of its design: the ability to subsume a whole clause within another. With subordination, we can produce expressions of increasing complexity that nevertheless remain coherent and comprehensible:

I must have told you about that seal

I must have told you about that seal[which was eyeing a fish]

I must have told you about that seal[which was eyeing a fish[that kept

jumping in and out of the icy water]]

And there is no need to stop there, because in theory the mechanisms of subordination allow the sentence to go on and on for as long as there is breath to spare:

I must have told you about that quarrelsome seal [which was eyeing a disenchanted but rather attractive fish [that kept jumping in and out of the icy water [without paying the least attention to the heated debate [being conducted by a phlegmatic walrus and two young oysters [who had recently been tipped off by a whale with connections in high places [that the government was about to introduce speed limits on swimming in the reef area [due to the overcrowding [caused by the recent influx of new tuna immigrants from the Indian Ocean [where temperatures rose so much last year [that . . .]]]]]]]]]]

Subordination makes it possible to convey elaborate information in a compact way, by weaving different assertions on multiple levels into one intricate whole while keeping each of these levels under control. The paragraph above, for instance, has just one simple sentence at its primary level: 'I must have already told you about that seal.' But from there downwards, more and more information is interlaced using different types of subordinate clause.

There are no reliable reports about any language that lacks subordination altogether.* But although all known languages use some subordination, languages vary greatly in the range of subordinate clauses they have at their disposal and in the extent to which they rely on them.

For instance, if you have nothing better to do with your time than pore over ancient texts, you will soon notice that the narrative style of ancient languages such as Hittite, Akkadian, or biblical Hebrew often seems soporifically repetitive. The reason is that the mechanisms of subordination were less developed in these languages, so the coherence of their narrative relied to a much greater extent on a simple type of 'and . . . and . . .' concatenation, in which the clauses merely followed the temporal order of events. Here, for instance, is a short Hittite text, a report by King Murshili II, who reigned in the fourteenth century BC from his imperial capital of Hattusha, in what is today central Turkey. Murshili is describing in dramatic tones how he came to be afflicted by a severe illness that impaired his ability to speak (a stroke?). But to mod-

---

* There has been a lot of brouhaha in the last few years about Pirahã, a language from the Brazilian Amazon, and its alleged lack of subordination. But a few Pirahã subordinate clauses have recently managed to escape from the jungle and telegraph reliable linguists to say that reports of their death have been greatly exaggerated. (See notes for more information.)

ern ears the vivid substance of the report contrasts starkly with the monotonous staccato of the style:

This is what Murshili, the Great King, said:

Kunnuwa nannaḫḫun	I drove (in a chariot) to Kunnu
nu ḫaršiḫarši udaš	and a thunderstorm came
namma Tarḫunnaš ḫatuga tetḫiškit	then the Storm-God kept thundering terribly
nu nāḫun	and I feared
nu-mu-kan memiaš išši anda tepawešta	and the speech in my mouth became small
nu-mu-kan memiaš tepu kuitki šarā iyattat	and the speech came up a little bit
nu-kan aši memian arḫapat paškuwānun	and I forgot this matter completely
maḫḫan-ma uēr wittuš appanda pāir	but afterwards the years came and went
nu-mu wit aši memiaš tešḫaniškiuwān tiyat	and this matter came to appear repeatedly in my dreams
nu-mu-kan zazḫia anda keššar šiunaš araš	and God's hand seized me in my dreams
aišš-a-mu-kan tapuša pait	then my mouth went sideways
nu . . .	and . . .

Today, we would tend to use various subordinate clauses and thus would not need to follow the order of events so punctiliously. For example, we might say: 'There was once a terrible thunderstorm when I was driving to Kunnu. I was so terrified of the Storm-God's thundering that I lost my speech, and my voice came up only a little. For a while, I forgot about the matter completely, but as the years went by, this episode began to appear in my dreams, and while dreaming, I was struck by God's hand and my mouth would go sideways.'

Here is another example, this time from Akkadian, the language of the Babylonians and Assyrians of ancient Mesopotamia. This document, written sometime before 2000 BC, reports the result of a legal proceeding. We are told that a certain Ubarum proved before the inspectors that he had told a Mr Iribum to take the field of Kuli, and that he (Ubarum) didn't know that Iribum, on his own initiative, had instead taken the field of someone else, Bazi. But while this is the gist of what the document says, the Akkadian text doesn't put it quite like that. What it actually says is:

ana Iribum Ubarum eqel Kuli šūlu'am iqbi	Ubarum told Iribum to take Kuli's field
šū libbiššuma	he (Iribum) on his own initiative
eqel Bazi uštēli	took the field of Bazi
Ubarum ula īde	Ubarum didn't know
mahar laputtî ukīnšu	he proved (this against) him
	in front of the inspectors

The difference between the Akkadian formulation and the way we would naturally describe the situation in English lies mainly in our pervasive use of constructions such as 'he didn't know that [...]' or 'he proved that [...]'. This particular type of subordinate clause is called 'finite complement', but although the name is rather a mouthful, the construction itself is the bread and butter of English prose. In both written and spoken registers, we can take practically any sentence (let's say 'Iribum took the field') and, without altering anything in the sentence itself, make it a subordinate part of another sentence:

He didn't know that [Iribum took the field]

And since it is so easy to set up this hierarchical relation once, we can do it again:

Ubarum proved that [he didn't know that [Iribum took the field]]

And again:

The tablet explained that [Ubarum proved that [he didn't know that [Iribum took the field]]]

And again:

The epigrapher discovered that [the tablet explained that [Ubarum proved that [he didn't know that [Iribum took the field]]]]

The Akkadian report does not use such finite complements. In fact, most of its clauses are not hierarchically ordered but simply juxtaposed according to the temporal order of the events. This is not a coincidence of just one text. While we may take finite complements for granted today, this construction was missing in the oldest attested stages of Akkadian (and of Hittite). And there are living languages that do not have this construction even today.

Not that linguistic textbooks will divulge this information, mind you. In fact, some will ardently profess the opposite. Take that flagship of linguistic education, the *Introduction to Language* by Fromkin and Rodman that I mentioned earlier, and its twelve articles of faith that constitute 'what we know about language'. The second affirmation, as you will recall, is that all languages are equally complex. A little further below, affirmation eleven asserts:

Syntactic universals reveal that every language has a way of forming sentences such as:

- Linguistics is an interesting subject.
- I know that linguistics is an interesting subject.
- You know that I know that linguistics is an interesting subject.
- Cecelia knows that you know that I know that linguistics is an interesting subject.
- Is it a fact that Cecelia knows that you know that I know that linguistics is an interesting subject?

Unfortunately, the textbook does not disclose the precise identity of the 'syntactic universals' that have revealed that every language has such constructions. Nor does it specify when and where this revelation was handed down to mankind. But is the claim actually true? I have never had the privilege of communing with a syntactic universal myself, but the evidence from more mundane sources, namely descriptions of actual languages, leaves no doubt that some languages do not have a way of forming such sentences (and not just because they don't have a word for 'linguistics'). Many Australian aboriginal languages, for example, lack a construction equivalent to the finite complements of English, and so do some Indian languages of South America, including one, Matses, that we will meet in the next chapter. In such languages, one simply cannot form sentences such as:

> It is a fact that many students don't realise that their linguistics text-books don't know that some languages do not have finite complements.

Instead, this state of affairs would have to be expressed by other means. For example, in the early stages of Akkadian, one would do it along these lines:

> Some languages do not have finite complements. Some linguistics text-books don't know that. Many students don't realise their textbooks' ignorance. This is a fact.

While systematic statistical surveys on subordination have not yet been conducted, impressionistically it seems that languages that have restricted use of complements (or even lack them altogether) are mostly spoken in simple societies. What is more, ancient languages such as Akkadian and Hittite show that this type of 'syntactic technology' developed at a period when the societies in question were growing in complexity. Is this just coincidence?

I have argued elsewhere that it is not. Finite complements are a more effective tool for conveying elaborate propositions, especially when less information can be left to the context and more explicitness and accuracy are required. Recall the sequence of events described in the Akkadian legal document on page 122. Of course, it is possible to convey the set of propositions described there just as the Akkadian text organises it, with a simple juxtaposition of clauses: X told Y to do something; Y did something different; X didn't know that; X proved it in front of the inspectors. But when the dependence between the clauses is not explicitly marked, some ambiguity remains. What exactly did X prove? Did he prove that Y did something different from what he was told? Or did X prove that he didn't *know* that Y did something different? The juxtaposition does not make that clear, but the hierarchical structure of finite complements can easily do so.

The language of legal proceedings, with its zealous insistence on accurate, explicit, and context-independent statements, is an extreme example of the type of elaborate communicative patterns that are more likely to arise in a complex society. But it is not the only example. As I mentioned earlier, in a large society of strangers there will be many more occasions where elaborate information has to be conveyed without reliance on shared background and knowledge. Finite complements are better equipped to convey such information than alternative constructions, so it is plausible that finite complements are more likely to emerge under the communicative pressures of a more complex society. Of course, as no statistical surveys about subordination have been conducted yet, speculations about correlations between subordination and the complexity of a society necessarily have to remain on an impressionistic level. But there are signs that things might be changing.

For decades, linguists have elevated the hollow slogan that 'all languages are equally complex' to a fundamental tenet of their discipline, zealously suppressing as heresy any suggestion that the complexity of any areas of grammar could reflect aspects of society. As a consequence, relatively little work has been done on the subject. But a flurry of publications from the last couple of years shows that more linguists are now daring to explore such connections.

The results of this research have already revealed some significant statistical correlations. Some of these, such as the tendency of smaller societies to have more complex word structure, may seem surprising at first sight, but look plausible on closer examination. Other connections, such as the greater reliance on subordination in complex societies, still require detailed statistical surveys, but nevertheless seem intuitively convincing. And finally, the relation between the complexity of the sound system and the structure of society awaits a satisfactory explanation. But now that the taboo is lifting and more research is being done, there are undoubtedly more insights in store. So watch this space.

⌒

We have come a long way from the Aristotelian view of how nature and culture are reflected in language. Our starting point was that only the labels (or, as Aristotle called them, the 'sounds of speech') are cultural conventions, while everything behind those labels is a reflection of nature. By now culture has emerged as a considerable force whose influence extends far beyond merely bestowing labels on a preordained list of concepts and a preordained system of grammatical rules.

In the second part of the book, we move on to a question that may seem a fairly innocuous corollary to the conclusions of the first part: does our mother tongue influence the way we think? Since the conventions of the culture we were born into affect the way we carve up the world into concepts and the way we organise these concepts into elaborate ideas, it seems only natural to ask whether our culture can affect our thoughts *through* the linguistic idiosyncrasies it has imposed on us. But while raising the question appears harmless enough in theory, among serious researchers the subject has become a pariah. The following chapter explains why.

PART II

The LANGUAGE LENS

6

Crying Whorf

In 1924, Edward Sapir, the leading light of American linguistics, was entertaining no illusions about the attitude of outsiders towards his field: 'The normal man of intelligence has something of a contempt for linguistic studies, convinced as he is that nothing can well be more useless. Such minor usefulness as he concedes to them is of a purely instrumental nature. French is worth studying because there are French books which are worth reading. Greek is worth studying – if it is – because a few plays and a few passages of verse, written in that curious and extinct vernacular, have still the power to disturb our hearts – if indeed they have. For the rest, there are excellent translations. . . . But when Achilles has bewailed the death of his beloved Patroclus and Clytaemnestra has done her worst, what are we to do with the Greek aorists that are left on our hands? There is a traditional mode of procedure which arranges them into patterns. It is called grammar. The man who is in charge of grammar and is called a grammarian is regarded by all plain men as a frigid and dehumanized pedant.'

In Sapir's own eyes, however, nothing could be further from the truth. What he and his colleagues were doing did not remotely resemble the pedantic sifting of subjunctives from aorists, mouldy ablatives from rusty instrumentals. Linguists were making dramatic, even world-view-changing discoveries. A vast unexplored terrain was being opened up, the languages of the American Indians, and what was revealed there had the power to turn on its head millennia's wisdom about the natural ways of organising thoughts and ideas. For the Indians expressed them-selves in unimaginably strange ways and thus demonstrated that many aspects of familiar languages, which that had previously been assumed to be simply natural and universal, were in fact merely accidental traits of European tongues. The close study of Navajo, Nootka, Paiute, and a panorama of other native languages catapulted Sapir and his col-leagues to vertiginous heights, from where they could now gaze down on the languages of the Old World like people who see their home patch from the air for the first time and suddenly recognise it as just one little spot in a vast and varied landscape. The experience was exhilarating. Sapir described it as the liberation from 'what fetters the mind and benumbs the spirit . . . the dogged acceptance of absolutes'. And his student at Yale Benjamin Lee Whorf enthused: 'We shall no longer be able to see a few recent dialects of the Indo-European fam-ily . . . as the apex of the evolution of the human mind. They, and our own thought processes with them, can no longer be envisioned as spanning the gamut of reason and knowledge but only as one constel-lation in a galactic expanse.'

It was difficult not to get carried away by the view. Sapir and Whorf became convinced that the profound differences between languages must have consequences that go far beyond mere grammatical organi-sation and must be related to profound divergence in modes of thought. And so in this heady atmosphere of discovery, a daring idea about the power of language shot to prominence: the claim that our mother tongue determines the way we think and perceive the world. The idea itself was not new – it had been lying around in a raw state for more than a century – but it was distilled in the 1930s into a powerful con-coction that then intoxicated a whole generation. Sapir branded this idea the principle of 'linguistic relativity', equating it with nothing less than Einstein's world-shaking theory. The observer's perceptions of the world – so ran Sapir's emendation of Einstein – depend not only on his inertial frame of reference but also on his mother tongue.

The following pages tell the story of linguistic relativity – a history of an idea in disgrace. For as loftily as it had once soared, so precipitously did the theory then crash, when it transpired that Sapir and especially his student Whorf had attributed far-fetched cognitive consequences to what were in fact mere differences in grammatical organisation. Today, any mention of linguistic relativity will make most linguists shift uneasily in their chairs, and 'Whorfianism' has largely become an intellectual tax haven for mystical philosophers, fantasists, and post-modern charlatans.

Why then should one bother telling the story of a disgraced idea? The reason is not (just) to be smug with hindsight and show how even very clever people can sometimes be silly. Although there is undeniable pleasure in such an exercise, the real reason for exposing the sins of the past is this: although Whorf's wild claims were largely bogus, I will try to convince you later that the notion that language can influence thoughts should not be dismissed out of hand. But if I am to make a plausible case that some aspects of the underlying idea are worth salvaging and that language may after all function as a lens through which we per-ceive the world, then this salvaging mission must steer clear of previous errors. It is only by understanding where linguistic relativity went astray that we can turn a different way.

WILHELM VON HUMBOLDT

The idea of linguistic relativity did not emerge in the twentieth century entirely out of the blue. In fact, what happened at Yale – the over-reaction of those dazzled by a breathtaking linguistic landscape – was a close rerun of an episode from the early 1800s, during the high noon of German Romanticism.

The prevailing prejudice towards the study of non-European lan-guages that Edward Sapir gently mocked in 1924 was nothing to poke fun at a century earlier. It was simply accepted wisdom – not just for the 'ordinary man of intelligence' but also among philologists themselves

– that the only languages worthy of serious study were Latin and Greek. The Semitic languages Hebrew and Aramaic were occasionally thrown into the bargain because of their theological significance, and Sanskrit was grudgingly gaining acceptance into the club of classical worthies, but only because it was so *similar* to Greek and Latin. But even the modern languages of Europe were still widely viewed as merely degenerate forms of the classical languages. Needless to say, the languages of illiterate tribes, without great works of literature or any other redeeming features, were seen as devoid of any interest, primitive jargons just as worthless as the primitive peoples who spoke them.

It was not that scholars at the time were unconcerned about the question of what is common to all languages. In fact, from the seventeenth century onwards, the writing of learned treatises on 'universal grammar' was very much in vogue. But the universe of these universal grammars was rather limited. Around 1720, for instance, John Henley published in London a series of grammars called *The Compleat Linguist; or, An Universal Grammar of All the Considerable Tongues in Being*. All the considerable tongues in being amounted to nine: Latin, Greek, Italian, Spanish, French, Hebrew, Chaldee (Aramaic), Syriac (a later dialect of Aramaic), and Arabic. This exclusive universe offered a somewhat distorted perspective, for – as we know today – the variations among European languages pale in significance compared with the otherness of more exotic tongues. Just imagine what misleading ideas one would get on 'universal religion' or on 'universal food' if one limited one's universe to the stretch between the Mediterranean and the North Sea. One would travel in the different European countries and be impressed by the great divergences between them: the architecture of the churches is entirely different, the bread and cheese do not taste at all the same. But if one never ventured to places further afield, where there were no churches, cheese, or bread, one would never realise that these intra-European differences are ultimately minor variations in essentially the same religion and the same culinary culture.

In the second half of the eighteenth century, the view was beginning to widen slightly, as various attempts were made to compile 'universal dictionaries' – lists of equivalent words in languages from different continents. But although the scope and ambition of these catalogues gradually grew, they didn't go much beyond a linguistic cabinet of curiosities showcasing weird and wonderful words. In particular, the dictionaries revealed little of value about the *grammar* of exotic languages. Indeed, for most philologists at the time, the notion that the grammar of a barbarian language could be a worthwhile subject of study seemed perverse. Studying grammar meant the study of Greek and Latin, because 'grammar' *was* the grammar of Greek and Latin. So when remote languages were described (not by philologists but by missionaries who needed them for practical purposes), the descriptions usually consisted of a list of Latin paradigms on one side and the allegedly corresponding forms in the native language on the other side. The nouns in an American Indian language, for example, would be shown in six forms, corresponding to the six cases of the Latin noun. Whether or not the language in question made any case distinctions was irrelevant – the noun would still be duly frogmarched into nominative, genitive, dative, accusative, vocative, and ablative. The French writer Simon-Philibert de La Salle de l'Étang demonstrates this frame of mind in his 1763 dictionary of Galibi, a now extinct language of the Caribbean, when he complains that 'the Galibis have nothing in their language that makes distinctions of case, for which there should be six in the declension of each word'. Such descriptions seem to us today like clumsy parodies, but they were conceived in complete earnestness. The notion that the grammar of an American Indian language might be organised on fundamentally different principles from those of Latin was simply beyond the intellectual horizon of the writers. The problem was much deeper than the failure to understand a particular feature of the grammar of a particular New World language. It was that many of the missionaries didn't even understand that there was something there to understand.

Enter Wilhelm von Humboldt (1767–1835), linguist, philosopher, diplomat, educational reformer, founder of the University of Berlin, and one of the stellar figures of the early nineteenth century. His education – the best of what the Berlin Enlightenment scene had to offer – imbued him with unbounded admiration for classical culture and for the classical

Wilhelm von Humboldt, 1767–1835

languages. And until he reached the age of thirty-three, there was little to show that he would one day break out of the mould or that his linguistic interests would ever extend beyond the revered Latin and Greek. His first publication, at the age of nineteen, was about Socrates and Plato; he then wrote about Homer and translated Aeschylus and Pindar. A happy life-time of classical scholarship seemed to stretch in front of him.

His linguistic road to Damascus led through the Pyrenees. In 1799, he travelled to Spain and was greatly taken with the Basque people, their culture, and their landscape. But above all, it was their language that aroused his curiosity. Here was a language spoken on European soil but entirely unlike all other European tongues and clearly from a different stock. Back from the journey, Humboldt spent months read-ing through everything he could find about the Basques, but as there wasn't very much in the way of reliable information, he returned to the Pyrenees to do serious fieldwork and learn the language firsthand. As his knowledge deepened, he realised the extent to which the structure of this language – rather than merely its vocabulary – diverged from everything else he knew and from what he had previously taken as the only natural form of grammar. The revelation gradually dawned on him that not all languages were made in the image of Latin.

Once Humboldt's curiosity was aroused, he tried to find descriptions of even more remote tongues. There was almost nothing published at the time, but the opportunity to discover more presented itself when he became the Prussian envoy to the Vatican in 1802. Rome was teeming with Jesuit missionaries who had been expelled from their missions in Spanish South America, and the Vatican library contained many manuscripts with descriptions of South and Central American languages that these missionaries had brought with them or written once back in Rome. Humboldt trawled through such grammars, and with his eyes now wide open after his experience with Basque, he could make out how distorted a picture they presented: structures that deviated from the European type had either passed unnoticed or been coerced to fit the European mould. 'It is sad to see,' he wrote, 'what violence these missionaries exerted both on themselves and on the languages, in order to force them into the narrow rules of Latin grammar.' In his determination to understand how the American languages actually worked, Humboldt completely rewrote many of these grammars, and gradually the real structure of the languages emerged from behind the facade of Latin paradigms.

Humboldt set linguists on a steep learning curve. Of course, the second-hand information that he was able to glean about American Indian languages was nothing like the deep first-hand knowledge that Sapir developed a century later. And considering what we know today about how the grammars of different languages are organised, Humboldt was barely scratching the surface. But the dim ray of light that shone from his materials felt dazzling nonetheless because of the utter darkness in which he and his contemporaries had languished.

For Humboldt, the elation of breaking new ground was mixed with frustration at the need to impress the value of his discoveries upon an uncomprehending world, which persisted in regarding the study of primitive tongues as an activity fit only for butterfly collectors. Humboldt went to great lengths to explain why the profound dissimilarities among grammars were in fact a window into far greater things. 'The difference between languages,' he argued, 'is not only in sounds and signs but in world-view. Herein is found the reason and ultimate goal of all the study of language.' But this was not all. Humboldt also claimed that grammatical differences not only reflect pre-existing differences in thought but are responsible for shaping these differences in the first place. The mother tongue 'is not just the means for representing a truth already recognised but much more to discover the truth that had not been recognised previously'. Since 'language is the forming organ of thought', there must be an intimate relation between the laws of grammar and the laws of thinking. 'Thinking,' he concluded, 'is dependent not just on language in general but to a certain extent on each individual language.'

A seductive idea was thus tossed into the air, an idea that in the 1930s would be taken up (and up and up) at Yale. Humboldt himself never went as far as alleging that our mother tongue can entirely constrain our thoughts and intellectual horizons. He explicitly acknowledged something that in the hullabaloo around Whorf a century later tended to be overlooked, namely that, in principle, any thought can be expressed in any language. The real differences between languages, he argued, are not in what a language is *able* to express but rather in 'what it encourages and stimulates its speakers to do from its own inner force'.

What exactly this 'inner force' is, what ideas precisely it 'stimulates' speakers to formulate, and how in practical terms it might do so always remained rather elusive in Humboldt's writings. As we'll see, his basic intuition may have been sound, but despite the detailed knowledge that he amassed about many exotic languages, his statements on the subject of the mother tongue's influence on the mind always remained in the higher stratosphere of philosophical generalities and never really got down to the nitty-gritty of detail.

In fact, in his voluminous musings on this subject, Humboldt abided by the first two commandments for any great thinker: (1) Thou shalt be vague, (2) Thou shalt not eschew self-contradiction. But it may have been exactly this vagueness that struck a chord with his contemporaries. Following Humboldt's lead, it now became fashionable among the great and the good to pay tribute to language's influence on thought, and as long as one didn't feel the urge to provide any particular examples, one could freely indulge in resonant but ultimately hollow imagery. The renowned Oxford professor of philology Max Müller declared in 1873 that 'the words in which we think are channels of thought which we have not dug ourselves, but which we found ready made for us'. And his nemesis across the Atlantic, the American linguist William Whitney, may have concurred with Müller in nothing else but agreed neverthe-less that 'every single language has its own peculiar framework of estab-lished distinctions, its shapes and forms of thought, into which, for the human being who learns that language as his mother-tongue, is cast the content and product of his mind, his store of impressions, . . . his expe-rience and knowledge of the world'. The mathematician and philoso-pher William Kingdon Clifford added a few years later that 'it is the thought of past humanity imbedded in our language which makes Nature to be what she is for us'.

Throughout the nineteenth century, however, such statements remained on the level of occasional rhetorical flourishes. It was only in the twentieth century that the slogans began to be distilled into specific claims about the alleged influence of particular grammatical phenom-ena on the mind. The Humboldtian ideas now underwent a rapid pro-cess of fermentation, and as the spirit of the new theory grew more powerful, the rhetoric became less sober.

LINGUISTIC RELATIVITY

What was it in the air that catalysed this reaction? One reason must have been the great (and wholly justified) excitement about the enormous advances that linguists were making in understanding the outlandish nature of Amerindian languages. Linguists in America did not need to pore over manuscripts from the Vatican library to unearth the struc-ture of the native languages of the continent, as there were still dozens of living native languages to be studied in situ. What is more, in the century that separated Sapir from Humboldt, the science of language had experienced a meteoric rise in sophistication, and the analytic tools at linguists' disposal became incomparably more powerful. When these advanced tools began to be applied in earnest to the treasure hoard of Native American languages, they revealed grammatical landscapes that Humboldt could not have dreamed of.

Edward Sapir, like Humboldt a century before him, started his lin-guistic career far from the open vistas of American languages. His studies at Columbia concentrated on Germanic philology and consisted of things rather reminiscent of the pedantic collections of obscure verbal forms in ancient tongues that he derided in the passage I quoted earlier. Sapir credited his conversion from the dusty armchair of Germanic philology to the great outdoors of Indian languages to the influence of Franz Boas, the charismatic professor of anthropology at Columbia who was also the pioneer in the scientific study of the native languages of the continent. Years later, Sapir reminisced about a life-changing meeting at which Boas summoned counter-examples from this, that, or the other Indian tongue to every generalisation about the structure of language that Sapir had previously believed in. Sapir began to feel that Germanic philology had taught him very little and that he still had 'everything to learn about language'. Henceforth, he was to apply his legendary sharpness of mind to the study of Chinook, Navajo, Nootka, Yana, Tlingit, Sarcee, Kutchin, Ingalik, Hupa, Paiute, and other native languages, producing analyses of unmatched clarity and depth.

In addition to the exhilaration of discovering weird and exotic grammars, there was something else in the air that pushed Sapir towards the formulation of his linguistic relativity principle. This was the radical trend in the philosophy of the early twentieth century. At the time, philosophers such as Bertrand Russell and Ludwig Wittgen-

Edward Sapir, 1884–1939

stein were busy decrying the pernicious influences of language on the metaphysics of the past. Russell wrote in 1924: 'Language misleads us both by its vocabulary and by its syntax. We must be on our guard in both respects if our logic is not to lead to a false metaphysic.'

Sapir translated the claims about language's influence on philosophical ideas into an argument about the influence of the mother tongue on everyday thoughts and perceptions. He started talking about the 'tyrannical hold that linguistic form has upon our orientation in the world', and as opposed to anyone before him, he went on to inject such slogans with actual content. In 1931 he advanced the following example for how one specific linguistic difference should affect speakers' thoughts. When we observe a stone moving through space towards the earth, Sapir explained, we involuntarily divide this event into two separate concepts: a stone and the action of falling, and we declare that 'the stone falls'. We assume that this is the only way to describe such an event. But the inevitability of the division into 'stone' and 'fall' is just an illusion, because the Nootka language, which is spoken on Vancouver Island, does things in a very different way. There is no verb in Nootka that corresponds to our general verb 'fall' and that can describe the action independently of a specific falling object. Instead, a special verb, 'to stone,' is used to refer to the motion of a stone in particular. To describe the event of a stone *falling*, this verb is combined with the element 'down'. So the state of affairs that we break up into 'stone' and 'fall' is described in Nootka as something like '[it] stones down'.

Such concrete examples of 'incommensurable analysis of experience in different languages', Sapir says, 'make very real to us a kind of relativity that is generally hidden from us by our naïve acceptance of fixed habits of speech. . . . This is the relativity of concepts or, as it might be called, the relativity of the form of thought.' This type of relativity, he adds, may be easier to grasp than Einstein's, but to understand it one needs the comparative data of linguistics.

Unfortunately for Sapir, it is exactly by forsaking the cosy vagueness of philosophical slogans and venturing into the freezing draughts of specific linguistic examples that he exposes the thin ice on which his theory stands. The Nootka expression 'it stones down' is undoubtedly a very different way of describing the event, and it certainly sounds strange, but does this strangeness mean that Nootka speakers necessarily have to *perceive* the event in a different way? Does the fusion of verb and noun in Nootka necessarily imply that Nootka speakers do not have separate images of the action and the object in their minds?

We can test this if we apply Sapir's argument to a slightly more familiar language. Take the English phrase 'it rains'. This construction is actually quite similar to the Nootka 'it stones down', because the action (falling) and the object (water drops) are combined into one verbal concept. But not all languages do it in this way. In my mother tongue, the object and the action are kept apart, and one says something like 'rain falls'. So there is a profound difference in the way our languages express the event of raining, but does this mean that you and I have to *experience* rain in a different way? Do you feel you are prevented by the grammar of your mother tongue from understanding the distinction between the watery substance and the action of falling? Do you find it hard to relate the falling raindrops to other things that fall down? Or are the differences in the way our languages express the idea of 'raining' no more than merely differences in grammatical organisation?

At the time, no one thought of stumbling over such molehills. The excitement about the – largely factual – strangeness of expression in American Indian languages was somehow taken as sufficient to deduce the – largely fictional – differences in their speakers' perceptions and thoughts. In fact, the party was just beginning, for onto the stage now steps Sapir's most creative student, Benjamin Lee Whorf.

Whereas Sapir still kept a few toes on the ground and on the whole was reluctant to spell out the exact form of the alleged tyrannical hold of linguistic categories on the mind, his student Whorf suffered no such qualms. Whorf was to boldly go where no man had gone before, and in a series of ever wilder claims he expounded the power of our mother tongue to influence not just our thoughts and perceptions but even the physics of the cosmos. The grammar of each language, he wrote, 'is not merely a reproducing instrument for voicing ideas, but rather is itself the shaper of ideas, the programme and guide for the individual's mental activity, for his analysis of impressions. . . . We dissect nature along lines laid down by our native languages.'

The general structure of Whorf's arguments was to mention an out-landish grammatical feature and then, with a fateful 'hence', 'so', or 'therefore', to conclude that this feature must result in a very different way of thinking. From the frequent fusion of noun and verb in Ameri-can Indian languages, for example, Whorf concluded that such lan-guages impose a 'monistic view of nature' rather than our 'bipolar division of nature'. Here is how he justifies such claims: 'Some lan-guages have means of expression in which the separate terms are not so separate as in English but flow together into plastic synthetic creations. *Hence* such languages, which do not paint the separate-object picture of the universe to the same degree as English and its sister tongues, point towards possible new types of logic and possible new cosmical pictures.'

If you find yourself getting swept away by the prose, just remember the English phrase 'it rains', which combines the raindrops and the action of falling into one 'plastic synthetic creation'. Is your 'separate-object picture of the universe' affected? Do you and speakers of 'rain falls' languages operate under a different type of logic and different cos-mical pictures?

HOPI TIME

What surprises most is to find that various grand generalisations of the Western world, such as time, velocity and matter, are not essential to the construction of a consistent picture of the universe.

(Benjamin Lee Whorf, *Science and Linguistics*)

Even the stork in the heavens knows her times. And the turtledove, the swallow, and crane keep the time of their coming. But My people know not the ordinance of the Lord.

(Jeremiah 8:7)

By far the most electrifying of Whorf's arguments concerned a differ-ent area of grammar and a different language: Hopi from north-eastern

Arizona. Today the Hopi number about six thousand and are known especially for the 'snake dance', in which the performers dance with live snakes between their teeth. The snakes are then released and spread the word among their peers that the Hopi are in harmony with the spiritual and natural world. But Whorf made Hopi famous for a different reason: the Hopi language, he said, had no concept of time. Whorf claimed to have made a 'long and careful study' of the Hopi language, although he never actually got round to visiting them in Arizona and his research was exclusively based on his conversations with one Hopi informant who lived in New York City. At the start of his investigations, Whorf argued that Hopi time 'has zero dimensions; i.e., it cannot be given a number greater than one. The Hopi do not say, "I stayed five days", but "I left on the fifth day". A word referring to this kind of time, like the word day, can have no plural'. From this fact he concluded that 'to us, for whom time is a motion on a space, unvarying repetition seems to scatter its force along a row of units of that space, and be wasted. To the Hopi, for whom time is not a motion but a "getting later" of everything that has ever been done, unvarying repetition is not wasted but accumulated.' Whorf thus found it 'gratuitous to assume that a Hopi who knows only the Hopi language and the cultural ideas of his own society has the same notions . . . of time and space that we have'. The Hopi, he said, would not understand our idiom 'tomorrow is another day', because for them the return of the day is 'felt as the return of the same person, a little older but with all the impresses of yesterday, not as "another day," i.e. like an entirely different person.'

But this was only the beginning. As his investigations of Hopi deepened, Whorf decided that his previous analysis had not gone far enough and that the Hopi language in fact contains no reference to time at all. Hopi, he explained, contains 'no words, grammatical forms, constructions or expressions that refer directly to what we call "time," or to past, present, or future'. Thus a Hopi 'has no general notion or intuition of TIME as a smooth flowing continuum in which everything in the universe proceeds at an equal rate'.

This spectacular revelation outshone anything that anyone had previously been able to imagine, and it shot Whorf to the attention of the world. The fame of his claims quickly spread far beyond linguistics, and within a few years Whorf's ideas were in every mouth. Needless to say, the stakes were raised with each retelling. A 1958 book called *Some Things Worth Knowing: A Generalist's Guide to Useful Knowledge* reported that the English language makes it impossible for 'us laymen' to understand the scientific concept of time as a fourth dimension. But 'a Hopi Indian, thinking in the Hopi language – which does not treat time as a flow – has less trouble with the fourth dimension than do we'. A few years later, one anthropologist explained that for the Hopi 'time seems to be that aspect of being which is the knife-edge of now as it is in the process of becoming both "past" and "future." Viewed thus, we have no present either, but our linguistic habits make us feel as if we had.'

There was only one hitch. In 1983, the linguist Ekkehart Malotki, who did extensive fieldwork on the Hopi language, wrote a book called *Hopi Time*. The first page of the book is largely blank, with only two short sentences printed in the middle, one below the other:

> After long and careful study and analysis, the Hopi language is seen to contain no words, grammatical forms, constructions, or expressions that refer directly to what we call 'time.'
>
> (Benjamin Lee Whorf, 'An American Indian Model of the Universe,' 1936)

> *pu' antsa pay qavongvaqw pay su'its talavay kuyvansat, pàasatham pu' pam piw maanat taatayna*
>
> Then indeed, the following day, quite early in the morning at the hour when people pray to the sun, around that time then, he woke up the girl again
>
> (Ekkehart Malotki, Hopi Field Notes, 1980)

Malotki's book goes on to describe, in 677 pages of small print, the numerous expressions for time in the Hopi language, as well as the tense and aspect system on its 'timeless verbs'. Incredible how much a language can change in forty years.

It is not difficult to comprehend why the principle of linguistic relativity, or the 'Sapir–Whorf hypothesis', as it has also come to be known, has sunk into such disrepute among respectable linguists. But there are others – philosophers, theologians, literary critics – who carry the torch regardless. One idea has proved particularly resilient to the onslaught of fact or reason: the argument that the tense system of a language determines the speakers' understanding of time. Biblical Hebrew has offered particularly rich picking, as its allegedly tenseless verbal system could be relied on to explain anything from the Israelites' conception of time to the nature of Judaeo-Christian prophecy. In his 1975 cult book *After Babel*, George Steiner follows a long line of great thinkers in attempting to 'relate grammatical possibilities and constraints to the development of such primary ontological concepts as time and eternity'. While always careful to avoid any formulation that could be nailed to a specific sense, Steiner nevertheless informs us that 'much of the distinctive Western apprehension of time as a linear sequence and vectorial motion is set out in and organised by the Indo-European verb system'. But biblical Hebrew, according to Steiner, never developed such tense distinctions at all. Is this difference between the elaborate tense system of the Indo-European Greek and the tenselessness of Hebrew, he asks, responsible for the 'contrasting evolution of Greek and Hebrew thought'? Or does it merely reflect pre-existing thought patterns? 'Is the convention that spoken facts are strictly contemporaneous with the presentness of the speaker – a convention which is crucial to Hebraic-Christian doctrines of revelation – a generator or a consequence of grammatical form?' Steiner concludes that the influence must go in both directions: the verbal system influences thought, which in turn influences the verbal system, all in 'manifold reciprocity'.

Above all, Steiner argues, it is the future tense that has momentous consequences for the human soul and mind, as it shapes our concept of time and rationality, even the very essence of our humanity. 'We can be defined as the mammal that uses the future of the verb "to be,"' he explains. The future tense is what gives us hope for the future, and without it we are all condemned to end 'in Hell, that is to say, in a gram-mar without futures'.

Before you rush to get rid of your psychiatrist and hire a grammar-ian instead, try this quick reality check. First, on a point of order, one should mention that no one fully understands the niceties of the bibli-cal Hebrew verbal system. There are two main verbal forms in Hebrew, and the difference between them seems to depend on some elusive mix of both tense and what linguists call aspect – the distinction between completed actions (e.g. 'I ate') and ongoing actions ('I was eating'). But let's even grant for the sake of argument that the Hebrew verb does not express the future tense, or any other tenses at all. Need this absence have any constraining effect on the speakers' understanding of time, future, and eternity? Here is a verse from a delightful prophecy about impending doom, where a wrathful Jehovah promises his enemies imminent retribution:

לִי נָקָם וְשִׁלֵּם לְעֵת תָּמוּט רַגְלָם כִּי קָרוֹב יוֹם אֵידָם וְחָשׁ עֲתִדֹת לָמוֹ

Vengeance is mine, and recompense, at the time when their foot **shall slip**; for the day of their calamity is near, and the things to come **hasten** upon them.

(The Song of Moses, Deuteronomy 32:35)

There are two verbs in the Hebrew original, and as it happens, the first, 'slip', is in one of the two main verbal forms I have just mentioned, and the second, 'hasten', is in the other. In the English translation, these two verbs appear in two different tenses: 'shall slip' and 'hasten'. But while scholars can argue until vengeance comes home whether the difference between the Hebrew verbal forms expresses primarily aspect or tense, does any of this matter two hoots to the meaning of this verse? Would the meaning of the English translation change in any way if we changed the verb 'slip' to the present tense: 'at the time when their foot *slips*'? And can you detect any nebulousness about the concept of the future in the spine-chilling image of the things to come *hastening* upon the sinners?

Or think about it another way: when you ask someone, in perfect

English prose and in the present tense, something like 'are you coming tomorrow?' do you feel your grasp of the concept of futurity is slipping? Your idea of time changing in manifold reciprocity? The hope and resilience of your spirit and the fabric of your humanity beginning to fail? If Jeremiah were alive today, he might say (or do I mean 'he might have said'?): Even the stork in the heavens knows her times. And the turtledove, the swallow, and crane keep the time of their coming. But My scholars know not the ordinance of the World.

You may feel you have heard enough about linguistic relativity by now, but let me treat you to one final bit of burlesque. In 1996, the American journal *Philosophy Today* featured an article entitled 'Linguistic Relativity in French, English, and German Philosophy' in which the author, William Harvey, asserted that the grammar of French, English, and German can explain the differences between the three philosophical traditions. For example, 'English philosophy being largely, according to our thesis, determined by English grammar, we should find it to be, like the language, a fusion of the French and the German.' The point is then proved by showing that English theology (Anglican) is a cross between (French) Catholicism and (German) Protestantism. There are further gems. German's case system 'is part of the explanation for German philosophy's orientation towards system construction', whereas 'if English thought is in some ways more open to ambiguity and lack of system, it might be attributed in part to the relative variability and looseness of English syntax'.

It might. It might also be attributable to the irregular shape of hot cross buns. More appropriately, however, it should be attributed to the habit of English-language journals to allow the likes of Mr Harvey free range. (Incidentally, I know that hot cross buns are not particularly irregular. But then again, neither is English syntax particularly 'variable and loose'. It is more rigid in its word order, for instance, than German.)

THE PRISON-HOUSE OF LANGUAGE

By far the most famous claim that Nietzsche never made was: 'We have to cease to think if we refuse to do so in the prison-house of language.'

What he actually said was: 'We cease to think if we do not want to do it under linguistic constraints' (*Wir hören auf zu denken, wenn wir es nicht in dem sprachlichen Zwange thun wollen*). But the English mistranslation has turned into a catchphrase, and as it happens, this phrase neatly summarises everything that is so wrong about linguistic relativity. For there is one toxic fallacy that runs like quicksilver through all the arguments we have encountered so far, and this is the assumption that the language we happen to speak is a prison-house that limits the concepts we are able to understand. Whether it is the claim that the lack of a tense system constrains speakers' understanding of time, or the allegation that when a verb and an object are fused together speakers do not understand the distinction between action and thing – what unites all these contentions is a premise that is as crude as it is false, namely that 'the limits of my language mean the limits of my world', that the concepts expressed in a language are the same as the concepts its speakers are able to understand, and that the distinctions made in a grammar are the same as the distinctions the speakers are able to conceive.

It is barely comprehensible that such a ludicrous notion could have achieved such currency, given that so much contrary evidence screams in the face wherever one looks. Do ignorant folk who have never heard of 'Schadenfreude' find it difficult to understand the concept of relishing someone else's misfortune? Conversely, do Germans, whose language uses one and the same word for 'when' and 'if' (*wenn*), fail to understand the logical difference between what might happen under certain conditions and what will happen regardless? Did the ancient Babylonians, who used the same word (*arnum*) for both 'crime' and 'punishment,' not understand the difference? If so, why did they write thousands of legal documents, law codes, and court protocols to determine exactly what punishment should be given for what crime?

The list of examples could easily be extended. The Semitic languages require different verbal forms for the masculine and the feminine ('you eat' would have different forms depending on whether you are female or male), whereas English does not make gender distinctions on verbs. George Steiner concludes from this that 'an entire anthropology of sexual equality is implicit in the fact that our verbs, in distinction from those of Semitic tongues, do not indicate the gender of the agent'. Really? There are some languages that are so sexually enlightened that they make no gender distinctions even on pronouns, so that even 'he' and 'she' are fused into one unisex plastic synthetic creation. Which languages might these be? Turkish, Indonesian, and Uzbek, to name a few examples – not exactly languages of societies renowned for their anthropology of sexual equality.

Of course, no list of such blunders could be complete without George Orwell's novel *1984*, where the political rulers have such faith in the power of language that they assume political dissent could be entirely eliminated if only all offending words could be expunged from the vocabulary. 'In the end we shall make thoughtcrime literally impossible, because there will be no words in which to express it.' But why stop there? Why not abolish the word 'greed' as a quick fix for the world's economy, or do away with the word 'pain' to save billions on paracetamol, or confine the word 'death' to the dustbin as an instant formula for universal immortality?

⌒

My ultimate aim, proclaimed earlier on, was to convince you that there might after all be something worth salvaging from the idea that our mother tongue can influence our thoughts and perceptions. This aim may now seem more like a suicide mission. But although the prospects for linguistic relativity do not look terribly promising right at the moment, the good news is that, having reached the intellectual nadir, things can only look up from here. In fact, the bankruptcy of Whorfianism has been beneficial for the progress of science, because by setting such an appalling example it has exposed the two cardinal errors that any responsible theory about the influence of language on thought must avoid. First, Whorf's addiction to fantasies unfettered by facts has taught us that any alleged influence of a language on speakers' minds must be demonstrated, not just assumed. One cannot just say 'language X does things differently from language Y, and *hence* speakers of X must think differently from speakers of Y'. If there are reasons to suspect that speakers of X might think differently from speakers of Y, this has to be shown empirically. In fact, even that is not quite enough, since when differences in thought patterns can be demonstrated, a convincing case still has to be made that it was really language that *caused* these differences, rather than other factors in the speakers' cultures and environments.

The second major lesson from the errors of Whorfianism is that we must escape from the prison-house of language. Or rather, what we must escape from is the delusion that language is a prison-house for thought – that it constrains its speakers' ability to reason logically and prevents them from understanding ideas that are used by speakers of other languages.

Of course, when I say that a language does not prevent its speakers from understanding any concepts, I do not mean one that can talk about any subject in any language in its current state. Try to translate a dishwasher operating manual into the language of a tribe from the Papuan highlands, and you will get stuck fairly quickly, since there are no words for forks, or plates, or glasses, or buttons, or soap, or rinsing programmes, or flashing fault indicators. But it's not the deep nature of the language that prevents the Papuans from understanding such concepts; it's simply the fact that they are not acquainted with the relevant cultural artefacts. Given enough time, you could perfectly well explain all these things to them in their mother tongue.

Likewise, try to translate an introduction to metaphysics or to algebraic topology or, for that matter, many passages of the New Testament into our Papuan language, and you are unlikely to get very far, because you will not have words equivalent to most of the abstract concepts that are required. But again, you could create the vocabulary for such abstract concepts in any language, either by borrowing it or by extending the use of existing words to abstract senses. (European languages used both strategies.) These brave claims about the theoretical possibility of expressing complex ideas in any language are not merely wishful thinking; they have been proved countless times in practise. Admittedly, the experiment has not been conducted so often with dishwasher manuals or with metaphysics textbooks, but it has been conducted very often with the New Testament, which contains theological and philosophical arguments on extremely high levels of abstraction.

And if you are still tempted by the theory that the inventory of ready-made concepts in our mother tongue determines the concepts we are able to understand, then just ask yourself how one would ever manage to learn any new concepts if that theory were true. Take this example: if you are not a professional linguist, the word 'factivity' will probably not be part of your language. But does this mean that your mother tongue (ordinary English, that is) precludes you from understanding the distinction between 'factive' and 'non-factive' verbs? Let's see. The verbs 'realise' and 'know', for example, are called 'factive', because if you say something like 'Alice realised that her friends had left', you are implying that what Alice realised was a true fact. (So it would be very odd to say 'Alice realised that her friends had left, but in fact they hadn't'.) On the other hand, non-factive verbs such as 'assume' do not imply a true fact: when you say 'Alice assumed that her friends had left', you can continue equally naturally with either 'and indeed they had' or 'but in fact they hadn't'. So there we are. I have just explained a new and highly abstract concept to you, factivity, that was not part of your language before. Was your mother tongue a barrier?

Since there is no evidence that any language forbids its speakers from thinking anything, as Humboldt himself recognised two hundred years ago, the effects of the mother tongue cannot be sought in what different languages *allow* their speakers to think. But where then? Humboldt went on to say, in somewhat mystical terms, that languages nevertheless differ in what they 'encourage and stimulate to do from their own inner force'. He seems to have had the right sort of intuition, but he was clearly struggling to pin it down and never managed to get beyond the metaphors. Can we turn his hazy imagery into something more transparent?

I believe we can. But to do so, we need to abandon the so-called Sapir–Whorf hypothesis, the assumption that languages limit their speakers' ability to express or understand concepts, and turn instead to a fundamental insight that can be dubbed the Boas–Jakobson principle.

FROM SAPIR-WHORF TO BOAS-JAKOBSON

We have already encountered the anthropologist Franz Boas as the person who introduced Edward Sapir to the study of Native American

Franz Boas, 1858–1942   Roman Jakobson, 1896–1982

languages. In 1938, Boas made an acute observation about the role of grammar in language. He wrote that, in addition to determining the relationship between the words in a sentence, 'grammar performs another important function. It determines those aspects of each experience that *must* be expressed.' And he went on to explain that such obligatory aspects vary greatly between languages. Boas's observation was rather inconspicuously placed in a little section about 'grammar' within a chapter entitled 'Language' within an introduction to *General Anthropology,* and its significance does not seem to have been fully appreciated until two decades later, when the Russian-American linguist Roman Jakobson encapsulated Boas's insight into a pithy maxim: 'Languages differ essentially in what they *must* convey and not in what they *may* convey.' The crucial differences between languages, in other words, are not in what each language allows its speakers to express – for in theory any language could express anything – but in what information each language obliges it speakers to express.

Jakobson gives the following example. If I say in English 'I spent yesterday evening with a neighbour', you may well wonder whether my companion was male or female, but I have the right to tell you politely that it's none of your business. But if we are speaking French or German or Russian, I don't have the privilege to equivocate, because I am obliged by the language to choose between *voisin* or *voisine*, *Nachbar* or *Nachbarin*, *sosed* or *sosedka*. So French, German, and Russian would compel me to inform you about the sex of my companion whether or not I felt it was your business. This does not mean, of course, that English speakers are oblivious to the differences between evenings spent with male or female neighbours. Nor does it mean that English speakers cannot express the distinction should they want to. It only means that English speakers are not obliged to specify the sex each time the neighbour is mentioned, while speakers of some languages are.

On the other hand, English does oblige you to specify certain bits of information that can be left to the context in some other languages. If I want to tell you in English about a dinner with my neighbour, I may not have to tell you the neighbour's sex, but I do have to tell you something about the timing of the event: I have to decide whether we *dined, have been dining, are dining, will be dining*, and so on. Chinese, on the other hand, does not oblige its speakers to specify the exact time of the action each time they use a verb, because the same verbal form can be used for past or present or future actions. Again, this does not mean that Chinese speakers are unable to express the time of the action if they think it is particularly relevant. But as opposed to English speakers, they are not obliged to do so every time.

Neither Boas nor Jakobson was highlighting such grammatical differences in relation to the influence of language on the mind. Boas was concerned primarily with the role that grammar plays in language, and Jakobson was dealing with the challenges that such differences pose for translation. Nevertheless, it seems to me that the Boas–Jakobson principle is the key to unlocking the actual effects of a particular language on thought. If different languages influence their speakers' minds in varying ways, this is not because of what each language allows people to think but rather because of the kinds of information each language habitually obliges people to think *about*. When a language forces its speakers to pay attention to certain aspects of the world each time they open their mouths or prick up their ears, such habits of speech can eventually settle into habits of mind with consequences for memory, or perception, or associations, or even practical skills.

If this all still sounds a little too abstract, then the contrast between the Sapir–Whorf hypothesis and the Boas–Jakobson principle can be

1. Kit of wools for the Holmgren colour-blindness test (see page 47).

2. A rainbow.

3. The difference between these two pictures demonstrates Magnus's revised theory (see page 48). The picture on the top is what Europeans see, and the picture on the bottom is what Magnus argued the ancients would have seen: the red hues are just as vivid, but the cooler colours green and blue are much less so.

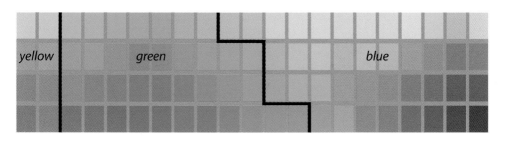

4a. The English colours 'yellow', 'green' and 'blue' (see page 84).

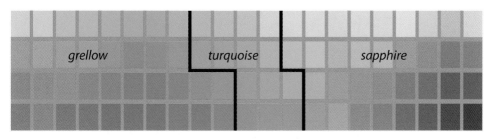

4b. An alternative division? 'Grellow', 'turquoise', and 'sapphire'.

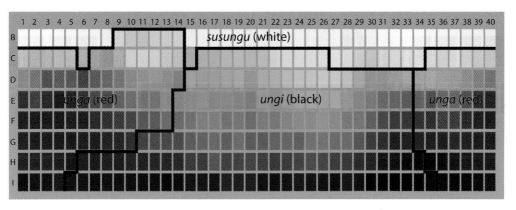

5a. The Bellonese 3-colour system (see page 84).

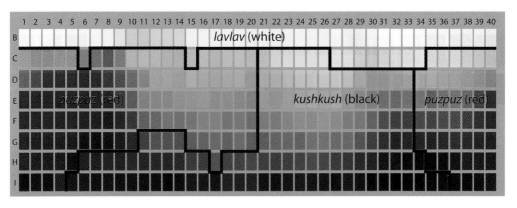

5b. The Ziftish 3-colour system (see page 84).

6. The set of 320 coloured chips used by Berlin and Kay (in 40 equally spaced hues and 8 degrees of brightness. All chips are at maximum saturation). (See page 85.)

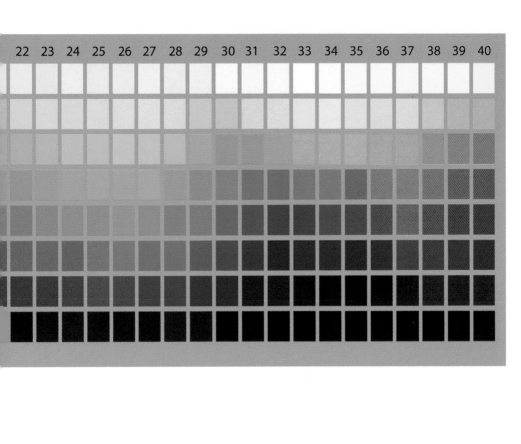

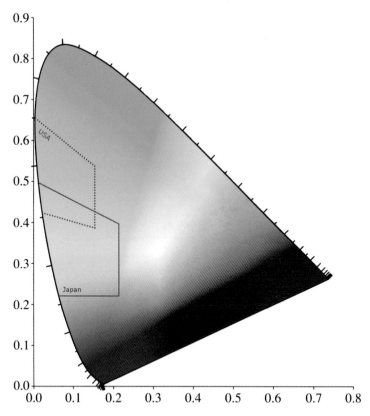

7. Official specifications for the approved hues of green traffic lights in Japan and the United States, defined as regions of the standard CIE 1931 chromaticity diagram (see page 217).

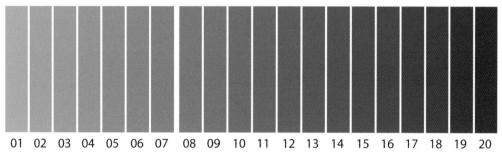

01 02 03 04 05 06 07 08 09 10 11 12 13 14 15 16 17 18 19 20

8. The 'Russian blues' experiment (see page 222).

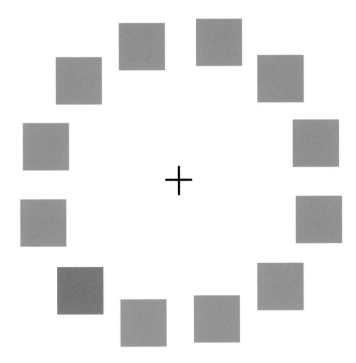

9. Circle of squares in green and blue shades (see page 228).

Easy-to-name colours

Difficult-to-name colours

10. Easy-to-name and difficult-to-name colours in Chinese (see page 230).

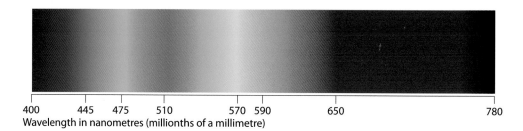

400   445   475   510   570 590   650   780
Wavelength in nanometres (millionths of a millimetre)

11. The visible spectrum.

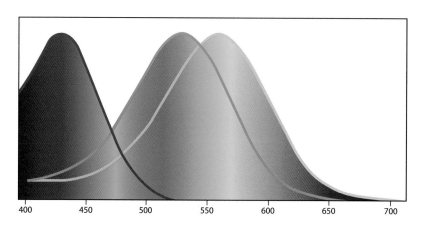

400   450   500   550   600   650   700

12. The (normalised) sensitivity of the short-wave, middle-wave, and long-wave cones
as a function of wavelength (see page 243).

brought into focus with another example. Chinese may seem to us rather
lax in allowing its speakers to equivocate about the time of the action,
but just try to imagine what a speaker of Matses from Peru might feel
upon hearing about the incredibly crude and careless tense distinctions
of English.

The Matses are a 2,500-strong tribe, and they live in the tropical rainforest along the Javari River, a tributary of the Amazon. Their language,
which was recently described by the linguist David Fleck, compels them
to make distinctions of mind-blowing subtlety whenever they report
events. To start with, there are three degrees of pastness in Matses: you
cannot just say that someone 'passed by there'; you have to specify with
different verbal endings whether this action took place in the recent past
(roughly up to a month), distant past (roughly from a month to fifty
years), or remote past (more than fifty years ago). In addition, the verb has
a system of distinctions that linguists call 'evidentiality,' and as it happens, the Matses system of evidentiality is the most elaborate that has
ever been reported for any language. Whenever Matses speakers use a
verb, they are obliged to specify – like the finickiest of lawyers – exactly
how they came to know about the facts they are reporting. The Matses, in
other words, have to be master epistemologists. There are separate verbal
forms depending on whether you are reporting direct experience (you
saw someone passing by with your own eyes), something inferred from
evidence (you saw footprints on the sand), conjecture (people always pass
by at that time of day), or hearsay (your neighbour told you he had seen
someone passing by). If a statement is reported with the incorrect evidentiality form, it is considered a lie. So if, for instance, you ask a Matses man
how many wives he has, unless he can actually see his wives at that very
moment, he would answer in the past tense and would say something like
daëd ikoşh: 'two there were [directly experienced recently]'. In effect, what
he would be saying is, 'There were two last time I checked.' After all, given
that the wives are not present, he cannot be absolutely certain that one of
them hasn't died or run off with another man since he last saw them, even
if this was only five minutes ago. So he cannot report it as a certain fact in
the present tense.

But finding the right verbal form for directly experienced events is child's play compared with the hair-splitting precision required when you report an event that has only been inferred. Here, Matses obliges you to specify not just how long ago you assume the event occurred but also how long ago you made the inference. Suppose you saw wild pigs' footprints on the ground somewhere outside the village, and you want to tell your friends that the animals passed by at that place. In English, saying 'wild pigs passed by there' is exactly as much information as you have to specify. But in Matses, you have to reveal both how long ago you found out about the event (that is, how long ago you saw the footprints) and how long before that you think the event itself (pigs passing by) actually occurred. For example, if a short time ago you discovered tracks that were still fresh, you assume that the wild pigs passed by only shortly before you saw the tracks, so you would have to say:

kuen–ak–o–ṣh
passed by–HAPPENED SHORTLY BEFORE EXPERIENCED–EXPERIENCED RECENTLY–they
they passed by' (I found out a short time ago, it had happened shortly before that)

If a short time ago you discovered tracks that were already old, you would have to say:

kuen–nëdak–o–ṣh
passed by–HAPPENED LONG BEFORE EXPERIENCED–EXPERIENCED RECENTLY–they
they passed by' (I found out a short time ago, it had happened long before that)

If a long time ago you discovered tracks that were still fresh, you would have to say:

kuen–ak–onda–ṣh
passed by–HAPPENED SHORTLY BEFORE EXPERIENCED–EXPERIENCED LONG AGO–they
they passed by' (I found out long ago, it had happened shortly before that)

And if a long time ago you discovered old tracks:

kuen–nëdak–onda–şh
passed by–HAPPENED LONG BEFORE EXPERIENCED–EXPERIENCED LONG AGO–they
'they passed by' (I found out long ago, it had happened long before that)

The Matses system is outlandish by any stretch of the imagination, and nothing quite as elaborate has yet been found elsewhere. Matses shows just how fundamentally languages can vary in the kinds of information they oblige their speakers to convey. But the weirdness of Matses also helps to clarify exactly where credible influences of language on thought may and may not be sought. One shudders to think what Whorf would have made of the Matses language if information about it had fallen into his hands, or, for that matter, what a Whorfian among the Matses would make of the unfathomable vagueness of English verbs. 'I find it gratuitous to assume,' such a Matses sage would say, 'that an American who knows only the English language and the cultural ideas of his own society can have a proper grasp of epistemology. English speakers simply would not be able to understand the difference between directly experienced events and merely inferred facts, because their language imposes on them a monistic view of the universe that blends the event with how it was experienced into one plastic synthetic creation.'

But this is gobbledegook, because we have no problems understanding the Matses distinctions, and if we are so minded we can easily express them in English: 'I saw with my own eyes a short time ago that . . . ', 'I inferred a long time ago that . . . ', 'I guessed a very long time ago that . . .', and so on. When this kind of information is felt to be particularly relevant, for instance in the witness box, English speakers routinely use such expressions. The only real difference between English and Matses, therefore, is that Matses *forces* its speakers to supply all this information whenever they describe an event, whereas English does not.

Whether the requirement to specify evidentiality translates into habits of mind that affect more than language is something that no one has yet studied empirically. But all the credible claims from recent years about the influence of a particular language on thought run on similar lines. No one (in his or her right mind) would argue nowadays that the structure of a language limits its speakers' understanding to those concepts and distinctions that happen to be already part of the linguistic system. Rather, serious researchers have looked for the consequences of the *habitual* use from an early age of certain ways of expression. For example, does the need to pay constant attention to certain aspects of experience train speakers to be especially sensitive to certain details or induce particular types of memory patterns and associations? These are exactly the questions we shall explore in the next chapters.

For some critics, such as Steven Pinker, the fact that our mother tongue constrains neither our capacity to reason logically nor our ability to understand complex ideas is an irredeemable anticlimax. In his recent book, *The Stuff of Thought*, Pinker argues that since no one has ever managed to show that speakers of one language find it impossible, or even extremely difficult, to reason in a particular way that comes naturally to the speakers of another language, then any remaining effects of language on thought are mundane, unsexy, boring, even trivial. Obviously, what's sexy is a matter of personal taste. But in what follows, I hope to show that while the actual effects of language on thought are very different from the wild and woolly claims of the past, they are far from boring, mundane, or trivial.

7

Where the Sun Doesn't Rise in the East

DRESSED FOR DINNER

The Guugu Yimithirr language has one famous claim to fame, and is consequently celebrated throughout the wide world of trivial pursuits. The story runs roughly like this. In July 1770, Captain Cook's *Endeavour* was grounded off the north-eastern coast of Australia, near the mouth of a river soon to be named Endeavour, in a place that was later to become Cooktown. During the weeks when the ship was being repaired, Captain Cook and his crew made contact with the native population of the continent, both human and marsupial. With the former, relations were at first rather cordial. Cook writes in his diary on 10 July 1770: 'In the A.M. four of the Natives came down to the Sandy point on the North side of the Harbour, having along with them a small wooden Canoe with Outriggers, in which they seem'd to be employed striking fish. They were wholy naked, their Skins the Colour of Wood soot. Their Hair was black, lank, and cropt short, and neither wooly nor Frizled. Some part of their Bodys had been painted with red, and one of them had his upper lip and breast painted with Streakes of white. Their features were far from being disagreeable; their Voices were soft and Tunable.'

The other natives were treated with somewhat less respect. In the *Account of the Voyages*, which was based on the diaries of Cook and his officers, we read the following description for what unfolded later that week: 'Mr Gore, who went out this day with his gun, had the good fortune to kill one of the animals which had been so much the subject of our speculation. . . . The head, neck, and shoulders, are very small in proportion to the other parts of the body; the tail is nearly as long as the body, thick near the rump, and tapering towardss the end: the fore-legs of this individual were only eight inches long, and the hind-legs two and twenty: its progress is by successive leaps or hops, of a great length, in an erect posture; the skin is covered with a short fur, of a dark mouse or grey colour, excepting the head and ears, which bear a slight resemblance to those of a hare. This animal is called by the natives *Kanguroo*. The next day, our Kanguroo was dressed for dinner, and proved most excellent meat.'

The *Endeavour* returned to England the following year with the skins of two kangaroos, and the animal painter George Stubbs was commissioned to do a likeness. Stubbs's kangaroo immediately caught the public's imagination, and the animal shot into celebrity. Eighteen years later, the excitement reached fever pitch when the first living specimen, 'the wonderful Kanguroo from Botany Bay', arrived in London and was displayed in the Haymarket. English thus gained its first word of Australian aboriginal origin, and as the fame of the animal spread to other countries, 'kangaroo' became the most prominent feature of international vocabulary that was exported by a native language of Australia.

Or was it?

While the kangaroo's enduring popularity in the Old World was not a matter for doubt, the authenticity of the word's roots in Australia soon came under suspicion. For when later Australian explorers spotted the animal in other parts of the continent, the local Aborigines never came up with anything remotely similar to 'kangaroo'. Natives the length and breadth of Australia didn't even recognise the word, and some of them actually assumed they were being taught the English name for the animal when they heard it. Since many different native

George Stubbs's *The Kongouro from New Holland*, 1772

languages were spoken across the continent, the fact that the Aborigines in other parts of Australia did not recognise the word was not, in itself, so suspicious. But most damaging to the credibility of 'kangaroo' was the report of another explorer, Captain Philip Parker King, who visited the mouth of the very same Endeavour River in 1820, fifty years after Cook had left. When Captain King asked the Aborigines he met there what the animal was called, he was given a completely different name from what Cook had recorded. King transcribed the name in his own diary as 'minnar' or 'meenuah'.

So who were those natives with voices soft and tunable who had given Cook the word 'kanguroo' in 1770, and what was their language? Or had Cook simply been duped? By the mid-nineteenth century, scepticism about the authenticity of the word was rife. In 1850, John Crawfurd, a distinguished Orientalist and Stamford Raffles's successor as the resident of Singapore, wrote in the *Journal of the Indian Archipelago and Eastern Asia* that 'it is very remarkable that this word, supposed to be Australian, is not to be found as the name of this singular marsupial animal in any language of Australia. Cook and his companions, therefore, when they gave it this name, must have made some mistake, but of what nature cannot be conjectured.' Myths and legends of all kinds soon spread. The most famous version, beloved of comedians unto this day, is that 'kangaroo' was the phrase for 'I don't understand', the answer allegedly given by the bemused natives to Cook's question 'What is this animal called?'

More responsible lexicographers elected to remain cautious, and the *Oxford English Dictionary* hedges with appropriate elegance in the following definition, which – at the time I'm writing – still appears in the online edition: 'Kangaroo: stated to have been the name in a native Australian language. Cook and Banks believed it to be the name given to the animal by the natives at Endeavour River, Queensland.'

The mystery from Down Under was eventually resolved in 1971, when the anthropologist John Haviland began an intensive study of Guugu Yimithirr, a language spoken by an aboriginal community of about a thousand people who these days live some thirty miles north of Cooktown, but who previously occupied the territory near the Endeavour River. Haviland found that there is one particular type of large grey kangaroo whose name in Guugu Yimithirr is *gangurru*. The paternity of the name could thus no longer be in doubt. But if so, why wasn't Captain King given the same name by the speakers of the same language when he visited in 1820? As it happens, the large grey *gangurru* that Cook's party spotted is only rarely seen near the coast, so King probably pointed at a different type of kangaroo, which has a different name in Guugu Yimithirr. But we will never know which type of kangaroo it was that King saw, because the word he recorded, 'minnar' or 'meenuah', was no doubt *minha*, the general term that means 'meat' or 'edible animal'.

So Captain Cook was not duped. His linguistic observations are now rehabilitated, and in consequence, Guugu Yimithirr, the language that bequeathed to international vocabulary its most famous aboriginal icon, has won a place in the hearts and minds of trivia addicts all over the world.

EGOCENTRIC AND GEOGRAPHIC COORDINATES

'Then would you read a Sustaining Book, such as would help and comfort a Wedged Bear in Great Tightness?' So for a week

Christopher Robin read that sort of book at the North end of
Pooh, and Rabbit hung his washing on the South end.
('Pooh Goes Visiting and Pooh and Piglet Nearly Catch a Woozle')

There is an even better reason why Guugu Yimithirr deserves to be
famous, but this reason is unknown even to the most avid trainspotters
and is confined to the circles of professional linguists and anthropologists. The name of the language Guugu Yimithirr means something
like 'this kind of language' or 'speaking this way' (*guugu* is 'language',
and *yimi-thirr* means 'this way'), and this name is rather apt since
Guugu Yimithirr has a manner of talking about spatial relations that is
decidedly out of this way. Its method of describing the arrangements of
objects in space sounds almost incredibly odd to us, and when these
peculiarities in Guugu Yimithirr were uncovered they inspired a large-
scale research project into the language of space. The findings from this
research have led to a fundamental revision of what had been assumed
to be universal properties of human language, and have also supplied
the most striking example so far of how our mother tongue can affect
the way we think.

Suppose you want to give someone driving directions for getting to
your house. You might say something like: 'Just after the traffic lights,
take the first left and continue until you see the supermarket on your
left, then turn right and drive to the end of the road, where you'll see a
white house right in front of you. Our door is the one on the right.' You
could, in theory, also say the following: 'Just to the east of the traffic
lights, drive north and continue until you see a supermarket in the
west. Then drive east, and at the end of the road you'll see a white house
directly to the east. Ours is the southern door.' These two sets of directions are equivalent in the sense that they describe the same route, but
they rely on different systems of coordinates. The first system uses *egocentric* coordinates, whose two axes depend on our own body: a left–
right axis and a front–back axis orthogonal to it. This coordinate system
moves around with us wherever we turn. The axes always shift together
with our field of vision, so that what is in the front becomes behind if
we turn round, what was on our right is now on the left. The second

system of coordinates uses fixed geographic directions, which are based on the compass directions North, South, East, and West. These directions do not change with your movements – what is to your north remains exactly to your north no matter how often you twist and turn.

Of course, the egocentric and geographic systems do not exhaust the possibilities of talking about space and giving spatial directions. One could, for example, just point at a particular direction and say 'go that way'. But for simplicity, let's concentrate on the differences between the egocentric and the geographic systems. Each system of coordinates has advantages and disadvantages, and in practise we use both in our daily lives, depending on their appropriateness to the context. It would be most natural to use cardinal directions when giving instructions for hiking in the open countryside, for example, or more generally for talking about large-scale orientation. 'Oregon is north of California' is more natural than 'Oregon is to the right of California if you're facing the sea'. Even inside some cities, especially those with clear geographic axes, people use fixed geographic concepts such as 'uptown' or 'downtown'. But on the whole, when giving driving or walking directions in town, it is far more usual to use the egocentric coordinates: 'turn left, then take the third right', and so on. The egocentric coordinates are even more dominant when we describe small-scale spaces, especially inside buildings. The geographic directions may not be entirely absent (estate agents may wax lyrical about south-facing living rooms, for instance), but this usage is at best marginal. Just think how ridiculous it would be to say, 'When you get out of the lift, walk south and then take the second door to the east.' When Pooh gets wedged in Rabbit's front doorway and is forced to remain there for a whole week to reduce his girth, A. A. Milne refers to the 'North end' and 'the South end' of Pooh and thereby highlights the desperate fixity of his predicament. But think how absurd it would be for an aerobic trainer or a ballet teacher to say, 'How raise your north hand and move your south leg eastwards.'

Why does the egocentric system feel so much easier and more natural to handle? Simply because we always know where 'in front of' us is and where 'behind' and 'left' and 'right' are. We don't need a map or a compass to work this out, we don't need to look at the sun or the North Star, we just feel it, because the egocentric system of coordinates is based directly on our own body and our immediate visual field. The front–back axis cuts right between our two eyes: it is a long imaginary line that extends straight from our nose into the distance and which turns with our nose and eyes wherever and whenever they turn. And likewise, the left–right axis, which cuts through our shoulders, always obligingly adapts itself to our own orientation.

The system of geographic coordinates, on the other hand, is based on external concepts that do not adapt themselves to our own orientation and that need to be computed (or remembered) from the position of the sun or the stars or from features of the landscape. So on the whole, we revert to the geographic coordinates only when we really need to do so: if the egocentric system is not up to the task or if the geographic directions are specifically relevant (for instance, in evaluating the merits of south-facing rooms).

Indeed, philosophers and psychologists from Kant onwards have argued that all spatial thinking is essentially egocentric in nature and that our primary notions of space are derived from the planes that go through our bodies. One of the trump arguments for the primacy of the egocentric coordinates was of course human language. The universal reliance of languages on the egocentric coordinates, and the privileged position that all languages accord the egocentric coordinates over all other systems, was said to parade before us the universal features of the human mind.

But then came Guugu Yimithirr. And then came the astounding realisation that those naked Aborigines who two centuries ago gave the kangaroo to the world had never heard of Immanuel Kant. Or at least they had never read his famous 1768 paper on the primacy of the egocentric conception of space to language and mind. Or at the very least, if they had read it, they never got round to applying Kant's analysis to their language. As it turns out, their language does not make any use of egocentric coordinates at all!

CRYING NOSE TO THE SOUTH

In retrospect, it seems almost a miracle that when John Haviland started researching Guugu Yimithirr in the 1970s, he could still find anyone who spoke the language at all. For the Aborigines' brush with civilisation was not entirely conducive to the conservation of their language.

After Captain Cook departed in 1770, the Guugu Yimithirr were at first spared intense contact with Europeans, and for a whole century were largely left to their own devices. But when the forces of progress eventually did arrive, they came with lightning speed. Gold was discovered in the area in 1873, not far from the spot where Cook's *Endeavour* had once moored, and a town named after Cook was founded – quite literally – overnight. One Friday in October 1873, a ship full of prospectors sailed into a silent, lonely, distant river mouth. And on the Saturday, as one of the travellers later described, 'we were in the middle of a young diggings township – men hurrying to and fro, tents rising in all directions, the shouts of sailors and labourers landing more horses and cargo, combined with the rattling of the donkey-engine, cranes and chains'. Following in the footsteps of the diggers, farmers started taking up properties along the Endeavour River. The prospectors needed land for mining, and the farmers needed the land and the waterholes for their cattle. In the new order, there was not much space left for the Guugu Yimithirr. The farmers resented their burning of grass and chasing the cattle away from the waterholes, so the police were employed to remove the natives from the settlers' land. The Aborigines reacted with a certain degree of antagonism, and this in turn provoked the settlers to a policy of extermination. Less than a year after Cooktown was founded, the *Cooktown Herald* explained in an editorial that 'when savages are pitted against civilisation, they must go to the wall; it is the fate of their race. Much as we may deplore the necessity for such a state of things, it is absolutely necessary, in order that the onward march of civilisation may not be arrested by the antagonism of the aboriginals.' The threats were not empty, for the ideology was carried out through a policy of 'dispersion', which meant shooting aboriginal camps out of existence. Those natives who had not been 'dispersed' either retreated in isolated bands into the bush or were drawn to the town, where they were reduced to drink and prostitution.

In 1886, thirteen years after Cooktown was founded, Bavarian missionaries established a Lutheran mission at Cape Bedford, to the north of the town, to try to salvage the wrecked souls of the lost pagans. Later, the mission moved to a place christened Hopevale, further inland. The mission became a sanctuary for the remaining Aborigines from the entire region and beyond. Although people speaking many different aboriginal languages were brought to Hopevale, Guugu Yimithirr was dominant and became the language of the whole community. A Mr Schwartz, the head of the mission, translated the Bible into Guugu Yimithirr, and although his command of the language was moderate, his faulty Guugu Yimithirr eventually became enshrined as a kind of 'church language', which people can't easily understand but which enjoys an aura much like that of the English of the King James Bible.

In the following decades, the mission underwent further trials and tribulations. During World War II, the whole community was forcefully relocated to the south, and the septuagenarian missionary Schwartz, who had arrived in Cooktown aged nineteen and had lived among the Guugu Yimithirr for half a century, was interred as an enemy alien. And yet, defying the odds, the Guugu Yimithirr language somehow refused to give up the ghost. Well into the 1980s, there were still some older men around who spoke an authentic version of the language.

Haviland discovered that Guugu Yimithirr, as spoken by the older generation, does not have words for 'left' or 'right' as directions at all. Even more strangely, it does not even use terms such as 'in front of' or 'behind' to describe the position of objects. Whenever we would use the egocentric system, the Guugu Yimithirr use the four cardinal directions: *gungga* (North), *jiba* (South), *guwa* (West), and *naga* (East). (In practise, their directions are slightly skewed from the compass North, by about 17 degrees, but this is of not much consequence to our present concerns.)

If Guugu Yimithirr speakers want someone to move over in a car to make room, they will say *naga-naga manaayi*, which means 'move a bit to the east'. If they want to tell you to move a bit back from the table, they will say *guwa-gu manaayi*, 'move a bit to the west'. It is even unusual to say only 'move a bit that way' in Guugu Yimithirr. Rather, one has to add the correct direction 'move a bit that way to the south'. Instead of saying that John is 'in front of the tree,' they would say, 'John is just north of the tree'. If they want to tell you to take the next left turn, they would say, 'go south here.' To tell you where exactly they left something in your house, they would say, 'I left it on the southern edge of the western table.' To tell you to turn off the camping stove, they would say, 'turn the knob east.'

In the 1980s, another linguist, Stephen Levinson, also came to Hopevale, and he describes some of his outlandish experiences with Guugu Yimithirr direction giving. One day, while he was trying to film the poet Tulo telling a traditional myth, Tulo suddenly told him to stop and 'look out for that big ant just north of your foot'. In another instance, a Guugu Yimithirr speaker called Roger explained where frozen fish could be found in a shop some thirty miles away. You will find them 'far end this side', Roger said, gesturing to his right with two flicks of the hand. Levinson assumed that the movement indicated that when one entered the shop the frozen fish were to be found on the right-hand side. But no, it turned out that the fish were actually on the left when you entered the shop. So why the gesture to the right? Roger was not gesturing to the right at all. He was pointing to the north-east, and expected his hearer to understand that when he went into the shop he should look for the fish in the north-east corner.

It gets curiouser. When older speakers of Guugu Yimithirr were shown a short silent film on a television screen and then asked to describe the movements of the protagonists, their responses depended on the orientation of the television when they were watching. If the television was facing north and a man on the screen appeared to be approaching, the older men would say that the man was 'coming northwards'. One younger man then remarked that you always know which way the TV was facing when the old people tell the story.

The same reliance on geographic directions is maintained even when speakers of Guugu Yimithirr are asked to describe a picture inside a book. Suppose the book is facing top-side north. If a man is shown standing to the left of a woman, speakers of Guugu Yimithirr would say, 'the man is to the west of the woman.' But if you rotate the book top-side east, they will say, about exactly the same picture, 'the man is to the north of the woman.' Here, for instance, is how one Guugu Yimithirr speaker described the above picture (guess which way he was facing): *bula gabiir gabiir*, 'two girls,' *nyulu nubuun yindu buthiil naga*, 'the one has nose to the east,' *nyulu yindu buthiil jibaarr*, 'the other nose to the south,' *yugu gaarbaarr yuulili*, 'a tree stands in between,' *buthiil jibaarr nyulu baajiiljil*, 'she's crying nose to the south.'

If you are reading a book facing north, and a Guugu Yimithirr speaker wants to tell you to skip ahead, he will say, 'go further east,' because the pages are flipped from east to west. If you are looking at it facing south, the Guugu Yimithirr will of course say, 'go further west.' They even dream in cardinal directions. One person explained how he

entered heaven in a dream, going northwards, while the Lord was coming towards him southwards.

There are words for 'left hand' and 'right hand' in Guugu Yimithirr.
But they are used only to refer to the inherent properties of each hand
(for instance, to say 'I can lift this with my right hand but not with my
left hand'). Whenever the *position* of a hand in any particular moment
is to be indicated, an expression such as 'hand on the western side' is
used.

In our language, the coordinates rotate with us whenever and wherever we turn. For the Guugu Yimithirr, the axes always remain constant. One way of visualising this difference is to think of the two options
on the displays of satellite navigation systems. Many of these gadgets let
you choose between a 'north up' and a 'driving direction up' display. In
the 'driving direction up' mode, you always see yourself moving directly
upwards on the screen, but the streets around you keep rotating as you
turn. In the 'north up' mode, the streets always stay in the same position, but you see the arrow representing you turning in different directions, so that if you are driving south, the arrow will be moving
downwards. Our linguistic world is primarily in the 'driving direction
up' mode, but in Guugu Yimithirr one speaks exclusively in the 'north
up' mode.

A CRUMB ON YOUR SEAWARD CHEEK

The first reaction to these reports would be to dismiss them as an elaborate practical joke played by bored Aborigines on a few gullible linguists, not unlike the tall stories of sexual liberation that were told to
the anthropologist Margaret Mead by adolescent Samoan girls in the
1920s. The Guugu Yimithirr may not have heard of Kant, but they somehow must have got their hands on *My Adventures on the Remote Island
of Zift* and decided to invent something that would out-nonsense even
the Ziftish concepts 'bose' and 'rird.' But how on earth did they manage
to conjure up something so utterly unlikely and at odds with the rest of
the world?

Well, it turns out that Guugu Yimithirr is not quite as unusual as one might imagine. Once again, we have simply mistaken the familiar for the natural: the egocentric system could be paraded as a universal feature of human language only because no one had bothered to examine in depth those languages that happen to do things differently. In retrospect, it seems strange that such a striking feature of many languages could have gone unnoticed for such a long time, especially since clues had been littering the academic literature for a while. References to unusual ways of talking about space (such as 'your west foot' or 'could you pass me the tobacco there to the east') appeared in reports about various languages around the world, but it was not clear from them that such unusual expressions went beyond the occasional oddity. It took the extreme case of Guugu Yimithirr to inspire a systematic examination of the spatial coordinates in a large range of languages, and only then did the radical divergence of some languages from what had previously been considered universal and natural start sinking in.

To begin with, in Australia itself the reliance on geographic coordinates is very common. From the Djaru language of Kimberley in Western Australia, to Warlbiri, spoken around Alice Springs, to Kayardild, once spoken on Bentinck Island in Queensland, it seems that most Aborigines speak (or at least used to speak) in a distinctly Guugu Yimithirr style. Nor is this peculiar way merely an Antipodean aberration: languages that rely primarily on geographic coordinates turn out to be scattered around the world, from Polynesia to Mexico, from Bali and Nepal to Namibia and Madagascar.

Other than Guugu Yimithirr, the 'geographic language' that has received the most attention so far is found on the other side of the globe, in the highlands of south-eastern Mexico. In fact, we have already come across the Mayan language Tzeltal, in an entirely different context. (Tzeltal was one of the languages in Berlin and Kay's 1969 study of colour terms. The fact that its speakers chose either a clear green or a clear blue as the best example of their 'grue' colour was an inspiration for Berlin and Kay's theory of universal foci.) Tzeltal speakers live on a side of a mountain range that rises roughly towards the south and slopes down towards the north. Unlike in Guugu Yimithirr, their geographic axes are based not on the compass directions north–south and east–west but rather on this prominent feature of their local land-scape. The directions in Tzeltal are 'downhill', 'uphill', and 'across', which can mean either way on the axis perpendicular to uphill-downhill. When a specific direction on the across axis is required, Tzeltal speakers combine 'across' with a place-name and say 'across in the direction of X'.

Geographic coordinate systems that are based on prominent land-marks are also found in other parts of the world. In the language of the Marquesan Islands of French Polynesia, for example, the main axis is defined by the opposition sea-inland. A Marquesan would thus say that a plate on the table is 'inland of the glass' or that you have a crumb 'on your seaward cheek'. There are also systems that combine both cardinal directions and geographic landmarks. In the language of the Indonesian island of Bali, one axis is based on the sun (east–west) and the other axis is based on geographic landmarks: it stretches 'seaward' on one side and 'mountainward' on the other, towards the holy volcano Gunung Agung, the dwelling place of the Hindu gods of Bali.

Earlier on I said that it would be the height of absurdity for a dance teacher to say things like 'now raise your north hand and take three steps eastwards'. But the joke would be lost on some. The Canadian musicolo-gist Colin McPhee spent several years on Bali in the 1930s, researching the musical traditions of the island. In his book *A House in Bali*, he recalls a young boy called Sampih who showed great talent and enthusi-asm for dancing. As there was no suitable teacher in the boy's village, McPhee persuaded Sampih's mother to let him take the boy to a teacher in a different village, so that he could learn the rudiments of the art. Once McPhee had made all the arrangements, he travelled with Sampih to the teacher, left him there, and promised he would come back after five days to check how the boy was progressing. Given Sampih's talent, McPhee was sure that after five days he would be interrupting an advanced lesson. But when he returned, he found Sampih dejected, almost ill, and the teacher exasperated. It was impossible to teach the boy to dance, said the teacher, since Sampih simply did not understand any of the instructions. Why? Because Sampih did not know where 'mountainward', 'seaward', 'east', and 'west' were, so when he was told to take 'three steps mountainward' or to 'bend east' he didn't know what to do. Sampih would not have had the least trouble with these directions in his own village, but since he had never left his village before and since the landscape here was unfamiliar, he got disorientated and confused. No matter how often the teacher pointed at the mountainward direction, Sampih kept forgetting. It was all in vain.

Why didn't the teacher try to use different instructions? He would probably have replied that saying 'take three steps forward' or 'bend backwards' would be the height of absurdity.

PERFECT PITCH FOR DIRECTIONS

What I have reported so far are just facts. They may seem strange, and it is certainly strange that they were discovered only so recently, but the evidence collected by many researchers in different parts of the world no longer leaves room for doubt about their veracity. We venture onto riskier ground, however, when we move from the facts about language to their possible implications on the mind. Different cultures certainly make people *speak* about space in radically different ways. But does this necessarily mean that the speakers also *think* about space differently? By now red lights should be flashing and we should be on Whorf alert. It should be clear that if a language doesn't have a word for a certain concept, that does not necessarily mean its speakers cannot understand this concept.

Indeed, Guugu Yimithirr speakers are perfectly able to understand the concepts of left and right when they speak English. Ironically, it seems that some of them even entertained Whorfian notions about the alleged inability of English speakers to understand cardinal directions. John Haviland reports how he was once working with an informant on translating traditional Guugu Yimithirr tales into English. One story concerned a lagoon that lies 'west of the Cooktown airport' – a description that most English speakers would find perfectly natural and understand perfectly well. But his Guugu Yimithirr informant suddenly said: 'But white fellows wouldn't understand that. In English we'd better say, "to the right as you drive to the airport."'

Instead of searching in vain for how the lack of egocentric coordinates might constrain the Guugu Yimithirr's intellectual horizons, we should turn to the Boas–Jakobson principle and look for the difference in what languages *oblige* their speakers to convey rather than in what they *allow* them to convey. In this particular case, the relevant question is what habits of mind might develop in speakers of Guugu Yimithirr because of the necessity to specify geographic directions whenever spatial information is to be communicated.

When the question is framed in this way, the answer appears inescapable, but no less startling for all that. In order to speak Guugu Yimithirr, you need to know where the cardinal directions are at each and every moment of your waking life. You need to know exactly where the north, south, west, and east are, since otherwise you would not be able to impart the most basic information. It follows, therefore, that in order to be able to speak such a language, you need to have a compass in your mind, one that operates all the time, day and night, without lunch breaks or weekends.

And as it so happens, the Guugu Yimithirr have exactly this kind of an infallible compass. They maintain their orientation with respect to the fixed cardinal directions at all times. Regardless of visibility conditions, regardless of whether they are in thick forest or on an open plain, whether outside or indoors, whether stationary or moving, they have a spot-on sense of direction. Stephen Levinson relates how he took Guugu Yimithirr speakers on various trips to unfamiliar places, both walking and driving, and then tested their orientation. In their region, it is rarely possible to travel in a straight line, since the route often has to go around bogs, mangrove swamps, rivers, mountains, sand dunes, forests, and, if on foot, snake-infested grassland. But even so, and even when they were taken to dense forests with no visibility, even inside caves, they always, without any hesitation, could point accurately to the cardinal directions. They don't do any conscious computations: they don't look at the sun and pause for a moment of calculation before saying 'the ant is north of your foot'. They seem to have perfect pitch for directions. They simply feel where north, south, west, and east are, just as people with perfect pitch hear what each note is without having to calculate intervals.

Similar stories are told about Tzeltal speakers. Levinson relates how one speaker was blindfolded and spun round over twenty times in a darkened house. Still blindfolded and dizzy, he pointed without problem at the direction of 'true downhill'. A woman was taken into the market town for medical treatment. She had rarely if ever been in that town before, and certainly never in the house where she was staying. In the room, the woman spotted an unfamiliar contraption, a sink, and asked her husband: 'Is the hot water in the uphill tap?'

The Guugu Yimithirr take this sense of direction entirely for granted and consider it a matter of course. They cannot explain how they know the cardinal directions, just as you cannot explain how you know where in front of you is and where left and right are. One thing that can be ascertained, however, is that the most obvious candidate, namely the position of the sun, is not the only factor they rely on. Several people reported that when they travelled by plane to very distant places such as Melbourne, more than a three-hour flight away, they experienced the strange sensation that the sun did not rise in the east. One person even insisted that he had been to a place where the sun really did not rise in the east. This means that the Guugu Yimithirr's orientation does fail them when they are displaced to an entirely different geographic region. But more importantly, it shows that in their own environment they rely on cues other than the position of the sun, and that these cues can even take precedence. When Levinson asked some informants if they could think of clues that would help *him* improve his sense of direction, they volunteered such hints as the differences in brightness of the sides of trunks of particular trees, the orientation of termite mounds, wind directions in particular seasons, the flights of bats and migrating birds, the alignment of sand dunes in the coastal area.

⁓

But we are only just beginning, because the sense of orientation that is required to speak a Guugu Yimithirr-style language has to extend further than the immediate present. What about relating past experiences, for instance? Suppose I ask you to describe a picture you saw in a museum a long time ago. You would probably describe what you see in your mind's eye, say the milkmaid pouring the milk into a bowl on a table, the light coming from the window on the left and illuminating the wall behind her, and so on. Or suppose you are trying to remember a dramatic event from many years ago, when you capsized a sailing boat off the Great Barrier Reef. You jumped out to the right just before the boat rolled over to the left, and as you were swimming away you saw a shark in front of you, but . . . If you lived to tell the tale, you would probably describe it more or less as I just did now, by relaying everything from the vantage point of your orientation at the time: jumping 'to the right' of the boat, the shark 'in front of you'. What you will probably not remember is whether the shark was exactly to the north of you swimming south or to the west swimming east. After all, when there is a shark right in front of you, one of the last things you worry about is the cardinal directions. Similarly, even if at the time you visited the museum you could have worked out the orientation of the room in which the picture was hanging, it is extremely unlikely that you will remember now if the window in the picture was to the north or the east of the girl. What you will see in your mind's eye is the picture as it appeared when you stood in front of it, that's all.

But if you speak a Guugu Yimithirr-style language, that sort of memory will simply not do. You cannot say 'the window to the left of the girl' so you'll have to remember if the window was north of her or east or south or west. In the same way, you cannot say 'the shark in front of me'. If you want to describe the scene, you'd have to specify, even twenty years later, in which cardinal direction the shark was. So your memories of anything that you might ever want to report will have to be stored in your brain with cardinal directions as part of the picture.

Does this sound far-fetched? John Haviland filmed a Guugu Yimithirr speaker, Jack Bambi, telling his old friends the story of how in his youth he capsized in shark-infested waters but managed to swim safely ashore. Jack and another person were on a trip with a mission boat, delivering clothing and provisions to an outstation on the McIvor River. They were caught in a storm, and their boat capsized in a whirlpool. They both jumped into the water and managed to swim nearly three miles to the shore, only to discover, on returning to the mission, that Mr Schwartz was far more concerned at the loss of the boat than relieved at their miraculous escape. Except for its content, the remarkable thing about the story is that it was remembered throughout in cardinal directions: Jack Bambi jumped into the water on the western side of the boat, his companion to the east of the boat, they saw a giant shark swimming north, and so on.

Perhaps the cardinal directions were just made up for the occasion? Well, quite by chance, Stephen Levinson filmed the same person two years later, telling the same story. The cardinal directions matched exactly in the two tellings. Even more remarkable were the hand gestures that accompanied Jack's story. In the first film, shot in 1980, Jack is facing west. When he tells how the boat flipped over, he rolls his hands forward away from his body. In 1982, he is sitting facing north. Now, when he gets to the climactic point when the boat flips over, he makes a rolling movement from his right to his left. Only this way of representing the hand movements is all wrong. Jack was not rolling his hands from right to left at all. On both occasions, he was simply rolling his hands from east to west! He maintained the correct geographic direction of the boat's movement, without even giving it a moment's thought. And as it happens, at the time of year when the accident happened there are strong south-easterly winds in the area, so flipping from east to west seems very likely.

Levinson also relates how a group of Hopevale men once had to drive to Cairns, the nearest city, some 150 miles to the south, to discuss land-right issues with other aboriginal groups. The meeting was in a room without windows, in a building reached either by a back alley or through a car park, so that the relation between the building and the city layout was somewhat obscured. About a month later, back in Hopevale, he asked a few of the participants about the orientation of the meeting room and the positions of the speakers at the meeting. He got accurate responses, and complete agreement, about the orientation in cardinal directions of the main speaker, the blackboard, and other objects in the room.

TURNING THE TABLES

What we have established so far is that speakers of Guugu Yimithirr have to be able to recall anything they have ever seen with the criss-cross of the cardinal directions as part of the picture. It is almost a tautology to say, therefore, that they must commit to memory a whole extra layer of spatial information that we are blithely unaware of. After all, people who say 'the fish in the north-east corner of the shop' obviously have to remember that the fish was in the north-east corner of the shop. Since most of us do not remember whether fish are in north-east corners of shops (even if we could work it out at the time), this means that Guugu Yimithirr speakers register and remember information about space that we do not.

A more controversial question is whether this difference means that Guugu Yimithirr and English ever lead their speakers to remember different versions of the same reality. For example, could the crisscross of cardinal directions that Guugu Yimithirr imposes on the world make its speakers visualise and recall an arrangement of objects in space differently from us?

Before we can see how researchers tried to test such questions, let's first play a little memory game. I'm going to show you some pictures with a few toy objects arranged on a table. There are three objects in all, but you will see at most two at a time. What you have to do is try to remember their positions, in order to complete the picture later on. We start with picture 1, where you can see a house and a girl. Once you have memorised their positions, turn to the next page.

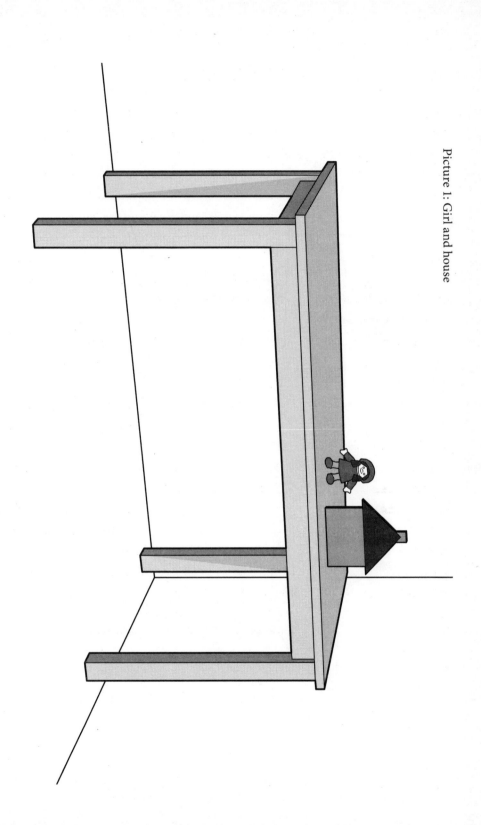

Picture 1: Girl and house

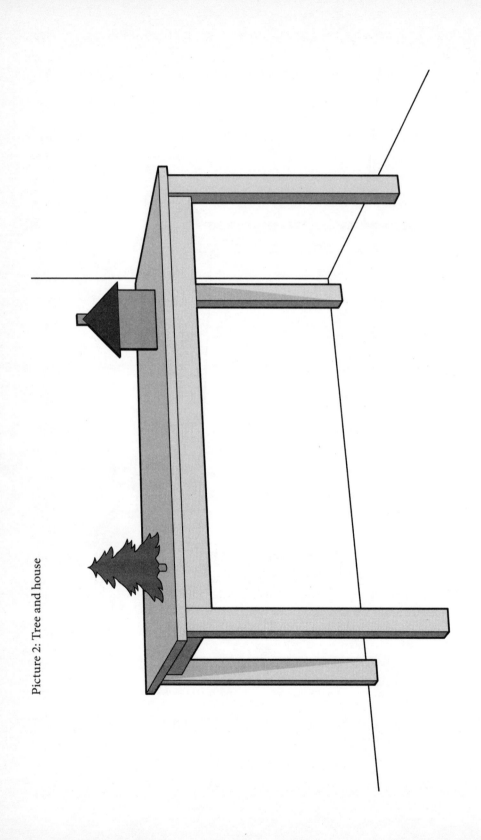

Picture 2: Tree and house

Now, in picture 2, you can see the house from the previous picture, and a new object, a tree. Try to remember the position of these two as well, and then turn to the next page.

Finally, in picture 3, you see just the girl on the table. Now imagine I gave you the toy tree and asked you to place this tree in a way that would complete the picture and would be consistent with the two layouts you saw before. Where would you put it? Make a small mark (mental or otherwise) on the table before you turn to the next page.

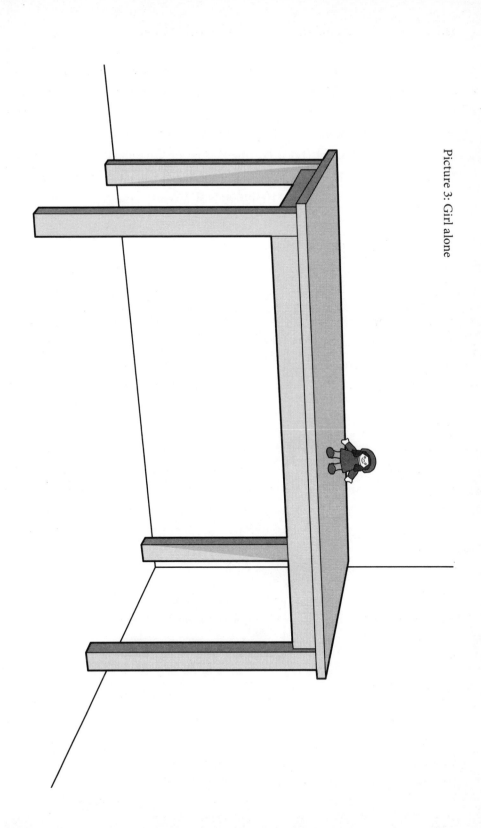

Picture 3: Girl alone

This is not a terribly difficult game, and it doesn't take prophetic powers to predict where you placed the tree. Your arrangement must have been more or less what is shown in picture 4, as you would have followed the obvious clues: earlier, the girl was standing immediately to the left of the house, whereas the tree was much further to the left. So this must mean that the tree was further to the left than the girl. If there is any difficulty here, it is only to understand what the point is in doing such obvious exercises.

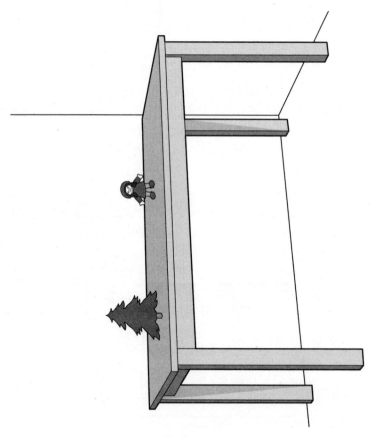

Picture 4

The point is that for speakers of Guugu Yimithirr or Tzeltal, the solution you have suggested does not seem obvious at all. In fact, when they were given tasks of this nature, they completed the picture in a

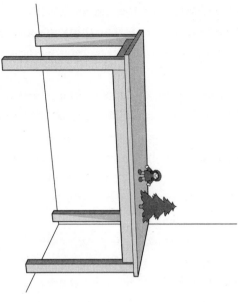

Picture 5

very different way. They did not put the tree anywhere to the left of the girl, but rather on her other side, to the right, as in picture 5.

But why should they get such a simple task so badly wrong? There was nothing wrong about their solution, thank you very much. But there was something wrong about the way I just described it, because contrary to what I said, they did not put the tree 'to the right of the girl'. They put it to the south of her. In fact, their solution makes perfect sense if one is thinking in geographic and not egocentric coordinates. To see why, let's assume that you are reading this book facing north. (You can always turn to face the north, if you know where it is, just to avoid confusion.) If you look back at picture 1, you'll see that the house was to the south of the girl. In picture 2, the tree was to the south of the house. Clearly, then, the tree must be south of the girl, since it is further south from the house, which is further south from the girl. So when completing the picture, it's perfectly sensible to put the tree to the south of the girl, as in picture 5.

The reason the two solutions diverge is that in this game the table in picture 2 was rotated 180 degrees from the other pictures. We, who think in egocentric coordinates, automatically factor out this rotation and ignore it, so it has no bearing on the way we remember the arrangement of the objects on the table. But those who think in geographic coordinates do not ignore the rotation, and so their memory of the same arrangement is different.

In the actual experiments conducted by Levinson and his colleagues from the Max Planck Institute in Nijmegen, the two tables were not on adjacent pages of a book but in adjacent rooms (as in the picture opposite). The participants were shown an arrangement on a table in one room, then moved to a facing room and shown the second arrangement on a second table, and then finally brought back to the first room to solve the puzzle and complete the picture on the first table. The rotation pattern was just as in the preceding pictures, only in real life and on real tables. Many varieties of such experiments have been conducted with speakers of different languages. And the results of these experiments show that the preferred coordinate system in the language correlates strongly with the solutions the participants tend to pick. Speakers of egocentric languages like English overwhelmingly chose the egocentric solution, whereas speakers of geographic languages like Guugu Yimithirr and Tzeltal chose the geographic solution.

On one level, the results of these experiments speak for themselves, but there has been some controversy in the last few years about how to interpret their significance. Whereas Levinson has claimed that the results demonstrate deep cognitive differences between speakers of languages with egocentric and geographic coordinates, some of his claims have been contested by other researchers. As usual in academic controversies, much of the debate boils down to bickering over ill-defined terms: is the effect of language strong enough to 'restructure cognition' (whatever that might mean exactly)? But on the factual level, the main argument levelled against the experiments was that the choice of solution can easily be biased by the physical environment in which they are conducted.

For example, participants might be encouraged to choose an egocentric solution if the two rooms are arranged so that they look the same from the egocentric perspective – say with the table on the right in both rooms and a cupboard to the left of the table in both rooms. On the other

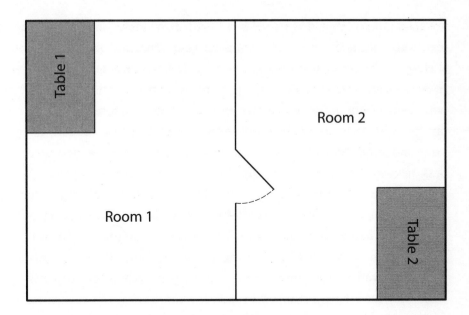

hand, a geographic solution might be encouraged if the environment is arranged to favour the geographic perspective – for instance, if the experiment is conducted in the open air, in view of a prominent geographic landmark. But while the point is well taken in general, in this particular experiment it serves only to strengthen the 'strangeness' of the solution chosen by speakers of Guugu Yimithirr-style languages, because the two rooms in Levinson's experiment were arranged to look exactly the same from the egocentric perspective. The table was on the right in both rooms (which meant it was in the north in one room and in the south in another), and all other furniture was arranged accordingly. And yet speakers of Guugu Yimithirr and Tzeltal overwhelmingly chose the geographic solution even under such 'adverse' conditions.

Does all this mean that we and speakers of Guugu Yimithirr sometimes remember 'the same reality' differently? The answer must be yes, at least to the extent that two realities that for us can look identical will appear different to them. We, who generally ignore rotations, will perceive two arrangements that differ only by rotation as the same reality, but they, who cannot ignore rotations, will perceive them as two different realities. One way of visualising this is to imagine the following situation. Suppose you are travelling with a Guugu Yimithirr friend and are staying in a large chain-style hotel, with corridor upon corridor of identical-looking doors. Your room is number 1264, and your friend is staying in the room just opposite yours, 1263. When you go to your friend's room, you see an exact copy of yours: the same little corridor with a bathroom on the left as you enter, the same mirrored wardrobe on the right, then the main room with the same bed on the left, the same indistinct-brown curtains drawn behind it, the same elongated desk next to the wall on the right, the same television set on the left corner of the desk and the same telephone and minibar on the right. In short, you have seen the same room twice. But when your Guugu Yim-ithirr friend comes into your room, he will see a room that is quite different from his, one where everything is reversed. Since the rooms face each other (rather like rooms 1 and 2 in the picture on page 185), and since they have been arranged to look the same from the egocentric perspective, they are actually north-side-south. In his room the bed was in the north, in yours it is in the south; the telephone that in his room was in the west is now in the east. So while you will see and remember the same room twice, the Guugu Yimithirr speaker will see and remember two different rooms.

CORRELATION OR CAUSATION?

One of the most tempting and most common of all logical fallacies is to jump from correlation to causation: to assume that just because two facts correlate, one of them was the cause of the other. To reduce this kind of logic ad absurdum, I could advance the brilliant new theory that language can affect your hair colour. In particular, I claim that speaking Swedish makes your hair go blond and speaking Italian makes your hair go dark. My proof? People who speak Swedish tend to have blond hair. People who speak Italian tend to have dark hair. QED. Against this epitome of tight logical reasoning you may come up with a few petty objections along these lines: yes, your facts about the correlation between language and hair colour are perfectly correct. But couldn't it be something other than language that caused the Swedes to have blond hair and the Italians dark? What about genes, for instance, or climate?

Now, as far as language and spatial thinking go, the only thing we have actually established is correlation between two facts: the first is that different languages rely on different coordinate systems; the second is that speakers of these languages perceive and remember space in different ways. Of course, my implication all along was that there is more than just correlation here and that the mother tongue is an important factor in *causing* the patterns of spatial memory and orientation. But how can we be sure that the correlation here is not as spurious as that between language and hair colour? After all, it is not as if language itself can *directly* create a sense of orientation in anyone. We may not know exactly what clues the Guugu Yimithirr rely on for telling where north is, but we can be absolutely certain that their remarkable surety about directions could have been achieved only through observation of cues from the physical environment.

Nevertheless, the argument advanced here is that a language like Guugu Yimithirr *indirectly* brings about the sense of orientation and geographic memory, because the convention of communicating only in geographic coordinates compels the speakers to be aware of directions all the time, forcing them to pay constant attention to the relevant environmental clues and to develop an accurate memory of their own changing orientation. John Haviland estimates that as many as one word in ten (!) in a normal Guugu Yimithirr conversation is north, south, west, or east, often accompanied by very precise hand gestures. Put another way, everyday communication in Guugu Yimithirr provides the most intense drilling in geographic orientation from the earliest imaginable age. If you have to know your bearings to understand the simplest things people say around you, you will develop the habit of calculating and remembering the cardinal directions at every second of your life. And as this habit of mind will be inculcated almost from infancy, it will soon become second nature, effortless and unconscious.

The causal link between language and spatial thinking thus seems far more plausible than the case of language and hair colour. Still, plausibility by no means constitutes proof. And as it happens, some psychologists and linguists, such as Peggy Li, Lila Gleitman, and Steven Pinker, have challenged the claim that it is primarily language that influences spatial memory and orientation. In *The Stuff of Thought*, Pinker argues that people develop their spatial thinking for reasons unrelated to language, and that languages merely *reflect* the fact that their speakers think in a certain coordinate system anyway. He points out that it is small rural societies that rely primarily on geographic coordinates, whereas all large urban societies rely predominantly on egocentric coordinates. From this undeniable fact he concludes that the system of coordinates used in a language is determined directly by the physical environment: if you live in a city you will spend much of your time indoors, and even when you venture outside, turning right and then left and then left again after the traffic lights will be the easiest way of orienting yourself, so the environment will encourage you to think primarily in egocentric coordinates. Your language will then simply reflect the fact that you think in the egocentric system anyway. On the other hand, if you are a nomad in the Australian bush, there are no roads or second-left turnings after the traffic lights to guide you, so ego-centric directions will be far less useful and you will naturally come to think in geographic coordinates. The way you then end up speaking about space will just be a symptom of the way you think anyway.

What is more, says Pinker, the environment determines not just the choice between egocentric and geographic coordinates but even the particular type of geographic coordinates that will be used in a language. It is surely not a coincidence that the Tzeltal system relies on a prominent geographic landmark, whereas the Guugu Yimithirr system uses compass directions. The environment of Tzeltal speakers is domi-nated by a visible landmark, the uphill–downhill slope, and so it is only natural for them to depend on this axis rather than on the more elusive compass directions. But as the environment of the Guugu Yimithirr lacks such prominent landmarks, it is no wonder that their axes are based on compass directions. In short, Pinker claims that the environ-ment has decreed for us what coordinates we think in, and it is spatial thinking that determines spatial language, not vice versa.

While Pinker's facts are hardly quibbleable with, his environmental determinism is unconvincing for several reasons. It makes sense, of course, that each culture would home in on a coordinate system suitable for its environment. Still, it is crucial to realise that different cultures have a considerable degree of freedom. For example, there is nothing in the physical environment of the Guugu Yimithirr that precludes their using *both* geographic coordinates (for large-scale space) *and* egocentric coordinates (for small-scale). There is no conceivable reason why a traditional hunter-gatherer existence would prevent anyone from saying 'there is an ant in front of your foot' instead of 'to the north of your foot'. After all, as a description of small-scale spatial relations, 'in front of your foot' is just as sensible and just as useful in the Australian bush as it is inside an office in London or Manhattan. This is not merely a theoretical argument – there are various languages of societies similar to Guugu Yimithirr that indeed use both egocentric and geographic coordinates. Even in Australia itself, there are aboriginal languages, such as Jaminjung in the Northern Territory, that do not rely only on geographic coordinates. So Guugu Yimithirr's exclusive use of geographic coordinates was not directly imposed by the physical environment or by the hunter-gatherer way of life. It is a cultural convention. The categorical refusal of Guugu Yimithirr ants ever to crawl 'in front of' Guugu Yimithirr feet is not a decree of nature but an expression of cultural choice.

What is more, there are odd pairs of languages around the world that are spoken in similar environments but have nevertheless chosen to rely on different coordinate systems. Tzeltal, as we have seen, uses geographic coordinates almost exclusively, but Yukatek, another Mayan language of a rural community from Mexico, predominantly employs egocentric coordinates. In the savannah of northern Namibia, the Hai‖om bushmen speak about space like the Tzeltal and Guugu Yimithirr, whereas the language of the Kgalagadi tribe from neighbouring Botswana, who live in a similar environment, relies heavily on egocentric coordinates. And when two anthropologists compared how Hai‖om and Kgalagadi speakers responded to rotation experiments of the type we saw earlier, most Hai‖om speakers offered geographic solutions (like the one that seemed counter-intuitive to us), whereas the Kgalagadi tended to give egocentric solutions.

So the coordinate system of each language cannot have been

completely determined by the environment, and this means that different cultures must have exercised some choice. In fact, all the evidence suggests that we should turn to the maxim 'freedom within constraints' as the best way to understand culture's influence on the choice of coordinate systems. Nature – in this case the physical environment – certainly places constraints on the types of coordinate system that can be used sensibly in a given language. But there is considerable freedom within these constraints to select from different alternatives.

There is another critical error in Pinker's environmental determinism, namely his glossing over the fact that the environment does not interact directly with a toddler or small child – it does so only through the mediation of upbringing. To clarify this point, we need to keep two different issues strictly apart. The first is the question of what the historical reasons were that caused a certain society to home in on a certain system of co-ordinates. The second issue, which is the one that is actually relevant for us here, is what happens to John Smith, an individual speaker of a Guugu Yimithirr–style language, when he grows up, and in particular what was mainly responsible for bringing about his perfect pitch for directions. Suppose we had evidence that John's skill developed only in late teens or early twenties, after he had been on countless hunting expeditions and has spent thousands of hours of trekking in the wild. The argument that language had much to do with creating this skill would have looked rather feeble, since it would have been far more plausible that this skill developed as a direct response to the environment, that the training and drilling came from his experiences of hunting and trekking and so on. But as it happens, we know that the geographic coordinate system is learned at a very early age. Studies of Tzeltal-speaking children show that they start using the geographic vocabulary by age two, that by age four they use geographic coordinates correctly to describe the arrangement of objects, and that they master the system by age seven. Alas, Guugu Yimithirr children no longer acquire the system at all, because the community is now dominated by English. But studies with Balinese children show similar results to Tzeltal: children in Bali use geographic coordinates by age three and a half and master the system by age eight.

At the age of two or three or even seven, John Smith has no idea about the reasons why his society, centuries or millennia ago, chose this or the other coordinate system, and whether that choice was suitable for the environment or not. He simply has to learn the system of his elders as given. And since constant and unfailing awareness of directions is required to use the geographic system correctly, John Smith must have developed his perfect pitch for directions at a very young age, long before it could have been a direct response to the needs of survival in the physical environment, the exigencies of hunting, and so on.

All this goes to show that the system of coordinates you speak and think in is determined for you not directly by the environment but rather by the way you were brought up – or, in other words, through the mediation of culture. Of course, one may still object that there is more to the way one is brought up than just language. So we cannot simply take for granted that language in particular, rather than anything else in a Tzeltal or Guugu Yimithirr speaker's upbringing, was the primary reason for inducing geographic thinking. I have argued that the main cause here is simply the constant need to calculate directions in order to speak and understand others. But at least in theory, one cannot rule out the possibility that children develop their geographic thinking for an entirely different reason, say because of intense explicit tuition in orientation from an early age.

In fact, there is one example in our own egocentric system of coordinates, the left–right asymmetry, which teaches us to be cautious. For most Western adults, left and right seem second nature, but children have great difficulties in mastering the distinction and generally manage it only at a very late age. Most children cannot cope with these concepts even passively until well into school age and don't use left and right actively in their own language until around the age of eleven. This late age of acquisition, and especially the fact that children often master the distinction only through the brute force of schooling (including, of course, the need to acquire literacy and master the inherent sidedness of letters), makes it unlikely that the left–right distinction was acquired simply through the requirements of daily communication.

But while the left–right distinction in our own egocentric system serves as a warning against jumping to conclusions about causation, the marked difference between the late acquisition of left–right and the early acquisition of geographic coordinates highlights exactly the reasons why, in the latter case, language is by far the most plausible cause. There is no evidence of formal tuition in geographic coordinates at an early age (although there is evidence from Bali of some geographically relevant religious practises, such as putting children to bed with the head pointing in a particular geographic direction). So the only imaginable mechanism that could provide such intense drilling in orientation at such a young age is the spoken language – the need to know the directions in order to be able to communicate about the simplest aspects of everyday life.

There is thus a compelling case that the relation between language and spatial thinking is not just correlation but causation, and that one's mother tongue affects how one thinks about space. In particular, a language like Guugu Yimithirr, which forces its speakers to use geographic coordinates at all times, must be a crucial factor in bringing about the perfect pitch for directions and the corresponding patterns of memory that seem so weird and unattainable to us.

Two centuries after Guugu Yimithirr bequeathed 'kangaroo' to the world, its last remaining speakers gave the world a harsh lesson in philosophy and psychology. Guugu Yimithirr proved – tongue on teeth – that a language can do perfectly well without concepts that had long been considered as universal building blocks of spatial language and thought. This recognition illuminated concepts of our own language, which our common sense would have sworn were simply decreed for us by nature, but which only seem so because our common sense happened to grow up in a culture that employs these concepts. Guugu Yimithirr provided a glaring example – brighter even than the language of colour – of cultural conventions that masquerade as nature.

What is more, the research that Guugu Yimithirr inspired has furnished the most striking example so far of how language can affect thought. It has shown how speech habits, imprinted from an early age, can create habits of mind that have far-reaching consequences beyond speaking, as they affect orientation skills and even patterns of memory. Guugu Yimithirr managed all this just in time, before finally going west. The 'unadulterated' language that John Haviland started recording from the oldest speakers in the 1970s has now gone the way of all tongues, together with the last members of that generation. While the sounds of Guugu Yimithirr are still heard in Hopevale, the language has undergone drastic simplification under the influence of English. Today's older speakers still use cardinal directions fairly frequently, at least when they speak Guugu Yimithirr rather than English, but most people younger than fifty have no real grasp of the system.

How many other features of mainstream European languages are there, which we still take as natural and universal even today simply because no one has yet properly understood the languages that do things differently? We may never know. Or put another way, if the prospect of having to make further uncomfortable adaptations to our world view seems daunting, the good news is that it is getting unlikelier by the minute that we will ever discover such features. Together with Guugu Yimithirr, hundreds of other 'tropical languages' are going to the wall, dispersed by the onward march of civilisation. The conventional predictions are that within two to three generations at least half the world's six thousand or so languages will have disappeared, especially those remote tribal tongues that are really different from what seems natural to us. With every year that passes, the notion that all languages do things essentially like English or Spanish is becoming closer to reality. Soon enough, it may be factually correct to argue that the 'standard average European' way is the only natural model for human language, because there are no languages that substantially diverge from it. But this will be a hollow truth.

Lest one fall under the impression, however, that it is only remote tribal languages that do things sufficiently strangely to induce noticeable differences in thinking, we shall now explore two areas where significant variation is to be found even among mainstream European languages, and where the influence of language on thought may thus be felt much closer to home.

8

Sex and Syntax

In one of his loveliest but most enigmatic poems, Heinrich Heine describes the yearning of a snowy pine tree for a sunburned oriental palm. In the original, the poem runs like this:

Ein Fichtenbaum steht einsam
Im Norden auf kahler Höh'.
Ihn schläfert; mit weißer Decke
Umhüllen ihn Eis und Schnee.

Er träumt von einer Palme,
Die, fern im Morgenland,
Einsam und schweigend trauert
Auf brennender Felsenwand.

The quiet despair of Heine's poem must have struck a chord with one of the great melancholics of the Victorian period, the Scottish poet James Thomson (1834–1882, not to be confused with the Scottish poet James Thomson, 1700–1848, who wrote *The Seasons*). Thomson was especially admired for his translations, and his rendering remains one of the most oft quoted of the many English versions:

> A pine-tree standeth lonely
> In the North on an upland bare;
> It standeth whitely shrouded
> With snow, and sleepeth there.
>
> It dreameth of a Palm Tree
> Which far in the East alone,
> In mournful silence standeth
> On its ridge of burning stone.

With its resonant rhymes and its interlocked alliteration, Thomson's rendering captures the isolation and the hopeless fixity of the forlorn pine and palm. His adaptation even manages to remain true to Heine's rhythm while apparently following the meaning of the poem very faithfully. And yet, despite all its artfulness, Thomson's translation entirely fails to reveal to an English reader a pivotal aspect of the original poem, perhaps the very key to its interpretation. It fails so decidedly because it glosses over one grammatical feature of the German language, which happens to be the basis of the whole allegory, and without which Heine's metaphor is castrated. If you haven't guessed what that grammatical feature is, the following translation by the American poet Emma Lazarus (1849–87) will make it clearer:

> There stands a lonely pine-tree
> In the north, on a barren height;
> He sleeps while the ice and snow flakes
> Swathe him in folds of white.
>
> He dreameth of a palm-tree
> Far in the sunrise-land,
> Lonely and silent longing
> On her burning bank of sand.

In Heine's original, the pine tree (**der** *Fichtenbaum*) is masculine while the palm (**die** *Palme*) is feminine, and this opposition of grammatical gender gives the imagery a sexual dimension that is repressed in Thomson's translation. But many critics believe that the pine tree conceals far more under his folds of white than merely the conventional romantic lament of unrequited love, and that the palm may be the object of an altogether different kind of desire. There is a tradition of Jewish love poems addressed to the distant and unattainable Jerusalem, which is always personified as a female beloved. This genre goes all the way back to one of Heine's favourite psalms: 'By the rivers of Babylon, there we sat down and wept when we remembered Zion. . . . If I forget thee [feminine], O Jerusalem, may my right hand wither, may my tongue cling to the roof of my mouth.' Heine may be alluding to this tradition, and his lonely palm on her ridge of burning stone may be a coded reference to the deserted Jerusalem, perched high up in the Judaean hills. More specifically, Heine's lines may be alluding to the most famous of all odes to Jerusalem, written in twelfth-century Spain by Yehuda Halevy, a poet whom Heine revered. The pine tree's object of desire 'far in the East' may be echoing Halevy's opening line, 'My heart is in the East, and I am in the furthest West.'

Whether or not the poem is really about Heine's despair at reconciling his roots in the Germanic North with the distant homeland of his Jewish soul is a mystery that may never be resolved. But there is no doubt that the poem cannot be unlocked without the genders of the two protagonists. Emma Lazarus's translation transfers this sexual basis into English, by employing the pronouns 'he' for the pine tree and 'her' for the palm. The price Lazarus pays for this faithfulness is that her translation sounds somewhat arch, or at least artificially poetic, since in English it is not natural to speak of trees in this way. But unlike English, which treats inanimate objects uniformly as 'it', German assigns thousands of objects to the masculine or feminine gender as a matter of course. In fact, in German there is nothing the slightest bit poetic about calling inanimate objects 'he' or 'she'. You would simply refer to a *Palme* as 'she' whenever you spoke of her, even in the most mundane chit-chat. You'd explain to your neighbours how you got her half price in the garden centre a few years ago and then unfortunately planted her too close to a eucalyptus, how his roots have disturbed her growth, and how she's given you no end of trouble since, with her fungus and her ganoderma butt rot. And all this would be related without a hint of poetic inspiration, or even of self-consciousness. It's just how one speaks if one speaks German – or Spanish, or French, or Russian, or a host of other languages with similar gender systems.

Gender is perhaps the most obvious area where significant otherness is found not just between 'us' and exotic tropical languages, but also much closer to home. You may spend nine lives without ever meeting a speaker of Tzeltal or Guugu Yimithirr. But you would have to go to great lengths to avoid meeting speakers of Spanish, French, Italian, German, Russian, Polish, or Arabic, to name just a few examples. Some of your best friends may even be gendered. Are their thought processes affected by this aspect of their language? Could it be that the feminine gender of the German *Palme* affects how a German thinks of a palm tree even beyond the artifice of poetry? As surprising as it may seem, we shall soon see that the answer is yes and that there is now solid evidence that gender systems can exert a powerful hold on speakers' associations.

'Gender' is a loaded word these days. It may not be quite as risqué as 'sex', but it runs the risk of engendering serious misunderstandings, so it is helpful to start by clarifying how linguists' rather dry use of this word diverges from that of everyday English and also from that of some of the trendier academic disciplines. The original sense of 'gender' had nothing to do with sex: it meant 'type', 'kind', 'race' – in fact, 'gender' has exactly the same origin as the words 'genus' and 'genre'. Like most serious problems in life, the latter-day diversity of meanings for 'gender' has its roots in ancient Greece. The Greek philosophers started using their noun *génos* (which meant 'race' or 'type') to refer to one particular division of things into three specific 'types': males (humans and animals), females, and inanimate things. And from Greek, this sense passed via Latin to other European languages.

In English, both senses of 'gender' – the general meaning 'type' and the more specific grammatical distinction – coexisted happily for a long time. As late as the eighteenth century, 'gender' could still be used in an entirely sexless way. When the novelist Robert Bage wrote in 1784, 'I also am a man of importance, a public man, Sir, of the patriotic gender', he meant nothing more than 'type'. But later on, this general sense of the word fell into disuse in everyday English, the 'neuter' category also beat a retreat, and the masculine–feminine division came to dominate the meaning of the word. In the twentieth century, 'gender' became simply a euphemism for 'sex', so if you find on some official form a request to fill in your 'gender', you are unlikely nowadays to write 'patriotic'.

In some academic disciplines, notably 'gender studies', the sexual connotations of 'gender' developed an even more specific sense and started being used to denote the social (rather than biological) aspects of the difference between women and men. 'Gender studies' are thus concerned with the social roles played by the two sexes rather than with the differences between their anatomies.

Linguists, on the other hand, veered in exactly the opposite direction: they returned to the original meaning of the word, namely 'type' or 'kind', and nowadays use it for any division of nouns according to some essential properties. These essential properties *may* be based on sex, but they do not have to be. Some languages, for example, have a gender distinction that is based only on 'animacy', the distinction between animate beings (people and animals of both sexes) and inanimate things. Other languages draw the line differently and make a gender distinction between human and non-human (animals and inanimate things). And there are also languages that divide nouns into much more specific genders. The African language Supyire from Mali has five genders: humans, big things, small things, collectives, and liquids. Bantu languages such as Swahili have up to ten genders, and the Australian language Ngan'gityemerri is said to have fifteen different genders, which include, among others, masculine human, feminine human, canines, non-canine animals, vegetables, drinks, and two different genders for spears (depending on size and material).

In short, when a linguist talks about 'gender studies' she is just as likely to mean 'animal, mineral, and vegetable' as the difference between men and women. Nevertheless, since the research on the influence of grammatical gender on the mind has so far been conducted exclusively on European languages, in which the distinction between masculine and feminine nouns dominates the gender system, our focus in the following pages will be on the masculine and feminine, and more exotic genders will make only a passing appearance.

⌀

The discussion so far may have given the impression that grammatical gender actually makes sense. The idea of grouping together objects with similar vital properties seems eminently reasonable in itself, so it would be only natural to assume that whatever criteria a language has chosen for making gender distinctions, it will abide by its own rules. We would expect, therefore, that a feminine gender would include all, and only all, female human beings or animals, that an inanimate gender would include all inanimate things, and only them, that a vegetable gender would include, well, vegetables.

There are in fact a handful of languages that do behave like that. In Tamil, there are three genders – masculine, feminine, and neuter – and you can pretty much tell which gender any noun belongs to given its obvious properties. Nouns denoting men (and male gods) are masculine; those denoting women and goddesses are feminine; everything else – objects, animals (and infants) – is neuter. Another straightforward case was Sumerian, the language spoken on the banks of the Euphrates some five thousand years ago by the people who invented writing and kick-started history. The Sumerian gender system was based not on sex but on the distinction between human and non-human, and nouns were assigned consistently to the appropriate gender. The only point of indecision was with the noun 'slave', which was sometimes deemed human and sometimes assigned to the non-human gender. Another language that can be said to belong to the elite club of logical gender is English. Gender is marked only on pronouns in English ('he', 'she', 'it'), and in general such pronouns are used transparently: 'she' refers to women (and occasionally to female animals), 'he' to men and to a few male animals, and 'it' to everything else. The exceptions, such as 'she' for a ship, are few and far between.

There are also some languages, such as Manambu from Papua New Guinea, where genders might not be entirely consistent, but where one can at least discern some basic threads of rationality in the system. In Manambu, masculine and feminine genders are assigned to inanimate objects, not just to men and women. But apparently there are reasonably transparent rules for the assignment. For instance, small and rounded things are feminine, while big and longish things are masculine. A belly is feminine, for example, but a pregnant woman's belly is spoken of in the masculine gender once it has become really big. Intense things are masculine, less intense things feminine. Darkness is feminine when it's not yet completely dark, but when it becomes pitch black it turns masculine. You don't have to agree with the logic, but at least you can follow it.

Finally, there are those languages, such as Turkish, Finnish, Estonian, Hungarian, Indonesian, and Vietnamese, that are entirely consistent about gender simply because they have no grammatical gender at all. In such languages, even pronouns referring to human being do not bear gender distinctions, so there aren't separate pronouns for 'he' and 'she'. When a Hungarian friend of mine is tired, he sometimes lets slip things like 'she is Emma's husband'. This is not because speakers of Hungarian are blind to the difference between men and women, only because they are not in the habit of specifying the sex of a person each and every time the person is mentioned.

If genders were always as straight as they are in English or Tamil, there would be little point in asking whether a gender system can affect people's perception of objects. For if the grammatical gender of every object merely reflected its real-world properties (man, woman, inanimate, vegetable, etc.), it could add nothing to anyone's associations that was not there objectively. But as it happens, languages with a consistent and transparent gender system are very much in the minority. The great majority of languages have wayward genders. Most European languages belong in this degenerate group: French, Italian, Spanish, Portuguese, Romanian, German, Dutch, Swedish, Norwegian, Danish, Russian, Polish, Czech, Greek.

Even in the most erratic gender systems, there is usually a core group of nouns that are assigned grammatical gender in a consistent way. In particular, male human beings almost always have masculine gender. Women, on the other hand, are much more often denied the privilege of belonging to the feminine gender and are relegated to the neuter gender instead. In German, there is a whole range of words for women that are treated as 'it': *das Mädchen* (girl, the diminutive form of 'maid'), *das Fräulein* (unmarried woman, the diminutive of *Frau*), *das Weib* (woman, cognate with English 'wife'), or *das Frauenzimmer* (woman, but literally 'lady chamber': the original meaning referred to the living chambers of the lady, but the word started to be used for the entourage of a noble lady, then for particular members of the entourage, and hence to increasingly less distinguished women).

The Greeks treat their women a little better: while their word for girl, *korítsi*, is, just as you would expect, of the neuter gender, if one speaks about a pretty buxom girl, one adds the augmentative suffix *-aros*, and the resulting noun, *korítsaros*, 'buxom girl', then belongs to the . . . masculine gender. (Heaven knows what Whorf, or for that matter Freud, would have made of that.) And if this seems the height of madness, consider that back in the days when English still had a real gender system, it assigned the word 'woman' not to the feminine gender, not even to the neuter, but, like Greek, to the masculine gender. 'Woman' comes from the Old English *wíf-man*, literally 'woman-human being'. Since in Old English the gender of a compound noun like *wíf-man* was determined by the gender of the last element, here the masculine *man*, the correct pronoun to use when referring to a woman was 'he'.

The habit of European languages to misplace human beings – especially from one sex – in the wrong gender may be the most offensive element about the system. But in terms of the number of nouns involved, this quirkiness is rather marginal. It is in the realm of inanimate objects that the party actually gets going. In French, German, Russian, and most other European languages, the masculine and feminine genders extend to thousands of objects that are by no stretch of the imagination male or female. What, for instance, is particularly feminine about a Frenchman's beard (*la barbe*)? Why is Russian water a

'she', and why does she become a 'he' once you have dipped a tea bag
into her? Why does the German feminine sun (*die Sonne*) light up the
masculine day (*der Tag*), and the masculine moon (*der Mond*) shine in
the feminine night (*die Nacht*)? After all, in French, he (*le jour*) is actually illuminated by him (*le soleil*), whereas she (*la nuit*) by her (*la lune*).
German cutlery famously spans the whole gamut of gender roles: *Das
Messer* (knife) may be an it, but on the opposite side of the plate lies the
spoon (*der Löffel*) in his resplendent masculinity, and next to him,
bursting with sex appeal, the feminine fork (*die Gabel*). But in Spanish,
it's the fork (*el tenedor*) that has a hairy chest and gravelly voice, and
she, the spoon (*la cuchara*), a curvaceous figure.

For native speakers of English, the rampant sexing of inanimate
objects and occasional desexing of humans are a cause of frustration
and merriment in equal measure. The erratic gender system was
the main charge in Mark Twain's famous indictment of 'The Awful
German Language':

> In German, a young lady has no sex, while a turnip has. Think what
> overwrought reverence that shows for the turnip, and what callous
> disrespect for the girl. See how it looks in print – I translate this from a
> conversation in one of the best of the German Sunday-school books:
>
> GRETCHEN: Where is the turnip?
> WILHELM: She has gone to the kitchen.
> GRETCHEN: Where is the accomplished and beautiful English
>   maiden?
> WILHELM: It has gone to the opera.

Twain was inspired by German grammar to write his famous 'Tale of
the Fishwife and Its Sad Fate', which he pretended to have translated
from German quite literally. It begins like this:

> It is a bleak Day. Hear the Rain, how he pours, and the Hail, how he
> rattles; and see the Snow, how he drifts along, and of the Mud, how
> deep he is! Ah the poor Fishwife, it is stuck fast in the Mire; it has

dropped its Basket of Fishes; and its Hands have been cut by the Scales as it seized some of the falling Creatures; and one Scale has even got into its Eye, and it cannot get her out. It opens its Mouth to cry for Help; but if any Sound comes out of him, alas he is drowned by the raging of the Storm. And now a Tomcat has got one of the Fishes and she will surely escape with him. No, she bites off a Fin, she holds her in her Mouth – will she swallow her? No, the Fishwife's brave Mother-dog deserts his Puppies and rescues the Fin – which he eats, himself, as his Reward. O, horror, the Lightning has struck the Fish-basket; he sets him on Fire; see the Flame, how she licks the doomed Utensil with her red and angry Tongue; now she attacks the helpless Fishwife's Foot– she burns him up, all but the big Toe, and even SHE is partly consumed; and still she spreads, still she waves her fiery Tongues; she attacks the Fishwife's Leg and destroys IT; she attacks its Hand and destroys HER also; she attacks the Fishwife's Leg and destroys HER also; she attacks its Body and consumes HIM; she wreathes herself about its Heart and IT is consumed; next about its Breast, and in a Moment SHE is a Cinder; now she reaches its Neck – He goes; now its Chin – IT goes; now its Nose – SHE goes. In another Moment, except Help come, the Fishwife will be no more. . . .

The thing is, for Germans none of this is even remotely funny. It is so natural, in fact, that German translators struggle to render the passage's particular brand of humour. One translator solved the problem by substituting the tale with another one, which he called 'Sehen Sie den Tisch, es ist grün' – literally 'look at the table, it is green'. If you find you are having a sense of humour failure yourself, then remember that what one really ought to say in German is 'look at the table, *he* is green'.

Twain believed that there was something specially debauched about the German gender system and that among all languages it was unusually and peculiarly irrational. But that belief was based on ignorance, because if anything it is English that is unusual in *not* having an irrational gender system. And at this point, I ought to declare a conflict of interest, since my mother tongue, Hebrew, assigns inanimate objects to the feminine and masculine genders just as erratically as German or

French or Spanish or Russian. When I go into a (masculine) house, the feminine door opens onto a masculine room with a masculine carpet (be he ever so pink), a masculine table, and feminine bookcases full of masculine books. Out of the masculine window I can see the masculine trees and on them the birds, which are feminine regardless of the accidents of their anatomy. If I knew more about (feminine) ornithology, I could tell by looking at each bird what biological sex she was. I would point at her and explain to the less initiated: 'You can tell she is a male because of that red spot on her chest and also because she is larger than the females.' And I would not feel there was anything remotely strange about that.

Wayward genders are not confined to Europe and the Mediterranean basin. If anything, languages further afield, which have a larger number of gender categories, have even more scope for erratic assignments, and hardly any such language fails to make ample use of the opportunity. In the Australian language Dyirbal, water is assigned to the feminine gender, but in another aboriginal language, Mayali, water belongs to the vegetable gender. The vegetable gender of the neighbouring Gurr-goni language includes the word *erriplen*, 'aeroplane'. In the African language Supyire, the gender for 'big things' includes, as one would expect, all the big animals: horse, giraffe, hippopotamus, and so on. All? Well, almost: one animal wasn't considered big enough to be included and was assigned instead to the human gender – the elephant. The problem is not how to find more such examples, it is how to stop.

⸺

Why do so many languages develop irregular genders? We don't know much about the infancy of gender systems, because in most languages the origin of gender markers is entirely opaque.* But the few clues we do

---

* Gender markers are the elements that indicate the gender of a noun. Sometimes, the gender markers can be suffixes on the noun itself, as in Italian *ragazz-o*, 'boy', and *ragazz-a*, 'girl'. Alternatively, the gender marker can appear on adjectives that modify the noun or on definite and indefinite articles. In Danish, for example, one cannot see on the nouns *dag*, 'day', and *hus*, 'house', themselves that they belong to separate genders, but the difference appears on the indefinite article and the adjective: **en** *kold dag*, 'a cold day', but **et** *koldt hus*

have make the ubiquitous irrationality of mature gender systems appear particularly peculiar, because all the signs suggest that in their early days genders were perfectly logical. There are a few languages, especially in Africa, in which the feminine gender marker looks rather like a shortened version of the noun 'woman' itself, and the inanimate gender marker resembles the noun 'thing'. Likewise, the vegetable gender marker in some Australian languages looks rather similar to the noun . . . 'vegetable'. It stands to reason, therefore, that gender markers started out in life as generic nouns such as 'woman', 'man', 'thing', or 'vegetable'. And if so, it seems plausible that they would have originally been applied only to women, men, things, and vegetables, respectively.

But with time the gender markers may start being extended to nouns beyond their original remit, and through a series of such extensions a gender system can quickly be brought out of kilter. In Gurr-goni, for example, the vegetable gender came to include the noun 'aeroplane' through a perfectly natural sequence of little steps: the original 'vegetable' gender marker must first have been extended to plants more generally, and hence to all kinds of wooden objects. Since canoes are made of wood, another natural step would have included them in the vegetable gender as well. Since canoes happened to be the main means of transport for the speakers of Gurr-goni, the vegetable gender was then widened to include means of transportation more generally. And so, when the borrowed word *erriplen* entered the language, it was quite naturally assigned to the vegetable gender. Each step in this chain was natural and made perfect sense in its own local context. But the end result seems entirely arbitrary.

The Indo-European languages may also have started with a transparent gender system. But suppose, for instance, that the moon came to be included in the masculine gender because he was personified as a male god. Later, the word 'month' developed from the word 'moon', so it was only natural that if the moon was a 'he' a 'month' would also be a

'a cold house'. Gender can also be marked on verbs: in Slavic languages such as Russian or Polish, a suffix -a is added to some verbs when the subject is feminine. And in Semitic languages such as Maltese, a prefix t shows that the subject of the verb is feminine (*tikteb*, 'she writes'), while the prefix j indicates that the subject is masculine (*jikteb*, 'he writes').

'he'. But if so, then words for other time units, such as 'day', can also come to be included in the masculine gender. While each step in this chain of extensions may be perfectly natural in itself, after two or three steps the original logic has become opaque, and so masculine and feminine genders can find themselves applied to a range of inanimate objects for no intelligible reason.

The worst thing about this loss of transparency is that it is a self-propelling process: the less consistent the system becomes, the easier it is to mess it up even further. Once there are enough nouns with arbitrary genders, children struggling to learn the language may stop expecting to find reliable rules based on the real-world properties of objects, so they may start looking for other types of clues. For example, they can start guessing what gender a noun has on the basis of what it *sounds* like (if X sounds like Y, and Y is feminine, then maybe X is feminine as well). Incorrect guesses by children may initially be perceived as errors, but with time such errors can stick and so before too long any trace of the original logic can be lost.

Finally, it is ironic that when a language loses one gender out of three the result may actually increase the waywardness of the system rather than decrease it. Spanish, French, and Italian, for instance, lost the original neuter gender of their Latin forebear, when the neuter coalesced with the masculine. But the result only ensured that *all* inanimate nouns are randomly assigned to the masculine or feminine genders.

Nevertheless, the syndrome of *genus erraticum* is not always an incurable illness in a language. As the history of English can attest, when a language manages to lose not just one gender but two, the result can be a radical overhaul that eliminates the erratic system altogether. Until the eleventh century, English had a full-blown three-gender system just like German. English speakers from the eleventh century would not have understood what Mark Twain was bemoaning in his 'Tale of the Fishwife and Its Sad Fate', since for them a wife (*wīf*) was an 'it', a fish (*fisc*) was a 'he', whereas fate (*wyrd*) was a 'she'. But all this changed during the twelfth century.

The collapse of the Old English irregular genders had little to do with improving standards of sex education. The reason was rather that the gender system had critically depended on the doomed system of case endings. Originally, English had a complex case system similar to that of Latin, where nouns and adjectives appeared with different endings depending on their role in the sentence. Nouns of different genders had different sets of such case endings, so one could tell from the endings which gender a noun belonged to. But the system of endings rapidly disintegrated in the century after the Norman Conquest, and once the endings had disappeared, the new generation of speakers hardly had any clues left to tell them which gender each noun was supposed to belong to. These new speakers, who grew up into a language that no longer gave them sufficient information to decide whether a carrot, for example, should be addressed as a 'he' or a 'she', fell back on a radical and highly innovative idea, and started to call it an 'it' instead. So over a period of just a few generations, the original arbitrary gender system was replaced by a new one with transparent rules, whereby (almost) all inanimate objects came to be referred to simply as 'it'.

Still, a few wily nouns, especially feminine ones, managed to escape the mass sterilisation. Mark Twain, who was outraged by the bestowal of femininity upon German turnips, would have been surprised to learn that the same custom was still practised in England only three centuries earlier. A medicinal manual published in London in 1561, *The Most Excellent and Perfecte Homish Apothecarye or Homely Physick Booke for all the Grefes and Diseases of the Bodye*, offers the following confection against hoarseness: 'He that is become hoorse lately, let him roste a rape [turnip] in ashes or upon the fyre till she be all black, then pare her clene and eate her as warm thou canst.'

In dialectal varieties of English, some gendered nouns survived for much longer, but in the standard language a great tide of neuters flooded the inanimate world, leaving only a few isolated nouns bobbing about in their femininity. The slow but sure iticisation of English can be said to have come to its final mooring on 20 March 2002. For the maritime world, that particular Wednesday seemed no more eventful than any other Wednesday. *Lloyd's List*, the newspaper of the shipping industry, published its daily pageful of dispatches on casualties, accidents, and acts of piracy at sea. Among others, it mentioned the ferry *Baltic Jet* en route from Tallinn to Helsinki, which 'had a fire in her port side engine room at 0814, local time'; the tanker *Hamilton Energy* departed from Port Weller Docks in Canada after 'repairs were made to damage suffered when she was in contact with a Saltie. The accident snapped the rudder post and drove her propeller shaft through her gearbox and smashed her engine casting off.' Elsewhere in Canada, a shrimp trawler got stuck in pack ice, but the owner said that 'there is a possibility she can be started up and steamed under her own power'. A day, in short, like any other.

The real ocean-shaking news was reported on a different page, stowed away in the editorial column. Kissed by the punning muse, the editor announced under the headline 'Her today, gone tomorrow' that 'we have taken the simple yet significant decision to change our style from the start of the next month and start referring to ships as neuter rather than female. It brings this paper into line with most other reputable international business titles.' Reactions from the public were stormy, and the paper was overwhelmed by letters to the editor. An irate Greek reader wrote: 'Sir, only a bunch of crusty, out of touch, stuck up Englishmen would dream of trying to change the way we've spoken of ships for thousands of years as "she". Get out of there and go tend to your gardens and hunt foxes, you arrogant ass holes. Sincerely yours, Stephen Komianos.' But not even this silver-tongued plea convinced *Lloyd's List* to change her course, and in April 2002 'she' fell by the quayside.

GENDER AND THOUGHT

Languages that treat inanimate objects as 'he' or 'she' force their speakers to talk about such objects with the same grammatical forms that are applied to men and women. This habit of he-ing and she-ing objects means that an association between an inanimate noun and one of the sexes is shoved down the speakers' ears whenever they hear the name of this object, and the same association is pushed up their throats whenever they have occasion to mention his or her name themselves. And as anyone whose mother tongue has a gender system will tell you, once the habit has taken hold and the masculine or feminine association has been established, it is very difficult to shake it off. When I speak English, I may *say* about a bed that 'it' is too soft, but I actually feel 'she' is too soft. She stays feminine all the way from the lungs up to the glottis and is neutered only when she reaches the tip of the tongue.

As a basis for serious investigation, however, my professed feelings towards beds hardly constitute reliable evidence. It is not just the anecdotal nature of this information that is the problem, but the fact that I have not provided any proof that the 'she' feeling is anything more than tongue-deep – a mere grammatical habit. The automatic association between an inanimate noun and a gendered pronoun does not, in itself, show that the grammatical gender has exercised any deeper effect on the speakers' thoughts. It does not show, in particular, whether speakers of Hebrew or Spanish, which treat beds as feminine, really associate with beds any womanly properties.

Over the last century, various experiments have been conducted with the aim of testing precisely this question: can the grammatical gender of inanimate objects influence speakers' associations? Probably the first such experiment was conducted at the Moscow Psychological Institute in pre-revolutionary Russia. In 1915, fifty people were asked to imagine each day of the week as a particular person, then to describe the person they had pictured for each day. It turned out that all participants envisaged Monday, Tuesday, and Thursday as men but Wednesday, Friday, and Saturday as women. Why should this be so? When asked to explain their choice, many of them could not give a satisfactory answer. But the researchers concluded that the answer could not be unrelated to the fact that the names for Monday, Tuesday, and Thursday have a masculine gender in Russian, whereas Wednesday, Friday, and Saturday are feminine.

In the 1990s, the psychologist Toshi Konishi conducted an experiment comparing the gender associations of speakers of German and of Spanish. There are quite a few inanimate nouns whose genders in the two languages are reversed. The German air is a she (*die Luft*) but *el aire* is he in Spanish; *die Brücke* (bridge) is also feminine in German but *el puente* is masculine; and the same goes for clocks, flats, forks, newspapers, pockets, shoulders, stamps, tickets, violins, the sun, the world, and love. On the other hand, *der Apfel* is masculine for Germans but *la manzana* is feminine in Spanish, and so are chairs, brooms, butterflies, keys, mountains, stars, tables, wars, rain, and rubbish. Konishi presented a list of such nouns with conflicting genders to German and to Spanish speakers and asked the participants for their opinions on the properties of those nouns: whether they were weak or strong, little or big, and so on. On average, the nouns that are masculine in German but feminine in Spanish (chairs and keys, for example) got higher marks for strength from the Germans, whereas bridges and clocks, which are masculine in Spanish but feminine in German, were judged stronger on average by the Spanish speakers.

The simple conclusion from such an experiment would be that bridges do have more manly connotations for Spanish speakers than for German speakers. However, one possible objection to this inference is that it may not be the bridge itself that carries such connotations – it may only have been hearing the name together with the masculine article *el* or *un*. In this interpretation, when Spanish and German speakers simply look at a bridge, their associations may not be affected at all, and it may be only in the moment of speech, only through the act of saying or hearing the gender marker itself, that a fleeting association with manliness or womanliness is created in the speaker's mind.

Is it possible, therefore, to get round the problem and check whether womanly or manly associations for inanimate nouns are present even when the gender markers in the relevant language are not explicitly mentioned? The psychologists Lera Boroditsky and Lauren Schmidt tried to do this by repeating a similar experiment with Spanish and German speakers, but this time communicating with the participants in English rather than in their respective mother tongue. Although the experiment was conducted in a language that treats inanimate objects uniformly as 'it', the Spanish and German speakers still showed marked differences in the attributes they chose for the relevant objects. German speakers tended to describe bridges as beautiful, elegant, fragile, peaceful, pretty, and slender; Spanish speakers as big, dangerous, long, strong, sturdy, towering.

A more radical way of bypassing the problem was designed by the psychologist Maria Sera and her colleagues, who compared the reactions of French and Spanish speakers but used pictures of objects instead of words. As two closely related languages, French and Spanish mostly agree on gender, but there are still sufficiently many nouns that diverge: the fork, for instance, is *la fourchette* in French but *el tenedor* in Spanish, and so are cars (*la voiture, el carro*) and bananas (*la banana, el plátano*); on the other hand, French beds are masculine (*le lit*) but Spanish ones are feminine (*la cama*), and the same goes for clouds (*le nuage, la nube*) and butterflies (*le papillon, la mariposa*). The participants in this experiment were asked to help in the preparation of a film in which some everyday objects come to life. Their task was to choose the appropriate voice for each object in the film. They were shown a series of pictures, and for each one they were asked to choose between a man's voice and a woman's voice. Although the names of the objects were never mentioned, when French speakers saw the picture of a fork, most of them wanted her to speak in a woman's voice, whereas the Spanish speakers tended to choose a male voice for him instead. With the picture of the bed, the situation was reversed.

∽

The experiments described above are certainly suggestive. They seem to show that the grammatical gender of an inanimate object affects the properties that speakers associate with this object. Or at least what the experiments demonstrate is that the grammatical gender affects the responses when speakers are actively requested to indulge their imaginations and come up with associations for such an object. But this last point is in fact a serious weakness. All the experiments described so far suffer from one underlying problem, namely that they *forced* the participants to exercise their imaginations. A sceptic could argue with some justification that the only thing the experiments proved was that grammatical genders affect associations when the participants are coerced unnaturally to dream up properties for various inanimate objects. In the worst case, one could parody what might be going on in a participant's mind as something like: 'Here I am being asked all sorts of ridiculous questions. Now they want me to think up properties for a bridge – goodness me, what's next? Well, I'd better come up with something, otherwise they'll never let me go home. So I'll say X.' Under such circumstances, the first property that comes to a Spanish speaker's mind is indeed likely to be more manlike than womanlike. In other words, if you force Spanish speakers to be on-the-spot poets, and extract properties of bridges out of them, the gender system will indeed affect their choice of properties. But how can we tell whether the masculine gender has any influence on speakers' spontaneous conceptions of bridges, even outside such exercises in poetry on demand?

In the 1960s, the linguist Susan Ervin tried to downplay the element of creativity with an experiment that involved Italian speakers. She relied on the fact that Italian has very diffuse dialects, so even a native speaker would not be at all surprised to encounter entirely unfamiliar words in an unfamiliar dialect. Ervin invented a list of nonsense words that sounded as if they could be the dialectal terms for various objects. Some of these ended in -o (masculine) and the others in -a (feminine). She wanted to check what associations these words would evoke in Italian speakers but did not want the participants to realise that they were indulging in creative imagination. So she told them they were going to see a list of words from an Italian dialect that they didn't know, and she pretended that the aim of the experiment was to check whether people could guess correctly the properties of words merely by the way they sound. The participants tended to attribute to the -o words similar properties to those they attributed to men (strong, big, ugly), whereas the -a words tended to be described with properties that were also used for women (weak, little, pretty). Ervin's experiment showed that associations were affected by the grammatical gender even when the participants did not realise they were indulging in creative imagination and assumed that the question before them had a correct solution. But while this experiment went some way towards overcoming the problem of subjective judgements, it still did not solve the problem completely, since even if the participants were not aware of being coerced to produce associations on demand, in practise this is exactly what they were required to do.

In fact, it is difficult to imagine how one could design any experiment that would completely bypass the influence of subjective judgements. For the task requires nothing less than having one's cake and eating it too: how can any experiment measure whether grammatical genders exert an influence on speakers' associations, without soliciting these speakers for their associations? A few years ago, Lera Boroditsky and Lauren Schmidt found a way to do exactly that. They asked a group of Spanish speakers and a group of German speakers to participate in a memory game (which was conducted wholly in English, in order to avoid any explicit mention of the genders). The participants were given a list of two dozen inanimate objects, and for each of these objects, they had to memorise a person's name. For example, 'apple' had the name Patrick associated with it, and 'bridge' had the name Claudia. The participants were given a fixed period of time to memorise the names associated with the objects, then tested on how well they had managed. A statistical analysis of the results showed that they were better at remembering the assigned names when the gender of the object matched the sex of the person, and that they found it more difficult to remember the names when the gender of the object clashed with the sex of the person. For example, Spanish speakers found it easier to remember the name associated with 'apple' (*la manzana*) if it was Patricia rather than Patrick, and they found it easier to remember the name for a bridge (*el puento*) if it was Claudio rather than Claudia.

Since Spanish speakers found it objectively more difficult to match a bridge with a woman than with a man, we can conclude that when inanimate objects have a masculine or feminine gender, the associations of manhood or womanhood for these objects are present in Spanish speakers' minds even when they are not actively solicited, even when the participants are not invited to opine on such questions as whether bridges are strong rather than slender, and even when they speak English.

Of course, one could still object that the memory task in question was fairly artificial and at some remove from the concerns of everyday life, where one is not often called upon to memorise whether apples or bridges are called Patrick or Claudia. But psychological experiments often have to rely on such narrowly circumscribed tasks in order to tease out statistically significant differences. The importance of the results is not in what they say about the particular task itself but in what they reveal about the effect of gender more generally, namely that manly or womanly associations of inanimate objects are strong enough in the minds of Spanish and German speakers to affect their ability to commit information to memory.

⟳

There is always room for refinement and improvement in psychological experiments, of course, and those reported above are no exception. But the evidence that has emerged so far leaves little doubt that the idiosyncrasies of a gender system exert a significant influence on speakers' thoughts. When a language treats inanimate objects in the same way as it treats women and men, with the same grammatical forms or with the same 'he' and 'she' pronouns, the habits of grammar can spill over to habits of mind beyond grammar. The grammatical nexus between object and gender is imposed on children from the earliest age and reinforced many thousands of times throughout their lives. This constant drilling affects the associations that speakers develop about inanimate objects and can clothe their notions of such objects in womanly or manly traits. The evidence suggests that sex-related associations are not only fabricated on demand but present even when they are not actively solicited.

Gender thus provides our second example of how the mother tongue influences thought. As before, the relevant difference between languages with and without a gender system is not in what they *allow* their speakers to convey but in what they habitually *force* their speakers to say. There is no evidence to suggest that grammatical gender affects anyone's ability to reason logically. Speakers of gendered languages are perfectly able to understand the difference between sex and syntax, and are not under the illusion that inanimate objects have biological sex. German women rarely mistake their husbands for a hat (even though hats are masculine), Spanish men are not known to confuse a bed with what might be lying in it, and animism does not seem to be more widespread in Italy or Russia than in Anglo-Saxonia. Conversely, there is no reason to suspect that speakers of Hungarian or Turkish or Indonesian, which do not make gender distinctions even on pronouns, are in any way constrained from understanding the finer points about the birds and the bees.

Nevertheless, even if grammatical gender does not restrict anyone's capacity for reasoning, that does not make its consequence any less severe for those immured in a gendered mother tongue. For a gender system may come close to being a prison-house nevertheless – a prison-house of associations. The chains of associations imposed by the genders of one's language are all but impossible to cast off.

But if you native speakers of English are tempted to feel sorry for those of us who are shackled by the heavy load of an irrational gender system, then think again. I would never want to change places with you. My mind may be weighed down by an arbitrary and illogical set of associations, but my world has so much to it that you entirely miss out on, because the landscape of my language is so much more fertile than your arid desert of 'it's'.

It goes without saying that genders are language's gift to poets. Heine's masculine pine tree longs for the feminine palm; Boris Pasternak's *My Sister Life* can work only because 'life' is feminine in Russian; English translations of Charles Baudelaire's 'L'homme et la mer', however inspired, can never hope to capture the tempestuous relationship of attraction and antagonism that he evokes between 'him' (the man) and 'her' (the sea); nor can English do justice to Pablo Neruda's 'Ode to the Sea', in which the (masculine) *el mar* strikes a stone (*una piedra*) and then 'he caresses her, kisses her, drenches her, pounds his chest, repeating his own name' – the English 'it caresses it, kisses it, drenches it, pounds its chest' is not quite the same.

Needless to say, genders cheer up the everyday life of ordinary mortals too. Genders may be a nightmare for foreign learners, but they do not seem to cause any serious trouble to native speakers, and they make the world a livelier place. How tedious it would be if bees weren't 'she's' and butterflies 'he's', if one didn't step from feminine pavements to masculine roads, if twelve masculine months didn't crowd inside one feminine year, if one couldn't greet Mr Cucumber and Lady Cauliflower in the proper way. I would never want to forfeit my genders. Along with Aunt Augusta, I would rather say to the English language that to lose one gender may be regarded as a misfortune; to lose both looks like carelessness.

9

Russian Blues

Visitors to Japan in possession of a sharp eye might notice something unusual about the colour of some traffic lights. Not that there is anything odd about the basic scheme: just like everywhere else, the red light in Japan means 'stop', green is for 'go', and an orange light appears in between. But those who take a good look will see that the green lights are a different shade of green from that of other countries, and have a distinct bluish tint. The reason why is not an Oriental superstition about the protective powers of turquoise or a spillage of blue toner in a Japanese plastic factory, but a bizarre twist of linguistic-political history.

Japanese used to have a colour word, *ao*, that spanned both green and blue. In the modern language, however, *ao* has come to be restricted mostly to blue shades, and green is usually expressed by the word *midori* (although even today *ao* can still refer to the green of freshness or unripeness – green apples, for instance, are called *ao ringo*). When the first traffic lights were imported from the United States and installed in Japan in the 1930s, they were just as green as anywhere else. Nevertheless, in common parlance the go light was dubbed *ao shingoo*, perhaps because the three primary colours on Japanese artists' palettes are traditionally *aka* (red), *kiiro* (yellow), and *ao*. The label *ao* for a green light did not appear so out of the ordinary at first, because of the remaining associations of the word *ao* with greenness. But over time, the discrepancy between the green colour and the dominant meaning of the word *ao* began to feel jarring. Nations with a weaker spine might have opted for the feeble solution of simply changing the official name of the go light to *midori*. Not so the Japanese. Rather than alter the name to fit reality, the Japanese government decreed in 1973 that reality should be altered to fit the name: henceforth, go lights would be a colour that better corresponded to the dominant meaning of *ao*. Alas, it was impossible to change the colour to real blue, because Japan is party to an international convention that ensures road signs have a measure of uniformity around the globe. The solution was thus to make the *ao* light as bluish as possible while still being officially green (see figure 7 in the insert).

The turquoising of the traffic light in Japan is a rather out-of-the-way example of how the quirks of a language can change reality and thus affect what people get to see in the world. But of course this is not the kind of influence of language that we have been concerned with in the previous few chapters. Our question is whether speakers of different languages might perceive the *same reality* in different ways, just because of their mother tongues. Are the colour concepts of our language a lens through which we experience colours in the world?

In returning to the subject of colour, this final chapter tries to discharge an old debt, by turning on its head the nineteenth-century question about the relation between language and perception. Recall that Gladstone, Geiger, and Magnus believed that differences in the vocabulary of colour resulted from pre-existing differences in colour perception. But could it be that cause and effect have been reversed here? Is it possible that linguistic differences can be the *cause* of differences in perception? Could the colour distinctions we routinely make in our language affect our sensitivity to certain colours? Could our sensation of a Chagall painting or the stained-glass windows of Chartres Cathedral depend on whether our language has a word for 'blue'?

⌒

Few thrills of later life can match the excitement of teenage philoso-
phising into the small hours of the morning. One particularly profound
insight that tends to emerge from these sessions of pimpled metaphysics
is the shattering realisation that one can never know how other people
really see colours. You and I may both agree that one apple is 'green' and
another 'red', but for all I know, when you say 'red' you may actually
experience my green, and vice versa. We can never tell, even if we compare notes until kingdom come, because if my sensation was in red–
green negative from yours, we would still agree on all colour descriptions
when we communicated verbally. We would agree on calling ripe toma-
toes red and unripe ones green, and we would even agree that red is a
warm colour and green is a cooler colour, for in my world flames look
green – which I call 'red' – so I would associate this colour with warm-
ness.

Of course, we are meant to be dealing with serious science here, not
with juvenile lucubrations. The only problem is that as far as understanding the actual sensation of colour is concerned, modern science
does not seem to have advanced substantially beyond the level of teenage metaphysics. A great deal is known today about the retina and its
three types of cones, each with peak sensitivity in a different part of the
spectrum. As explained in the appendix, however, the colour sensation
itself is formed not in the retina but in the brain, and what the brain
does is nothing remotely as simple as just adding up the signals from
the three types of cones. In fact, between the cones and our actual
sensation of colour there is a whirl of extraordinarily subtle and
sophisticated computation: normalisation, compensation, stabilisation, regularisation, even plain wishful seeing (the brain can make us
see a non-existent colour if it has reason to believe, based on its past
experience of the world, that this colour ought to be there). The brain
does all this computation and interpretation in order to give us a relatively stable picture of the world, one that doesn't change radically
under different lighting conditions. If the brain didn't normalise our

view in this way, we would experience the world as a series of pictures from cheap cameras, where colours of objects constantly change whenever the lighting is not optimal.

Beyond the realisation that the interpretation of the signals from the retina is enormously complex and subtle, however, scientists know fairly little about how the sensation of colour is really formed in anyone's brain, let alone how exactly it could vary between different people. So given the inability to approach the colour sensation directly, what hope is there of ever finding out whether different languages can affect their speakers' perception of colours?

In previous decades, researchers tried to overcome this obstacle by devising clever ways of making people describe in words what they experienced. In 1984, Paul Kay (of Berlin and Kay fame) and Willett Kempton tried to check whether a language like English, which treats blue and green as separate colours, would skew speakers' perception of shades near the green–blue border. They used a number of coloured chips in different shades of green and blue, mostly very close to the border, so that the greens were bluish green and the blues greenish blue. This meant that, in terms of objective distance, two green chips could be further apart from each other than if one of them was from a blue chip. The participants in the experiment were requested to complete a series of 'odd man out' tasks. They were shown three chips at a time and asked to choose which chip seemed most distant in colour from the other two. When a group of Americans were tested, their responses tended to exaggerate the distance between chips across the green–blue border and to underestimate the distance between chips on the same side of the border. For example, when two chips were green and the third was (greenish) blue, the participants tended to choose the blue as being furthest apart, even if in terms of objective distance one of the greens was actually further away from the other two. The same experiment was then conducted in Mexico, with speakers of an Indian language called Tarahumara, which treats green and blue as shades of one colour. Tarahumara speakers did not exaggerate the distance between chips on different sides of the green–blue border. Kay and Kempton concluded that the difference between the responses of

English and Tarahumara speakers demonstrated an influence of language on the perception of colour.

The problem with such experiments, however, is that they depend on soliciting subjective judgements for a task that seems vague or ambiguous. As Kay and Kempton conceded themselves, English speakers could have reasoned as follows: 'It's hard to decide here which one looks the most different, since all three are very close in hue. Are there any other kinds of clues I might use? Aha! A and B are both *called* "green" while C is *called* "blue." That solves my problem; I'll pick C as the most different.' So it is possible that English speakers simply acted on the principle 'If in doubt, decide by the name'. And if this is what they did, then the only thing the experiment proved was that English speakers rely on their language as a fallback strategy when they are required to solve a vague task for which there doesn't seem to be a clear answer. Tarahumara speakers cannot employ this strategy, as they don't have separate names for green and blue. But that does not prove the English speakers actually *perceive* the colours any differently from speakers of Tarahumara.

In an attempt to confront this problem head-on, Kay and Kempton repeated the same experiment with another group of English speakers, and this time the participants were told explicitly that they must not rely on the names of the colours when judging which chips were further apart. But even after this warning, the responses still exaggerated the distance between the chips across the green–blue border. Indeed, when asked to explain their choices, the participants insisted that these chips really *looked* further apart. Kay and Kempton concluded that if the names have an effect on speakers' choices, this effect cannot easily be brought under control or switched off at will, which suggests that language interferes in visual processing on a deep unconscious level. As we'll soon see, their hunch would metamorphose into something much less vague in later decades. But since the only evidence available in 1984 was based on subjective judgements for ambiguous tasks, it is no wonder that their experiment was not sufficient to convince.

For years it looked as if any attempt to determine in a more objective fashion whether language affects the perception of colour would always lead to the same dead end, because there is no way of measuring objectively how close different shades appear to different people. On the one hand, it's impossible to scan the sensation of colour directly off the brain. On the other, if one wants to tease out fine differences in perception by asking people to describe what they see, one necessarily has to devise tasks that involve the choice between very close variants. The tasks might then seem ambiguous and without a correct solution, so even if the mother tongue is shown to influence the choice of answers, it can still be questioned whether language has really affected visual perception or whether it has merely provided inspiration for choosing an answer to a vague question.

It is only recently that researchers managed to manoeuvre themselves out of this impasse. The method they hit upon is still very indirect, in fact it is positively roundabout. But for the first time, this method has allowed researchers to measure objectively *something* that is related to perception – the average time it takes people to recognise the difference between certain colours. The idea behind the new method is simple: rather than asking a vague question like 'Which two colours look closer to you?' the researchers set the participants a clear and simple task that has just one correct solution. What is actually tested, therefore, is not whether the participants get the right solution (they generally do) but rather their speed of reaction, from which one can draw inferences about brain processes.

One such experiment, published in 2008, was conducted by a team from Stanford, MIT, and UCLA – Jonathan Winawer, Nathan Witthoft, Michael Frank, Lisa Wu, Alex Wade, and Lera Boroditsky. We saw in chapter 3 that Russian has two distinct colour names for the range that English subsumes under the name 'blue': *siniy* (dark blue) and *goluboy* (light blue). The aim of the experiment was to check whether these two distinct 'blues' would affect Russians' perception of blue shades. The participants were seated in front of a computer screen and shown sets of three blue squares at a time: one square at the top and a pair below, as shown below and in colour in figure 8 in the insert.

One of the two bottom squares was always exactly the same colour as the upper square, and the other was a different shade of blue. The

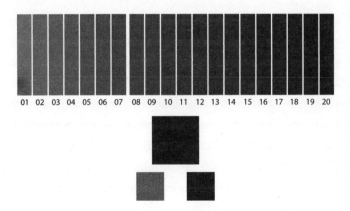

task was to indicate which of the two bottom squares was the same colour as the one on top. The participants did not have to say anything aloud, they just had to press one of two buttons, left or right, as quickly as they could once the picture appeared on the screen. (So in the picture above, the correct response would be to press the button on the right.) This was a simple enough task with a simple enough solution, and of course the participants provided the right answer almost all the time. But what the experiment was really designed to measure was how long it took them to press the correct button.

For each set, the colours were chosen from among twenty shades of blue. As was to be expected, the reaction time of all the participants depended first and foremost on how far the shade of the odd square out was from that of the other two. If the upper square was a very dark blue, say shade 18, and the odd one out was a very light blue, say shade 3, participants tended to press the correct button very quickly. But the nearer the hue of the odd one out came to the other two, the longer the reaction time tended to be. So far so unsurprising. It is only to be expected that when we look at two hues that are far apart, we will be quicker to register the difference, whereas if the colours are similar, the brain will require more processing work, and therefore more time, to decide that the two colours are not the same.

The more interesting results emerged when the reaction time of the Russian speakers turned out to depend not just on the objective distance between the shades but also on the borderline between *siniy* and *goluboy*! Suppose the upper square was *siniy* (dark blue), but immediately on the border with *goluboy* (light blue). If the odd square out was two shades along towards the light direction (and thus across the border into *goluboy*), the average time it took the Russians to press the button was significantly shorter than if the odd square out was the same objective distance away – two shades along – but towards the dark direction, and thus another shade of *siniy*. When English speakers were tested with exactly the same set-up, no such skewing effect was detected in their reaction times. The border between 'light blue' and 'dark blue' made no difference, and the only relevant factor for their reaction times was the objective distance between the shades.

While this experiment did not measure the actual colour sensation directly, it did manage to measure objectively the second-best thing, a reaction time that is closely correlated with visual perception. Most importantly, there was no reliance here on eliciting subjective judgements for an ambiguous task, because participants were never asked to gauge the distances between colours or to say which shades appeared more similar. Instead, they were requested to solve a simple visual task that had just one correct solution. What the experiment measured, their reaction time, is something that the participants were neither conscious of nor had control over. They just pressed the button as quickly as they could whenever a new picture appeared on the screen. But the average speed with which Russians managed to do so was shorter if the colours had different names. The results thus prove that there is something objectively different between Russian and English speakers in the way their visual processing systems react to blue shades.

And while this is as much as we can say with absolute certainty, it is plausible to go one step further and make the following inference: since people tend to react more quickly to colour recognition tasks the further apart the two colours appear to them, and since Russians react more quickly to shades across the *siniy–goluboy* border than what the objective distance between the hues would imply, it is plausible to conclude that neighbouring hues around the border actually *appear* further apart to Russian speakers than they are in objective terms.

Of course, even if differences between the behaviour of Russian and English speakers have been demonstrated objectively, it is always dangerous to jump automatically from correlation to causation. How can we be sure that the Russian language in particular – rather than anything else in the Russians' background and upbringing – had any causal role in producing their response to colours near the border? Maybe the real cause of their quicker reaction time lies in the habit of Russians to spend hours on end gazing intently at the vast expanses of Russian sky? Or in years of close study of blue vodka?

To test whether language circuits in the brain had any direct involvement with the processing of colour signals, the researchers added another element to the experiment. They applied a standard procedure called an 'interference task' to make it more difficult for the linguistic circuits to perform their normal function. The participants were asked to memorise random strings of digits and then keep repeating these aloud *while* they were watching the screen and pressing the buttons. The idea was that if the participants were performing an irrelevant language-related chore (saying aloud a jumble of numbers), the language areas in their brains would be 'otherwise engaged' and would not be so easily available to support the visual processing of colour.

When the experiment was repeated under such conditions of verbal interference, the Russians no longer reacted more quickly to shades across the *siniy–goluboy* border, and their reaction time depended only on the objective distance between the shades. The results of the interference task point clearly at language as the culprit for the original differences in reaction time. Kay and Kempton's original hunch that linguistic interference with the processing of colour occurs on a deep and unconscious level has thus received strong support some two decade later. After all, in the Russian blues experiment, the task was a purely visual-motoric exercise, and language was never explicitly invited to the party. And yet somewhere in the chain of reactions between the photons touching the retina and the movement of the finger muscles, the categories of the mother tongue nevertheless got involved, and they speeded up the recognition of the colour differences when the shades had different names. The evidence from the Russian blues experiment thus gives more credence to the subjective reports of Kay and Kempton's participants that shades with different names *looked* more distant to them.

An even more remarkable experiment to test how language meddles with the processing of visual colour signals was devised by four researchers from Berkeley and Chicago – Aubrey Gilbert, Terry Regier, Paul Kay (same one), and Richard Ivry. The strangest thing about the set-up of their experiment, which was published in 2006, was the unexpected number of languages it compared. Whereas the Russian blues experiment involved speakers of exactly two languages, and compared their responses to an area of the spectrum where the colour categories of the two languages diverged, the Berkeley and Chicago experiment was different, because it compared . . . only English.

At first sight, an experiment involving speakers of only one language may seem a rather left-handed approach to testing whether the mother tongue makes a difference to speakers' colour perception. Difference from what? But in actual fact, this ingenious experiment was rather dexterous, or, to be more precise, it was just as adroit as it was a-gauche. For what the researchers set out to compare was nothing less than the left and right halves of the brain.

Their idea was simple, but like most clever ideas, it appears simple only once someone has thought of it. They relied on two facts about the brain that have been known for a very long time. The first fact concerns the seat of language in the brain: for a century and a half now scientists have recognised that linguistic areas in the brain are not evenly divided between the two hemispheres. In 1861, the French surgeon Pierre Paul Broca exhibited before the Paris Society of Anthropology the brain of a man who had died on his ward the day before, after suffering from a debilitating brain disease. The man had lost his ability to speak years earlier but had maintained many other aspects of his intelligence. Broca's autopsy showed that one particular area of the man's brain had been completely destroyed: brain tissue in the frontal lobe of the left hemisphere had rotted away, leaving only a large cavity full of watery liquid.

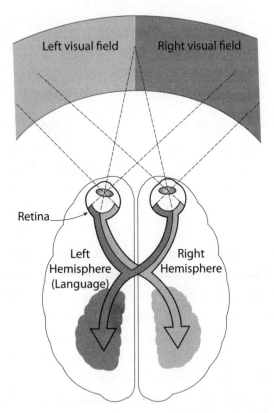

Processing of the left and right visual fields in the brain

Broca concluded that this particular area of the left hemisphere must be the part of the brain responsible for articulate speech. In the following years, he and his colleagues conducted many more autopsies on people who had lost their ability to speak, and the same area of their brains turned out to be damaged. This proved beyond doubt that the particular section of the left hemisphere, which later came to be called 'Broca's area', was the main seat of language in the brain.

The second well-known fact that the experiment relied on is that each hemisphere of the brain is responsible for processing visual signals from the opposite half of the field of vision. As shown in the illustration on the follwing page, there is an X-shaped crossing over between the two halves of the visual field and the two brain hemispheres: signals from our left side are sent to the right hemisphere to be processed, whereas signals from the right visual field are processed in the left hemisphere.

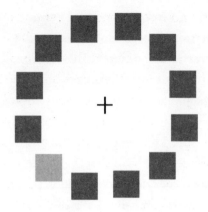

If we put the two facts together – the seat of language in the left hemi-sphere and the crossover in the processing of visual information – it follows that visual signals from our right side are processed in the same half of the brain as language, whereas what we see on the left is processed in the hemisphere without a significant linguistic component.

The researchers used this asymmetry to check a hypothesis that seems incredible at first (and even second) sight: could the linguistic meddling affect the visual processing of colour in the left hemisphere more strongly than in the right? Could it be that people perceive colours differently, depending on which side they see them on? Would English speakers, for instance, be more sensitive to shades near the green–blue border when they see these on their right-hand side rather than on the left?

To test this fanciful proposition, the researchers devised a simple odd-one-out task. The participants had to look at a computer screen and to focus on a little cross right in the middle, which ensured that whatever appeared on the left half of the screen was in their left visual field and vice versa. The participants were then shown a circle made out of little squares, as in the picture above (and in colour in figure 9 in the insert).

All the squares were of the same colour except one. The participants were asked to press one of two buttons, depending on whether the odd square out was in the left half of the circle or in the right. In the picture above, the odd square out is roughly at eight o'clock, so the correct response would be to press the left button. The participants were given a series of such tasks, and in each one the odd one out changed colour and position. Sometimes it was blue whereas the others were green, sometimes it was green but a different shade from all the other greens, sometimes it was green but the others were blue, and so on. As the task is simple, the participants generally pressed the correct button. But what was actually being measured was the time it took them to respond.

As expected, the speed of recognising the odd square out depended principally on the objective distance between the shades. Regardless of whether it appeared on the left or on the right, participants were always quicker to respond the further the shade of the odd one out was from the rest. But the startling result was a significant difference between the reaction patterns in the right and in the left visual fields. When the odd square out appeared on the right side of the screen, the half that is processed in the same hemisphere as language, the border between green and blue made a real difference: the average reaction time was significantly shorter when the odd square out was across the green–blue border from the rest. But when the odd square out was on the left side of the screen, the effect of the green–blue border was far weaker. In other words, the speed of the response was much less influenced by whether the odd square out was across the green–blue border from the rest or whether it was a different shade of the same colour.

So the left half of English speakers' brains showed the same response towards the blue–green border that Russian speakers displayed towards the *siniy–goluboy* border, whereas the right hemisphere showed only weak traces of a skewing effect. The results of this experiment (as well as a series of subsequent adaptations that have corroborated its basic conclusions) leave little room for doubt that the colour concepts of our mother tongue interfere directly in the processing of colour. Short of actually scanning the brain, the two-hemisphere experiment provides the most direct evidence so far of the influence of language on visual perception.

Short of scanning the brain? A group of researchers from the University of Hong Kong saw no reason to fall short of that. In 2008, they published the results of a similar experiment, only with a little twist. As before, the recognition task involved staring at a computer screen, recognising colours, and pressing one of two buttons. The difference was that the doughty participants were asked to complete this task while lying in the tube of an MRI scanner. MRI, or magnetic resonance imaging, is a technique that produces online scans of the brain by measuring the level of blood flow in its different regions. Since increased blood flow corresponds to increased neural activity, the MRI scanner measures (albeit indirectly) the level of neural activity in any point of the brain.

In this experiment, the mother tongue of the participants was Mandarin Chinese. Six different colours were used: three of them (red, green, and blue) have common and simple names in Mandarin, while three other colours do not (see figure 10 in the insert). The task was very simple: the participants were shown two squares on the screen for a split second, and all they had to do was indicate by pressing a button whether the two squares were identical in colour or not.

The task did not involve language in any way. It was again a purely visual-motoric exercise. But the researchers wanted to see if language areas of the brain would nevertheless be activated. They assumed that linguistic circuits would more likely get involved with the visual task if the colours shown had common and simple names than if there were no obvious labels for them. And indeed, two specific small areas in the cerebral cortex of the left hemisphere were activated when the colours were from the easy-to-name group but remained inactive when the colours were from the difficult-to-name group.

To determine the function of these two left-hemisphere areas more accurately, the researchers administered a second task to the participants, this time explicitly language-related. The participants were shown colours on the screen, and while their brains were being scanned they were asked to say aloud what each colour was called. The two areas that had been active earlier only with the easy-to-name colours now lit up as being heavily active. So the researchers concluded that the two specific areas in question must house the linguistic circuits responsible for finding colour names.

If we project the function of these two areas back to the results of the first (purely visual) task, it becomes clear that when the brain has to decide whether two colours look the same or not, the circuits responsible for visual perception ask the language circuits for help in making the decision, even if no speaking is involved. So for the first time, there is now direct neurophysiologic evidence that areas of the brain that are specifically responsible for name finding are involved with the processing of purely visual colour information.

In the light of the experiments reported in this chapter, colour may be the area that comes closest in reality to the metaphor of language as a lens. Of course, language is not a physical lens and does not affect the photons that reach the eye. But the sensation of colour is produced in the brain, not the eye, and the brain does not take the signals from the retina at face value, as it is constantly engaged in a highly complex process of normalisation, which creates an illusion of stable colours under different lighting conditions. The brain achieves this 'instant fix' effect by shifting and stretching the signals from the retina, by exaggerating some differences while playing down others. No one knows exactly how the brain does all this, but what is clear is that it relies on past memories and on stored impressions. It has been shown, for instance, that a perfectly grey picture of a banana can appear slightly yellow to us, because the brain remembers bananas as yellow and so normalises the sensation towards what it expects to see. (For further details, see the appendix.)

It is likely that the involvement of language with the perception of colour takes place on this level of normalisation and compensation, where the brain relies on its store of past memories and established distinctions in order to decide how similar certain colours are. And although no one knows yet what exactly goes on between the linguistic and the visual circuits, the evidence gathered so far amounts to a compelling argument that language does affect our visual sensation. In Kay and Kempton's top-down experiment from 1984, English speakers insisted that shades across the green–blue border *looked* further apart to them. The bottom-up approach of more recent experiments shows that the linguistic concepts of colour are directly involved in the processing of visual information, and that they make people react to colours of different names as if these were further apart than they are objectively. Taken together, these results lead to a conclusion that few would have been prepared to believe just a few years ago: that speakers of different languages may perceive colours slightly differently after all.

In one sense, therefore, the colour odyssey that Gladstone launched in 1858 has ended up, after a century and a half of peregrination, within spitting distance of his starting point. For in the end, it may well be that the Greeks did perceive colours slightly differently from us. But even if we have concluded the journey staring Gladstone right in the face, we are not entirely seeing eye to eye with him, because we have turned his story on its head and have reversed the direction of cause and effect in the relation between language and perception. Gladstone assumed that the difference between Homer's colour vocabulary and ours was a *result* of pre-existing differences in colour perception. But it now seems that the vocabulary of colour in different languages can be the *cause* of differences in the perception of colour. Gladstone thought that Homer's unrefined colour vocabulary was a reflection of the undeveloped state of his eye's anatomy. We know that nothing has changed in the eye's anatomy over the last millennia, and yet the habits of mind instiled by our more refined colour vocabulary may have made us more sensitive to some fine colour distinctions nonetheless.

More generally, the explanation for cognitive differences between ethnic groups has shifted over the last two centuries, from anatomy to culture. In the nineteenth century, it was generally assumed that there were significant inequalities between the hereditary mental faculties of different races, and that these biological inequalities were the main reason for their varying accomplishments. One of the jewels in the crown of the twentieth century was the recognition of the fundamental unity of mankind in all that concerns its cognitive endowment. So nowadays we no longer look primarily to the genes to explain variations in mental characteristics among ethnic groups. But in the twenty-first century, we are beginning to appreciate the differences in thinking that are imprinted by cultural conventions and, in particular, by speaking in different tongues.

Forgive Us Our Ignorances

Language has two lives. In its public role, it is a system of conventions agreed upon by a speech community for the purpose of effective communication. But language also has another, private existence, as a system of knowledge that each speaker has internalised in his or her own mind. If language is to serve as an effective means of communication, then the private systems of knowledge in speakers' minds must closely correspond with the public system of linguistic conventions. And it is because of this correspondence that the public conventions of language can mirror what goes on in the most fascinating and most elusive object in the entire universe, our mind.

This book set out to show, through the evidence supplied by language, that fundamental aspects of our thought are influenced by the cultural conventions of our society, to a much greater extent than is fashionable to admit today. In the first part, it became clear that the way our language carves up the world into concepts has not just been determined for us by nature, and that what we find 'natural' depends largely on the conventions we have been brought up on. That is not to say, of course, that each language can partition the world arbitrarily according to its whim. But within the constraints of what is learnable and sensible for communication, the ways in which even the simplest concepts are delineated can vary to a far greater degree than what plain common sense would ever expect. For, ultimately, what common sense finds natural is what it is familiar with.

In the second part, we saw that the linguistic conventions of our society can affect aspects of our thought that go beyond language. The demonstrable impact of language on thinking is very different from what was touted in the past. In particular, no evidence has come to light that our mother tongue imposes limits on our intellectual horizons and constrains our ability to understand concepts or distinctions used in other languages. The real effects of the mother tongue are rather the habits that develop through the *frequent use* of certain ways of expression. The concepts we are trained to treat as distinct, the information our mother tongue continuously forces us to specify, the details it requires us to be attentive to, and the repeated associations it imposes on us – all these habits of speech can create habits of mind that affect more than merely the knowledge of language itself. We saw examples from three areas of language: spatial coordinates and their consequences for memory patterns and orientation, grammatical gender and its impact on associations, and the concepts of colour, which can increase our sensitivity to certain colour distinctions.

According to the dominant view among linguists and cognitive scientists today, the influence of language on thought can be considered significant only if it bears on genuine reasoning – if, for instance, one language can be shown to prevent its speakers from solving a logical problem that is easily solved by speakers of another language. Since no evidence for such constraining influence on logical reasoning has ever been presented, this necessarily means – or so the argument goes – that any remaining effects of language are insignificant and that fundamentally we all think in the same way.

But it is all too easy to exaggerate the importance of logical reasoning in our lives. Such an overestimation may be natural enough for those reared on a diet of analytic philosophy, where thought is practically equated with logic and any other mental processes are considered beneath notice. But this view does not correspond with the rather mod-est role of logical thinking in our actual experience of life. After all, how many daily decisions do we make on the basis of abstract deductive rea-soning, compared with those guided by gut feeling, intuition, emotions, impulse, or practical skills? How often have you spent your day solving logical conundrums, compared with wondering where you left your socks? Or trying to remember where your car is in a multilevel car park? How many commercials try to appeal to us through logical syl-logisms, compared with those that play on colours, associations, allu-sions? And finally, how many wars have been fought over disagreements in set theory?

The influence of the mother tongue that has been demonstrated empirically is felt in areas of thought such as memory, perception, and associations or in practical skills such as orientation. And in our actual experience of life, such areas are no less important than the capacity for abstract reasoning, probably far more so.

The questions explored in this book are ages old, but the serious research on the subject is only in its infancy. Only in recent years, for example, have we understood the dire urgency to record and analyse the thou-sands of exotic tongues that are still spoken in remote corners of the globe, before they are all forsaken in favour of English, Spanish, and a handful of other dominant languages. Even in the recent past, it was still common for linguists to claim to have found a 'universal of human language' after examining a certain phenomenon in a sample that con-sisted of English, Italian, and Hungarian, say, and finding that all of these three languages agreed. Today, it is clearer to most linguists that the only languages that can truly reveal what is natural and universal are the hosts of small tribal tongues that do things very differently from what we are used to. So a race against time is now under way to record as many of these languages as possible before all knowledge of them is lost forever.

The investigations into the possible links between the structure of society and the structure of the grammatical system are in a much more embryonic stage. Having languished under the taboo of 'equal complexity' for decades, the attempts to determine to what extent the complexity of various areas in grammar depends on the complexity of society are still mostly on the level of discovering the 'how' and have barely began to address the 'why'.

But above all, it is the investigation of the influence of language on thought that is only just beginning as a serious scientific enterprise. (Its history as a haven for fantasists is of much longer standing, of course.) The three examples I presented – space, gender, and colour – seem to me the areas where the impact of language has been demonstrated most convincingly so far. Other areas have also been studied in recent years, but not enough reliable evidence has yet been presented to support them. One example is the marking of plurality. While English requires its speakers to mark the difference between singular and plural when-ever a noun is mentioned, there are languages that do not routinely force such a distinction. It has been suggested that the necessity (or otherwise) to mark plurality affects the attention and memory patterns of speakers, but while this suggestion does not seem implausible in theory, conclusive evidence is still lacking.

No doubt further areas of language will be explored when our experimental tools become less blunt. What about an elaborate system of evidentiality, for example? Recall that Matses requires its speakers to supply detailed information about their source of knowledge for every event they describe. Can the habits of speech induced by such a lan-guage have a measurable effect on the speakers' habits of mind beyond language? In years to come, questions such as this will surely become amenable to empirical study.

⌒

When one hears about acts of extraordinary bravery in combat, it is usually a sign that the battle has not been going terribly well. For when wars unfold according to plan and one's own side is winning, acts of exceptional individual heroism are rarely called for. Bravery is required mostly by the desperate side.

The ingenuity and sophistication of some of the experiments we have encountered is so inspiring that it is easy to mistake them for signs of great triumphs in science's battle to conquer the fortress of the human brain. But, in reality, the ingenious inferences made in these experiments are symptoms not of great strength but of great weakness. For all this ingenuity is needed only because we know so little about how the brain works. Were we not profoundly ignorant, we would not need to rely on roundabout methods of gleaning information from measures such as reaction speed to various contrived tasks. If we knew more, we would simply observe directly what goes on in the brain and would then be able to determine precisely how nature and culture shape the concepts of language, or whether any parts of grammar are innate, or how exactly language affects any given aspect of thought.

One may object, of course, that it is unfair to describe our present state of knowledge in such bleak terms, especially given that the very last experiment I reported was based on breathtaking technological sophistication. It involved, after all, nothing short of the online scanning of brain activity and revealed which specific areas are active when the brain performs particular tasks. How can that possibly be called ignorance? But try to think about it this way. Suppose you wanted to understand how a big corporation works and the only thing you were allowed to do was stand outside the headquarters and look at the windows from afar. The sole evidence you had to go on would be in which rooms the lights went on at different times of the day. Of course, if you kept watch very carefully, over a long time, there would be a lot of information you could glean. You would find out, for instance, that the weekly board meetings are held on floor 25, second room from the left, that in times of crisis there is great activity on floor 13, so there is probably an emergency control centre there, and so on. But how inadequate all this knowledge would be if you were never allowed to hear what was being said and all your inferences were based on watching the windows.

If you think this analogy is too gloomy, then remember that the most sophisticated MRI scanners do nothing more than show where the lights are on in the brain. The only thing they reveal is where there is increased blood flow at any given moment, and we infer from this that more neural activity is taking place there. But we are nowhere near being able to understand what is 'said' in the brain. We have no idea how any specific concept, label, grammatical rule, colour impression, orientation strategy, or gender association is actually coded.

When researching this book, I read quite a few latter-day arguments about the workings of the brain shortly after trawling through quite a few century-old discussions about the workings of biological heredity. And when these are read in close proximity, it is difficult not to be struck by a close parallel between them. What unites cognitive scientists at the turn of the twenty-first century and molecular biologists at the turn of the twentieth century is the profound ignorance about their object of investigation. Around 1900, heredity was a black box even for the greatest of scientists. The most they could do was make indirect inferences by comparing what 'goes in' on one side (the properties of the parents) and what 'comes out' on the other side (the properties of the progeny). The actual mechanisms in between were mysterious and unfathomable for them. How embarrassing it is for us, to whom life's recipe has been laid bare, to read the agonised discussions of these giants and to think about the ludicrous experiments they had to conduct, such as cutting the tails off generations of mice to see if the injury would be inherited by the offspring.

A century later, we can see much further into the mechanisms of genetics, but we are still just as short-sighted in all that concerns the workings of the brain. We know what comes in on one side (for instance, photons into the eye), we know what goes out the other side (a hand pressing a button), but all the decision-making in between still occurs behind closed doors. In the future, when the neural networks will have become as transparent as the structure of DNA, when scientists can listen in on the neurons and understand exactly what is said, our MRI scans will look just as sophisticated as cutting off mice's tails.

Future scientists will not need to conduct primitive experiments such as asking people to press buttons while looking at screens. They will simply find the relevant brain circuits and see directly how concepts are formed and how perception, memory, associations, and any other aspects of thought are affected by the mother tongue. If their historians of ancient science ever bother to read this little book, how embarrassing it will seem to them. How hard it will be to imagine why we had to make do with vague indirect inferences, why we had to see through a glass darkly, when they can just see face to face.

But ye readers of posterity, forgive us our ignorances, as we forgive those who were ignorant before us. The mystery of heredity has been illuminated for us, but we have seen this great light only because our predecessors never tired of searching in the dark. So if you, O subsequent ones, ever deign to look down at us from your summit of effortless superiority, remember that you have only scaled it on the back of our efforts. For it is thankless to grope in the dark and tempting to rest until the light of understanding shines upon us. But if we are led into this temptation, your kingdom will never come.

Colour: In the Eye of the Beholder

Humans can see light only at a narrow band of wavelength from 0.4 to 0.7 microns (thousandths of a millimetre), or, to be more precise, between around 380 and 750 nanometres (millionths of a millimetre). Light in these wavelengths is absorbed in the cells of the retina, the thin plate of nerve cells that line the inside of the eyeball. At the back of the retina there is a layer of photoreceptor cells that absorb the light and send neural signals that will eventually be translated into the colour sensation in the brain.

When we look at the rainbow or at light coming out of a prism, our perception of colour seems to change continuously as the wavelength changes (see figures 2 and 11 in the insert). Ultraviolet light at wavelengths shorter than 380 nm is not visible to the eye, but as the wavelength starts to increase we begin to perceive shades of violet; from around 450 nm we begin to see blue, from around 500 green, from 570 yellow, from 590 orange shades, and then once the wavelength increases above 620 we see red, all the way up to somewhere below 750 nm, where our sensitivity stops and infrared light starts.

A 'pure' light of uniform wavelength (rather than a combination of light sources in different wavelengths) is called monochromatic. It is natural to assume that whenever a source of light looks yellow to us, this is because it consists only of wavelengths around 580 nm, like the mono-chromatic yellow light of the rainbow. And it is equally natural to assume that when an object appears yellow to us, this must mean that it reflects light only of wavelengths around 580 nm and absorbs light in all other wavelengths. But both of these assumptions are entirely wrong. In fact, colour vision is an illusion played on us by the nervous system and the brain. We do not need any light at wavelength 580 nm to perceive yellow. We can get an identical 'yellow' sensation if pure red light at 620 nm and pure green light at 540 nm are superimposed in equal measures. In other words, our eyes cannot tell the difference between monochromatic yel-low light and a combination of monochromatic red and green lights. Indeed, television screens manage to trick us to perceive any shade of the spectrum by using different combinations of just three monochromatic lights – red, green, and blue. Finally, objects that appear yellow to us very rarely reflect only light around 580 nm and more usually reflect green, red, and orange light as well as yellow. How can all this be explained?

Until the nineteenth century, scientists tried to understand this phe-nomenon of 'colour matching' through some physical properties of light itself. But in 1801 the English physicist Thomas Young suggested in a famous lecture that the explanation lies not in the properties of light but rather in the anatomy of the human eye. Young developed the 'tri-chromatic' theory of vision: he argued that there are only three kinds of receptors in the eye, each particularly sensitive to light in a particular area of the spectrum. Our subjective sensation of continuous colour is thus produced when the brain compares the responses from these three different types of receptors. Young's theory was refined in the 1850s by James Clerk Maxwell and in the 1860s by Hermann von Helmholtz and is still the basis for what is known today about the functioning of the retina.

Colour vision is based on three kinds of light-absorbing pigment molecules that are contained within cells of the retina called cones. These three types of cells are known as long-wave, middle-wave, and short-wave cones. The cones absorb photons and send on a signal about the number of photons they absorb per unit of time. The short-wave cones have their peak sensitivity around 425 nm – that is, on the border between violet and blue. This does not mean that these cones absorb photons only at 425 nm. As can be seen from the diagram below (and in colour in figure 12), the short-wave cones absorb light at a range of wavelengths, from violet to blue and even some parts of green. But their sensitivity to light decreases as the wavelength moves away from the peak at 425 nm. So when monochromatic green light at 520 nm reaches the short-wave cones, a much smaller per centage of the photons are absorbed compared to light at 425 nm.

The second type of receptors, the middle-wave cones, have their peak sensitivity at yellowish green, around 530 nm. And again, they are sensitive (to a decreasing degree) to a range of wavelengths from blue to orange. Finally, the long-wave cones have their peak sensitivity quite close to the middle-wave cones, in greenish yellow, at 565 nm.

The cones themselves do not 'know' what wavelength of light they are absorbing. Each cone by itself is colour-blind. The only thing the cone registers is the overall intensity of light that it has absorbed. Thus, a short-wave cone cannot tell whether it is absorbing low-intensity violet light (at 440 nm) or high-intensity green light at (500 nm). And the middle-wave cone cannot tell the difference between light at 550 nm and light in the same intensity at 510 nm.

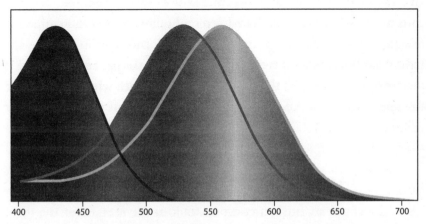

The (normalised) sensitivity of the short-wave, middle-wave, and long-wave cones as a function of wavelength.

The brain works out what colour it is seeing by comparing the rates at which photons are absorbed in the three different classes of cones. But there are infinitely many different spectral distributions that could give exactly the same ratios, and we cannot distinguish between them. For example, a monochromatic yellow light at wavelength 580 nm creates exactly the same absorption ratio between the cones as a combination of red light at 620 nm and green light at 540 nm, as mentioned earlier. And there are an infinite number of other such 'metameric colours,' different spectral distributions that produce the same absorption ratios between the three types of cones and thus look the same to the human eye.

It is important to realise, therefore, that our range of colour sensations is determined not directly by the range of monochromatic lights in the spectrum but rather by the range of possibilities of varying the ratios between the three types of cones. Our 'colour space' is three-dimensional, and it contains sensations that do not correspond to any colours of the rainbow. Our sensation of pink, for example, is created from an absorption ratio that corresponds not to any monochromatic light but rather to a combination of red and blue lights.

As the light fades at night, a different system of vision comes into play. The cones are not sensitive enough to perceive light in very low intensity, but there are other receptors, called rods, that are so sensitive they can register the absorption of even a single photon! The rods are most sensitive to bluish green light at around 500 nm. Our low-light vision, however, is colour-blind. This is not because the light itself 'forgets' its wavelength at night but simply because there is just one type of rod. As the brain has nothing with which to compare the responses from the single type of rod, no colour sensation can be produced.

SENSITIVITY TO DIFFERENT WAVELENGTHS

There are about six million cones in total in the retina, but the three types are not found in nearly equal numbers: there are relatively few short-wave (violet) cones, more than ten times as many middle-wave (green) cones, and even more long-wave cones. The far greater numbers of middle-wave and long-wave cones means that the eye is more efficient in absorbing light at the long-wave half of the spectrum (yellow and red) than at the short-wave half, so it takes lesser intensity of yellow light to be detected by the eye than blue or violet light. In fact, our day vision has a maximum sensitivity to light of 555 nm, at yellow–green. It is this idiosyncrasy of our anatomy that makes yellow appear brighter to us than blue or violet, rather than any inherent properties of the light itself, since blue light is not in itself less intense than yellow light. (In fact, wavelength and energy are inversely related: the long-wave red light has the lowest energy, yellow light has higher energy than red, but green and blue have higher energy than yellow. The invisible ultraviolet light has even higher energy, enough in fact to damage the skin.)

There is also a different type of unevenness in our sensitivity to colours: our ability to discriminate between fine differences in wavelength is not uniform across the spectrum. We are especially sensitive to wavelength differences in the yellow–green area, and the reason again lies in the accidents of our anatomy. Because the middle-wave (green) and long-wave (yellowish green) receptors are very close in their peak sensitivities, even very small variations in wavelength in the yellow–green area translate into significant changes in the ratios of light absorbed by the two neighbouring cones. Under optimal conditions, a normal person can discriminate between yellow hues differing in wavelength by just a single nanometre. But in the blue and violet area of the spectrum, our ability to discriminate between different wavelengths is less than a third of that. And with red hues near the edge of the spectrum, we are even less sensitive to wavelength differences than in the blues.

These two types of unevenness in our sensitivity to colour – the feeling of varying brightness and the varying ability to discriminate fine differences in wavelength – make our colour space asymmetric. And as mentioned in the footnote on page 91, this asymmetry makes certain divisions of the colour space better than others in increasing similarity within concepts and decreasing it across concepts.

COLOUR BLINDNESS

When one of the three types of cones fails, this reduces colour discrimination to two dimensions instead of three, and the condition is thus called dichromacy. The most frequent type of dichromacy is commonly called red–green blindness. It affects about 8 per cent of men and 0.45 per cent of women, who lack one of the two neighbouring types of cones (long-wave or middle-wave). Little is known about the actual colour sensations of people with colour blindness, because one cannot simply 'translate' the sensations of dichromats directly to those of trichromats. A few reports have been collected from the rare people with a red–green defect in one eye and normal vision in the other. Using their normal eye as a reference, such people say that their colour-blind eye has the sensation of yellow and blue. But since the neural wiring associated with the normal eye might not be normal in their cases, even the interpretation of such reports is not straightforward.

Other types of colour blindness are much rarer. A different type of dichromacy, called tritanopia, or in popular parlance blue–yellow blindness, arises in people who lack the long-wave (blue) cones. This condition affects only about 0.002 per cent of the population (two people in a hundred thousand). A more severe defect is the lack of two types of cones. Those affected are called monochromats, as they have only one functioning cone type. An even more extreme case is that of rod monochromats, who lack all three types of cone and rely only on the rods that serve the rest of us for night vision.

THE EVOLUTION OF COLOUR VISION

Human colour vision evolved independently from that of insects, birds, reptiles, and fish. We share our trichromatic vision with the apes and with Old World monkeys, but not with other mammals, and this implies that our colour vision goes back about thirty to forty million years. Most mammals have dichromatic vision: they have only two types of cones, one with peak sensitivity in the blue–violet area and one with peak sensitivity in green (the middle-wave cone). It is thought that the primate trichromatic vision emerged from a dichromatic stage through a mutation that replicated a gene and split the original middle-wave (green) receptor into two adjacent ones, the new one being a little further towards yellow. The position of the two new receptors was optimal for detecting yellowish fruit against a background of green foliage. Man's colour vision seems to have been a co-evolution with the development of bright fruits. As one scientist put it, 'with only a little exaggeration, one could say that our trichromatic colour vision is a device invented by certain fruiting trees in order to propagate themselves'. In particular, it seems that our trichromatic colour vision evolved together with a certain class of tropical trees that bear fruit too large to be taken by birds and that are yellow or orange when ripe. The tree offers a colour signal that is visible to the monkey against the masking foliage of the forest, and in return the monkey either spits out the undamaged seed at a distance or defecates it together with fertiliser. In short, monkeys are to coloured fruit what bees are to flowers.

It is not clear to what extent the passage from dichromacy to trichromacy was gradual or abrupt, mainly because it is not clear whether, once the third type of cone emerged, any additional neural apparatus was needed to take advantage of the signals coming from it. However, it is clear that the sensitivity to colour could not have evolved continuously along the spectrum from red towards the violet end, as Hugo Magnus argued it did. In fact, if viewed over a time span of hundreds of millions of years, the development went exactly the opposite way. The most ancient type of cone, which goes back to the premammalian period, is the one with peak sensitivity in the blue–violet end of the spectrum and with no sensitivity at all to yellow and red light. The second type of cone to emerge was the one with peak sensitivity in green, thus extending the eye's sensitivity much further towards the red end of the spectrum. And the youngest type of cone, from some thirty to forty million years ago, had peak sensitivity slightly further towards the red end, in yellow–green, and so increased the eye's sensitivity to the long-wave end of the spectrum even further.

THE BRAIN'S PHOTOSHOP

All the facts mentioned so far about the cones in the retina are correct to the best of my knowledge. But if you are under the impression that they actually explain our sensation of colour, then you have been coned! In fact, the cones are only the very first level in a highly complex and still largely unknown process of normalisation, compensation, and stabilisation – the brain's equivalent of the 'instant fix' function of picture-editing programmes.

Have you ever wondered why cheap cameras lie about colour all the time? Why is it, for example, that when you use them to take pictures in artificial light indoors, suddenly the colours look all wrong? Why does everything look unnaturally yellow and why do blue objects lose their lustre and become grey? Well, it's not the camera that is lying; it's your brain. In the yellowish light of incandescent lamps, objects actually do become more yellow and blues do become greyer – or at least they do to any objective measuring device. The colour of an object depends on the distribution of wavelengths that it reflects, but the wavelengths reflected naturally depend on the wavelengths of the light source. When the illumination has a greater proportion of light in a certain wavelength, for instance more yellow light, the objects inevitably reflect a greater proportion of yellow light. If the brain took the signals from the cones at face value, therefore, we would experience the world as a series of pictures from cheap cameras, with the colour of objects changing all the time depending on the illumination.

From an evolutionary perspective, it's easy to see why this would not be a very useful state of affairs. If the same fruit on a tree looked one colour at noon and a different colour in the evening, colour would not be a reliable aid in recognition – in fact, it would be a positive hindrance. In practise, therefore, the brain does an enormous amount of compensating and normalising in order to create for us a relatively stable sensation of colour. When the signals from the retina do not correspond to what it wants or expects, the brain normalises them with its 'instant fix' function, which is known as 'colour constancy'. This normalisation process, however, is far more sophisticated than the mechanical 'white balance' function of digital cameras, because it relies on the brain's general experience of the world and, in particular, on stored memories and habits.

It has been shown, for example, that long-term memory and object recognition play an important role in the perception of colour. If the brain remembers that a certain object should be a certain colour, it will go out of its way to make sure that you really see this object in this colour. A fascinating experiment that demonstrated such effects was conducted in 2006 by a group of scientists from the University of Giessen in Germany. They showed participants a picture on a monitor of some random spots in a particular colour, say yellow. The participants had four buttons at their disposal and were asked to adjust the colour of the picture by pressing these buttons until the spots appeared entirely grey, with no trace of yellowness or any other prismatic colour left. Unsurprisingly, the hue that they ended up on was indeed neutral grey.

The same set-up was then repeated, this time not with random spots on the screen but with a picture of a recognisable object such as a banana. The participants were again requested to adjust the hue by pressing buttons until the banana appeared grey. This time, however, the actual hue they ended up on was not pure grey but slightly bluish. In other words, the participants went too far to the other side of neutral grey before the banana really looked grey to them. This means that when the banana was already objectively grey, it still appeared to them slightly yellow! The brain thus relies on its store of past memories of what bananas look like and pushes the sensation of colour in this direction.

The involvement of language with the processing of visual colour information probably takes place on this level of normalisation and compensation. And while it is not clear how this works in practise, it seems plausible to assume that the concepts of colour in a language and the habit of differentiating between them contribute to the stored memories that the brain draws on when generating the sensation of colour.

NOTES

PROLOGUE: LANGUAGE, CULTURE, AND THOUGHT

page 1 'There are four tongues worthy of the world's use': Jerusalem Talmud, tractate *Soṭah,* p. 30a (אילו. ארבעה לשונות נאין להשתמש בהן העולם
הן לעז לזמר רומי לקרב סורסי לאיליי עברי לדיבור).

page 3 'significant marks of the genius and manners': Bacon 1861, 415 (*De
dignitate et augmentis scientiarum*, 1623, book 6: 'Atque una etiam
hoc pacto capientur signa haud levia [sed observatu digna quod for-
tasse quispiam non putaret] de ingeniis et moribus populorum et
nationum, ex linguis ipsorum').

page 3 'Everything confirms': Condillac 1822, 285.

page 3 'the intellect and the character of every nation': Herder 1812,
354–55.

page 3 'We infer the spirit of the nation in great measure': Emerson 1844a,
251.

page 3 'We may study the character of a people': Russell 1983, 34.

page 4 Cicero on *ineptus*: *De oratore* 2, 4.18.

page 4 'what the Romans speak is not so much a vernacular': Dante, *De
vulgari eloquentia* 1.11.

page 4 'the most logical, the clearest, and the most transparent language':
Brunetière 1895, 318.

page 4 Voltaire on the unique genius of French: *Dictionnaire phi-
losophique* (Besterman 1987, 102): 'Le génie de cette langue est la
clarté et l'ordre: car chaque langue a son génie, et ce génie consiste
dans la facilité que donne le langage de s'exprimer plus ou moins
heureusement, d'employer ou de rejeter les tours familiers aux autres
langues.'

page 4 Seventeenth-century French grammarians: Vaugelas, *Remarques
sur la langue françoise, nouvelles remarques*, 1647 (Vaugelas 1738,
470): 'la clarté du langage, que la Langue Françoise affecte sur toutes
les Langues du monde.' François Charpentier 1683, 462: 'Mais ne
conte-t-on pour rien cete admirable qualité de la langue Françoise,
qui possedant par excellence, la Clarté & la Netteté, qui sont les per-
fections du discours, ne peut entreprendre une traduction sans faire
l'office de commentaire?'

page 4 'we French follow in all our utterances': Le Laboureur 1669, 174.

page 4 'What is not clear may be English': Rivarol 1784, 49.

page 5 English is 'methodical, energetic, business-like': Jespersen 1955,
17.

page 5 'monistic view': Whorf 1956 (1940), 215.

page 5 'If our system of tenses was more fragile': Steiner 1975, 167, 161.

page 6 Anglican revolution due to English grammar: Harvey 1996.

page 6 Chomsky's Martian scientist: Piattelli-Palmarini 1983, 77.

page 9 'Taken in its wide ethnographic sense': Tylor 1871, 1.

page 13 'impressions of the soul': Aristotle, *De interpretatione* 1.16a.

page 14 'great store of words in one language': Locke 1849, 315.

page 15 Tagalog: Foley 1997, 109.

page 16 Body parts: See Haspelmath et al. 2005, 'Hand and Finger'. In
earlier Hebrew, there was a differentiation between יד (hand) and זרוע
(arm), and the latter is still used in some idiomatic expressions in
modern Hebrew. But in the spoken language, יד (hand) is regularly
used for both hand and arm. Likewise, English has a word, 'nape',
that refers to the back of the neck, but it's not in common use.

1: NAMING THE RAINBOW

page 25 'founded for the race': Gladstone 1877, 388.

page 26 'the most extraordinary phenomenon': Gladstone 1858, 1:13.

page 26 Gladstone's view of Homer: Wemyss Reid 1899, 143.

page 26 'You are so absorbed in questions about Homer': Myers 1958, 96.

page 27 *The Times* review of Gladstone: 'Mr Gladstone's Homeric Studies', published on 12 August 1858.

page 27 'There are few public men in Europe': John Stuart Blackie, reported in *The Times,* 8 November 1858.

page 27 'statesman, orator, and scholar': John Stuart Blackie, *Horae Hellenicae* (1874). E. A. W. Buchholz's *Die Homerischen Realien* (1871) was dedicated to 'dem eifrigen Pfleger und Förderer der Homerischen Forschung'.

page 27 'a little hobby-horsical': Letter to the Duke of Argyll, 28 May 1863 (Tennyson 1897, 493).

page 27 'Mr Gladstone may be a learned, enthusiastic': John Stuart Blackie, reported in *The Times,* 8 November 1858. On the reception of Gladstone's Homeric studies, see Bebbington 2004.

page 28 'characteristic of the inability of the English': Marx, letter to Engels, 13 August 1858.

page 28 'I find in the plot of the *Iliad*': Morley 1903, 544

page 28–29 Ilios, Wilusa, and the historical background of the *Iliad*: Latacz 2004; Finkelberg 2005.

page 29 Leto 'represents the Blessed Virgin': Gladstone 1858, 2:178; see also 2:153.

page 30 Gladstone's originality: Previous scholars, from as early as Scaliger in 1577, had commented about the paucity of colour descriptions in ancient writers (see Skard 1946, 166), but no one before Gladstone understood that the differences between us and the ancients went beyond occasional divergences in taste and fashion. In the eighteenth century, for example, Friedrich Wilhelm Doering wrote (1788, 88) that 'it is clear that in ancient times both Greeks and Romans could do without many names of colours, from which a later era was in no way able to abstain, once the tools of luxury had grown infinitely. For the austere simplicity of such unsophisticated men abhorred that great variety of colours used for garments and buildings, which in later times softer and more delicate men pursued with the greatest zeal.' ('Hoc autem primum satis constat antiquissimis temporibus cum graecos tum romanos multis colourum nominibus carere potuisse, quibus posterior aetas, luxuriae instumentis in infinitum auctis, nullo modo supersedere potuit. A multiplici enim et magna illa colourum in vestibus aedificiis et aliis operibus varietate, quam posthac summo studio sectati sunt molliores et delicatiores homines, abhorrebat austera rudium illorum hominum simplicitas.') And in his *Farbenlehre* (1810, 54), Goethe explained about the ancients that 'Ihre Farbenbenennungen sind nicht fix und genau bestimmt, sondern beweglich und schwankend, indem sie nach beiden Seiten auch von angrenzenden Farben gebraucht werden. Ihr Gelbes neigt sich einerseits ins Rote, andrerseits ins Blaue, das Blaue teils ins Grüne, teils ins Rote, das Rote bald ins Gelbe, bald ins Blaue; der Purpur schwebt auf der Grenze zwischen Rot und Blau und neigt sich bald zum Scharlach, bald zum Violetten. Indem die Alten auf diese Weise die Farbe als ein nicht nur an sich Bewegliches und Flüchtiges ansehen, sondern auch ein Vorgefühl der Steigerung und des Rückganges haben: so bedienen sie sich, wenn sie von den Farben reden, auch solcher Ausdrücke, welche diese Anschauung andeuten. Sie lassen das Gelbe röteln, weil es in seiner Steigerung zum Roten führt, oder das Rote gelbeln, indem es sich oft zu diesem seinen Ursprunge zurück neigt.'

page 31 sea red because of algae: Maxwell-Stuart 1981, 10.

page 32 'blue and violet reflects': Christol 2002, 36.

page 32 'if any man should say': Blackie 1866, 417.

page 32 'a born Chancellor of the Exchequer': 'Mr Gladstone's Homeric studies,' *The Times*, 12 August 1858.

page 33 violet iron: *Iliad* 23.850; violet wool: *Odyssey* 9.426; violet sea: *Odyssey* 5.56.

page 34 no one can be insensitive to the appeal of the colours: Goethe, *Beiträge zur Chromatik*.

page 34 'Homer had before him the most perfect example of blue': Gladstone 1858, 3:483.

page 35 'As obliterating fire lights up': *Iliad* 2.455–80.

page 35 'their head aslant': *Iliad* 8.306.

page 35 'blackening beneath the ripple of the West Wind': *Iliad* 7.64.

page 35 'have been determined for us by Nature': Gladstone 1858, 3:459.

page 36 'continued to be both faint and indefinite': Gladstone 1858, 3:493.

page 37 'only after submitting the facts': Gladstone 1877, 366.

page 37 'the organ of colour and its impressions': Gladstone 1858, 3:488.

page 38 'the perceptions so easy and familiar to us': Gladstone 1858, 3:496.

page 39 'The eye may require a familiarity': Gladstone 1858, 3:488.

page 39 'The organ was given to Homer': Gladstone 1877, 388.

page 40 Gladstone accurate and far-sighted: On the modernity of Gladstone's analysis, see also Lyons 1999.

2: A LONG-WAVE HERRING

page 41 Geiger's lecture: 'Ueber den Farbensinn der Urzeit und seine Entwickelung' (Geiger 1878).

page 42 Geiger's bold original theories: Many of these ideas, such as the discussion of the independent changes of sound and meaning, which anticipate Saussure's arbitrariness of the sign, or the systematic discussion of semantic developments from concrete to abstract, are found in Geiger 1868 and the posthumous Geiger 1872. See also Morpurgo Davies 1998, 176, for Geiger's ideas on accent in Indo-European. For assessments of Geiger's life and work, see Peschier 1871, Keller 1883, Rosenthal 1884.

page 42 Geiger's curiosity piqued by Gladstone's discoveries: It seems, however, that Geiger misread one aspect of Gladstone's analysis, since he seems to think (1878, 50) that Gladstone believed in the legend of Homer's blindness, whereas, as we have seen, Gladstone explicitly argued against this legend.

page 42 'These hymns, of more than ten thousand': Geiger 1878, 47.

page 43 biblical Hebrew does not have a word for 'blue': As various scholars from Delitzsch (1878, 260; 1898, 756) onwards as well as Geiger himself (1872, 318) have pointed out, there is one cryptic remark in the Old Testament, in Exodus 24:10 (also echoes in Ezekiel 1:26), that

seems, at least indirectly, to relate the sky to lapis lazuli. In Exodus
24, Moses, Aaron, and seventy of the elders of Israel climb up Mount
Sinai to see Yahweh: 'And then they saw the God of Israel. Beneath
his feet was something like a mosaic pavement of lapis lazuli, and
like the very essence of the heavens as regards purity.' There are two
descriptions of the 'pavement' beneath God's feet here: this surface is
first said to have the appearance of a pattern of bricks of lapis lazuli,
and second it is said to be pure 'like the very essence of the heavens'.
The sky itself is not *directly* compared to lapis lazuli, but it is hard to
escape the impression that the two descriptions are based on a close
association between the sky and this blue gemstone. On the interpretation of this passage, see Durham 2002, 344.

pages 44–45 Geiger quotes: 1878, 49, 57, 58.

page 44 Geiger's confusions about black and white: Geiger may have
assumed that black and white should be considered colours only if
they have separate names from dark and bright. This may explain his
obscure (and apparently conflicting) statements about the position
of white with respect to red. In his lecture (1878, 57) he says: 'Weiß
ist in [den ächten Rigvedalieder] von roth noch kaum gesondert.' But
in the table of contents for the second (unfinished and posthumously
published) volume of his *Ursprung und Entwickelung der menschlichen Sprache und Vernunft* (1872, 245), he uses the opposite order:
'Roth im Rigveda noch nicht bestimmt von weiß geschieden.' Unfortunately, the text of the unfinished volume stops before the relevant
section, so it is impossible to ascertain what exactly Geiger meant on
the subject of white.

page 45 tantalising hints in Geiger's own notes: In *Der Urpsrung der
Sprache* (1869, 242) he writes, 'Daß es sich auf niedrigen Entwicke-
lungsstufen noch bei heutigen Völkern ähnlich verhält, würde es
leicht sein zu zeigen.' And in his posthumously published notes, he
explicitly considers the possibility that language lags behind perception (1872, 317–18): '[Es] setzt sich eine ursprünglich aus völligem
Nichtbemerken hervorgegangene Gleichgültigkeit gegen die Farbe
des Himmels . . . fort. Der Himmel in diesen [Texten wird] nicht etwa
schwarz im Sinne von blau genant, sonder seine Bläue [wird] gänzlich
verschwiegen, und ohne Zweifel geschieht dies weil dieselbe [die

Bläue] nicht unmittelbar mit dem Dunkel verwechselt werden konnte. . . . Reizend ist es sodann, das Ringen eines unklaren, der Sprache und Vernunft überall um einige wenige Schritte vorauseilenden Gefühles zu beobachten, wie es . . . hie und da bloß zufällig einen mehr oder weniger nahe kommenden Ausdruck leiht.'

page 46 Lagerlunda crash: Olsén 2004, 127ff., Holmgren 1878, 19–22, but for a critical view see Frey 1975. The danger to the railways from colour-blind personnel was pointed out twenty years earlier, by George Wilson (1855), a professor of technology at the University of Edinburgh, but his book does not seem to have had much impact.

page 47 colour blindness in the newspapers: E.g., *New York Times*, 'Colour-blindness and its dangers' (8 July 1878); 'Color-blindness: How it endangers railroad travelers – some interesting experiments before a Massachusetts legislative committee' (26 January 1879); 'Color-blindness of railroad men' (23 May 1879); 'Color-blind railroad men: A large per centage of defective vision in the employees of a Massachusetts road' (17 August 1879); 'Color-blindness' (17 August 1879). See also Turner 1994, 177.

page 48 Magnus's treatise: In fact, Magnus published two more or less identical monographs in the same year (1877a, 1877b), one of a more academic and the other of a more popular nature.

page 48 Geiger's rousing speech: As described by Delitzsch 1878, 256.

page 48 Magnus's evolutionary model: 1877b, 50.

page 48 'the retina's performance was gradually increased': Magnus 1877a, 19. See also Magnus 1877b, 47.

page 48 'still just as closed and invisible': Magnus 1877a, 9.

page 49 Magnus's theory ardently discussed: According to Turner 1994, 178, the literature on the Magnus controversy exploded to more than 6 per cent of all publications on vision between 1875 and 1879.

page 49 Nietzsche on Greek colour vision: Nietzsche 1881, 261. Orsucci 1996, 244ff, has shown that Nietzsche followed the debate over Magnus's book in the first volume of the journal *Kosmos*.

page 49 Gladstone's review of Magnus: Gladstone 1877.

page 49 'if the capacity of distinguishing colours': Wallace 1877, 471n1. Wallace changed his mind the next year, however (1878, 246).

page 49 'the more delicate cones of the retina': Lecture delivered on

25 March 1878 (Haeckel 1878, 114).

page 51 'and the results of this habit': Lamarck 1809: 256–57

page 51 Wallace on the giraffe's neck: 1858, 61.

page 52 'when a boy, had the skin of both thumbs': Darwin 1881, 257.
Darwin also quotes approvingly 'Brown-Sequard's famous experiments' on guinea pigs, which were taken at the time to prove that the results of operations on certain nerves in the mother were inherited by the next generation.

page 52 the universal belief in the inheritance of acquired characteristics: Mayr 1991, 119. For an assessment of Weismann, see Mayr 1991, 111.

page 53 'Weismann began to investigate the point': Shaw, introduction to *Back to Methuselah* (1921, xlix). Shaw in fact had a strong aversion to (neo-) Darwinism and passionately believed in Lamarckian evolution.

page 53 Weismann reported on the still ongoing experiment: 1892, 523, n1, 514, 526–27.

page 54 Weismann's remained the minority view: For example, in 1907, Oskar Hertwig (1907, 37), the director of the Anatomical and Biological Institute in Berlin, still predicted that in the end the Lamarckian mechanism would prove the right one. See also Mayr 1991, 119ff.

page 54 'the acquired aptitudes of one generation': Gladstone 1858, 426, and similar formulation a few years later (1869, 539): 'the acquired knowledge of one generation becomes in time the inherited aptitude of another'.

page 54 Magnus's explicit reliance on the Lamarckian model: Magnus 1877b, 44, 50.

page 55 Criticism of Magnus: The earliest and most vocal critic of Magnus's theory was Ernst Krause, one of Darwin's first followers and popularisers in Germany (Krause 1877). Darwin himself felt that Magnus's scenario was problematic. On 30 June 1877, Darwin wrote to Krause: 'I have been much interested by your able argument against the belief that the sense of colour has been recently acquired by man.' Another vocal critic was the science writer Grant Allen (1878, 129–32; 1879), who argued that 'there is every reason to think that the perception of colours is a faculty which man shares with all the higher members of the animal world. In no other way can we account for the varied hues of flowers, fruits, insects, birds, and mammals, all of which seem to have been developed as allurements for the eye, guiding it towardss food or the opposite sex.' But the argument about the bright colours of animals was weakest exactly where it was most needed, because the colouring of mammals, as opposed to birds and insects, is extremely subdued, dominated by black, white, and shades of brown and grey. At the time, there was precious little direct evidence about which animals can see colours: bees and other insects had been shown to respond to colour, but the evidence petered out when it came to the higher animals and especially to mammals, whose sense of colour was shown (see Graber 1884) to be less developed than that of man. See also Donders 1884, 89–90, and, for a detailed account of the debate, Hochegger 1884, 132.

page 55 'we see in essence not with two eyes': Delitzsch 1878, 267.

page 56 a short visit to the British Museum: Allen 1879, 204.

page 57 'it does not seem plausible to us': Magnus 1877c, 427. See also Magnus 1880, 10; Magnus 1883, 21.

3: THE RUDE POPULATIONS INHABITING FOREIGN LANDS

page 58 Passers-by in the elegant Kurfürstendamm: Since 1925 this part of the street has been called Budapester Strasse.

page 58 Nubian display: Rothfels 2002, 84.

page 59 Nubians' sense of colour: Virchow 1878 (Sitzung am 19.10.1878), and Virchow 1879.

page 59 'rude populations inhabiting foreign lands': Gatschet 1879, 475.

page 59 'apologised once that he couldn't find a bottle': Bastian 1869, 89–90.

page 60 Relevance of the 'savages': Darwin, for instance, suggested in a letter to Gladstone (de Beer 1958, 89) that one should ascertain whether 'low savages' had names for shades of colour: 'I should expect that they have not, and this would be remarkable for the Indians of Chilee and Tierra del Fuego have names for every slight promontory and hill – even to a marvellous degree.'

page 61 'the colour of any grass, weed or plant': Gatschet 1879, 475, 477, 481.

page 61 Almquist's reports: Almquist 1883, 46–47. If pressed, the Chukchis also produced other terms, but these seemed to be variable. In Berlin, Rudolf Virchow reached a similar conclusion about the colour terminology of some of the Nubians (Virchow 1878, 353).

page 61 Nias in Sumatra: Magnus 1880, 8.

page 62 None of the Nubians failed to pick the right colours: Virchow 1878, 351n1.

page 62 Ovaherero: Magnus 1880, 9.

page 63 Magnus's revised theory: Magnus 1880, 34ff.; Magnus 1881, 195ff.

page 63 Rivers's life and work: Slobodín 1978.

page 64 'goodbye my friend – I don't suppose we shall ever meet again': Whittle 1997.

page 64 'Galileo of anthropology': Lévi-Strauss 1968, 162.

page 65 'For the first time trained experimental psychologists': Haddon 1910, 86.

page 66 'lively discussions were started': Rivers 1901a, 53.

page 67 'seemed almost inexplicable, if blue': Rivers 1901b, 51. See also Rivers 1901b, 46–47.

page 67 'certain degree of insensitiveness to blue': Rivers 1901a, 94. Rivers also tried to show experimentally, using a device called a Lovibond tintometre, that the thresholds at which the natives could recognise very pale blue glass were higher than those of Europeans. The serious problems with his experiments were pointed out by Woodworth 1910b, Titchener 1916, Bancroft 1924. Recently, two British scientists (Lindsey and Brown 2002) proposed a similar idea to Rivers's, suggesting that people closer to the equator suffer from stronger UV radiation, which causes their retina to lose sensitivity to green and blue. The severe problems with this claim were pointed out by Regier and Kay 2004.

page 68 'One cannot, however, wholly': Rivers 1901a, 94.

page 68 *siniy* and *goluboy* in Russian: Corbett and Morgan 1988.

page 70 'attended carefully to the mental development': C. Darwin to E.

Krause, 30 June 1877.

page 70 Acquisition of colours by children: Pitchford and Mullen 2002, 1362; Roberson et al. 2006.

page 70 Bellona: Kuschel and Monberg 1974.

page 75 Reviews of Rivers: Woodworth 1910b, Titchener 1916, Bancroft 1924.

4: THOSE WHO SAID OUR THINGS BEFORE US

page 78 'The life of yesterday': Lambert 1960, 244. The actual copy of this tablet is late, from Ashurbanipal's library (seventh century BC). But while no earlier copies of this particular proverb have so far been found, the Sumerian proverbs in general go back at least to the Old Babylonian period (2000–1600 BC).

page 78 'What is said is just repetition': Parkinson 1996, 649.

page 78 'Perish those who said our things before us': Donatus's phrase was mentioned by his student St Jerome in Jerome's commentrary on Ecclesiastes (Migne 1845, 1019): 'Comicus ait: Nihil est dictum, quod non sit dictum prius, unde et præceptor meum Donatus, cum ipsum versiculum exponeret, Pereant, inquit, qui ante nos nostra dixerunt.'

page 81 'The physical types chosen for representation': Francis 1913, 524.

page 82 'We are probably justified in inferring': Woodworth 1910a, 179.

page 83 Geiger's sequence may have been just a coincidence: Woodworth 1910b.

page 83 'Physicists view the colour-spectrum as a continuous scale': Bloomfield 1933, 140.

page 83 'arbitrarily sets its boundaries': Hjelmslev 1943, 48.

page 83 'there is no such thing as a "natural" division': Ray 1953; see also Ray 1952, 258.

page 84 Bellonese colour system: Kuschel and Monberg 1974.

page 85 Claims of arbitrariness in accounts before 1969: See Berlin and Kay 1969, 159–60n1.

page 85 'It seems no exaggeration to claim': Sahlins 1976, 1.

page 85 'Only very occasionally is a discovery': Newcomer and Faris 1971, 270.

page 87 Tzeltal foci: Berlin and Kay 1969, 32. Further detail (from Berlin's unpublished ms.) in Maclaury 1997, 32, 258–59, 97–104.

page 89 Alleged universality of the foci: Berlin and Kay's claims about the universality of the foci soon received a boost from the Berkeley psychologist Eleanor Rosch Heider (1972), who argued that the foci have a special status for memory, in that they are remembered more easily even by speakers of languages that do not have separate names for them. However, Rosch Heider's interpretation of her results has been questioned, and in recent years researches failed to replicate them (Roberson et al. 2005).

page 89 Foci that stray from Berlin and Kay's predictions: Roberson et al. 2000, 2005; Levinson 2000, 27.

page 90 majority of languages conform to Geiger's sequence or to the alternative of green before yellow: Kay and Maffi 1999.

page 91 Continued debate on whether colour concepts are determined primarily by culture or by nature: Roberson et al. 2000, 2005; Levinson 2000; Regier et al. 2005; Kay and Regier 2006a, 2006b. A related debate about infant colour categorisation: Özgen 2004; Franklin et al. 2005; Roberson et al. 2006.

page 91 Model for natural constraints: Regier et al. 2007; see also Komarovaa et al. 2007. In a few areas of the colour space, especially around blue/purple, the optimal partitions, according to Regier, Khetarpal, and Kay's model, deviate systematically from the actual systems found in the majority of the world's languages. This may be due either to imperfections in their model or to the override of cultural factors.

page 91 Red as an arousing colour: Wilson 1966, Jacobs and Hustmyer 1974, Valdez and Mehrabian 1994.

page 93 'crude conceptions of colour derived from the elements': Gladstone 1858, 3:491.

page 93 'Colours were for Homer not facts but images': Gladstone 1877, 386.

page 93 The Hanunoo: Conklin 1955, who does not refer to Gladstone. On the similarity between ancient Greek and Hanunoo, see also Lyons 1999.

page 93 from brightness to hue as a modern theory: MacLaury 1997; see also Casson 1997.

page 94 the acquired aptitudes of one generation: Gladstone 1858, 3:426.

page 94 'progressive education': Gladstone 1858, 3:495.

page 94 naturalness in concept learning: See Waxman and Senghas 1992.

page 96 Yanomamö kinship terms: Lizot 1971.

page 98 the innateness controversy: The most eloquent exposition of the nativist view is Steven Pinker's *The Language Instinct* (1994). Geoffrey Sampson's *The 'Language Instinct' Debate* (2005) offers a methodical refutation of the arguments in favour of innate grammar, as well as references to the voluminous academic literature on the subject.

5: PLATO AND THE MACEDONIAN SWINEHERD

page 99 the flaws of the equal-complexity dogma: For a fuller argument, see Deutscher 2009.

page 100 'You really mean the Aborigines have a language?': Dixon 1989, 63.

page 103 'Plato walks with the Macedonian swineherd': Sapir 1921, 219.

page 103 'Investigations of linguists date back': Fromkin et al. 2003, 15. (Full quotation: 'There are no primitive languages. All languages are equally complex and equally capable of expressing any idea in the universe.' The equal-complexity slogan is repeated also on p. 27.

page 104 'It is a finding of modern linguistics': Dixon 1997, 118.

page 104 'A *central* finding of linguistics has been': Forston 2004, 4.

page 105 'Objective measurement is difficult': Hockett 1958, 180. For a discussion of this passage, see Sampson 2009.

page 107 compensation in complexity between different sub-areas: Whenever linguists have tried, heuristically, to detect any signs of compensation in complexity between different areas they have failed to find them. See Nichols 2009, 119.

page 110 vocabulary size: Goulden et al. 1990 have estimated the vocabulary size of an average native-English-speaking university student at about seventeen thousand word families (a word family being a base word together with its derived forms, e.g., happy, unhappy, happiness), or as many as forty thousand different word types. Crystal

1995, 123, estimates the passive vocabulary of a university lecturer at seventy-three thousand words.

page 111 Sorbian dual: Corbett 2000, 20.

page 112 five categories of cultural complexity: Perkins 1992, 75.

page 113 recent studies on the relation between morphological complexity and size of society: See, e.g., Sinnemäki 2009; Nichols 2009, 120; Lupyan and Dale 2010.

page 114 Gothic verb *habaidedeima*: Schleicher 1860, 34.

page 115 communication among intimates: Givón 2002.

page 118 size of sound inventories: Maddieson 1984, 2005.

page 118 correlation between the number of speakers and the size of the sound inventory: Hay and Bauer 2007. For earlier discussions, see Haudricourt 1961; Maddieson 1984; and Trudgill 1992.

page 120 Pirahã: See most recently Nevins et al. 2009 and Everett 2009.

page 122 Ubarum told Iribum to dispossess Kuli: Foster 1990, who reads *šu li-pi₅-iš-ZU-ma* and translates 'that he might work it', but see Hilgert 2002, 484, and a near-identical form in Whiting 1987 no. 12:17, which proves the correctness of the translation given here.

page 124 absence of complement clauses in many Australian languages: See Dixon 2006, 263, and Dench 1991, 196–201. For Matses, see Fleck 2006. See also Deutscher 2000, ch. 10.

page 124 Finite complements are a more effective tool: Deutscher 2000, ch. 11.

page 125 a flurry of publications from the last couple of years: See most recently the collection of articles in Sampson et al. 2009.

6: CRYING WHORF

page 129 'The normal man of intelligence': Sapir 1924, 149.

page 130 'what fetters the mind and benumbs the spirit': Sapir 1924, 155.

page 130 'We shall no longer be able to see': Whorf 1956, 212.

page 132 Data collection in the eighteenth century: In 1710, Leibnitz called for the creation of a 'universal dictionary'. In 1713, he wrote to the Russian tsar Peter the Great, imploring him to gather word lists from the numerous undocumented languages spoken in his empire. The idea was taken up at the Russian court in all earnestness two generations later, when Catherine the Great started working on exactly such a project, personally collecting words from as many languages as she could find. She later commissioned others to continue her work, and the result was the so-called imperial dictionary (*Linguarum Totius Orbis Vocabularia Comparativa*) of 1787, which contained words from over two hundred languages of Europe and Asia. A second edition, published in 1790–91, added seventy-nine more languages. In 1800, the Spanish ex-Jesuit Lorenzo Hervás published his *Catálogo de las lenguas de las naciones conocidas*, which contained more than three hundred languages. And in the early nineteenth century, the German lexicographer Christoph Adelung started compiling his *Mithridates* (1806–17), which was to collect vocabularies and the text of the 'Our Father' from 450 different languages. On these compilations, see Müller 1861, 132ff.; Morpurgo Davies 1998, 37ff.; and Breva-Claramonte 2001.

page 133 the dictionaries revealed little of value about the *grammar* of exotic languages: There is one notable exception, Lorenzo Hervás's *Catálogo de las lenguas de las naciones conocidas*, which contained grammatical sketches. Humboldt befriended Hervás in Rome and received from him materials on American Indian languages. Nevertheless, Humboldt did not have a high opinion of Hervás's competence in grammatical analysis. In a letter to F. A. Wolf (19 March 1803), he writes: 'The old Hervás is a confused and unthorough person, but he knows a great deal, has an enormous amount of notes, and is therefore always useful.' As Morpurgo Davies (1998, 13–20, 37) points out, there is a natural tendency when assessing one's own achievement to underplay the achievements of one's predecessors. This may well be the case with Humboldt's assessment of Hervás. Even so, it is undeniable that Humboldt took comparative grammar to an entirely different level of sophistication.

page 133 missionary grammars: Jooken 2000.

page 135 'It is sad to see what violence': Humboldt 1821a, 237. See also Humboldt 1827, 172.

page 135 'The difference between languages': Humboldt 1820, 27. Humboldt did not invent this sentiment out of the blue, but previous claims to this effect were restricted mostly to observations about differences between the *vocabularies* of mainstream European languages. The French philosopher Étienne de Condillac, for example, commented on the difference between French and Latin in the connotations of words to do with agriculture. If grammatical differences were brought into the discussion at all, they never went beyond such banalities as Herder's claim that 'industrious nations have an abundance of moods in their verbs' (1812, 355).

page 136 'is not just the means for representing a truth': Humboldt 1820, 27. On precursors to the idea, most notably Johann David Michaelis's 1760 Prussian Academy prize essay, see Koerner 2000. Humboldt himself had already expressed the sentiment in vague form in 1798, before he had been exposed to non-Indo-European languages (Koerner 2000, 9).

page 136 'language is the forming organ of thought': Humboldt 1827, 191.

page 136 'Thinking is dependent not just on language in general': Humboldt 1820, 21.

page 136 'what it encourages and stimulates its speakers to do': Humboldt 1821b, 287. 'Sieht man bloß auf dasjenige, was sich in einer Sprache ausdrücken lässt, so wäre es nicht zu verwundern, wenn man dahin geriethe, alle Sprachen im Wesentlichen ungefähr gleich an Vorzügen und Mängeln zu erklären. . . . Dennoch ist dies gerade der Punkt, auf den es ankommt. Nicht, was in einer Sprache ausgedrückt zu werden vermag, sondern das, wozu sie aus eigner, innerer Kraft anfeuert und begeistert, entscheidet über ihre Vorzüge oder Mängel.' Admittedly, Humboldt made this famous pronouncement for the wrong reasons. He was trying to explain why, even if no language constrains the possibilities of thought in its speakers, some languages (Greek) are still much better than others, because they actively encourage speakers to form higher ideas.

page 136 'the words in which we think are channels of thought': Müller 1873, 151.

page 137 'every single language has its own peculiar framework': Whitney 1875, 22.

page 137 'it is the thought of past humanity imbedded': Clifford 1879, 110.

page 138 Boas's influence on Sapir: It is often suggested that Franz Boas may also have inspired Sapir's ideas about relativity. There are hints of this view in Boas 1910, 377, and a decade later (1920, 320) Boas made the argument more explicit in saying that 'the categories of language compel us to see the world arranged in certain definite conceptual groups which, on account of our lack of knowledge of linguistic processes, are taken as objective categories, and which, therefore, impose themselves upon the form of our thoughts'.

page 138 'everything to learn about language': Swadesh 1939. See also Darnell 1990, 9.

page 139 'Language misleads us both by its vocabulary and by its syntax': Russell 1924, 331. Sapir was introduced to such ideas by the book *The Meaning of Meaning: A Study in the Influence of Language upon Thought*, by Ogden and Richards (1923).

page 139 'tyrannical hold that linguistic form': Sapir 1931, 578.

page 139 'incommensurable analysis of experience in different languages': Sapir 1924, 155. Whorf (1956 [1940], 214) later elaborated the principle of relativity: 'We are thus introduced to a new principle of relativity, which holds that all observers are not led by the same physical evidence to the same picture of the universe, unless their linguistic backgrounds are similar.'

page 140 'is not merely a reproducing instrument for voicing ideas': Whorf 1956 (1940), 212.

page 141 'Some languages have means of expression': Whorf 1956 (1941), 241; 'monistic view of nature': Whorf 1956 (1940), 215.

page 141 'What surprises most is to find that various grand generalisations': Whorf 1956 (1940), 216.

page 142 'has zero dimensions; i.e., it cannot be given a number': Whorf 1956 (1940), 216; 'to us, for whom time is a motion': Whorf 1956 (1941), 151.

page 142 'no words, grammatical forms, constructions or expressions': Whorf 1956, 57.

page 143 'a Hopi Indian, thinking in the Hopi language': Chase 1958, 14.

page 143 'time seems to be that aspect of being': Eggan 1966.

page 144 'relate grammatical possibilities': This and the quotations that follow are from Steiner 1975, 137, 161, 165, 166.

page 147 *Wir hören auf zu denken*: Colli et al. 2001, 765.

page 147 'the limits of my language mean the limits of my world': Wittgenstein 1922, §5.6.

page 151 'grammar performs another important function': Boas 1938, 132–33. Boas also went on to explain that even when a grammar does not oblige speakers to express certain information, that does not imply obscurity of speech, since, when necessary, clarity can always be obtained by adding explanatory words.

page 151 'Languages differ essentially in what they *must* convey': Jakobson 1959a, 236; see also Jakobson 1959b and Jakobson 1972, 110. Jakobson (1972, 107–8) specifically rejects the influences of language on 'strictly cognitive activities'. He allows their influence only on 'everyday mythology, which finds its expression in divagations, puns, jokes, chatter, jabber, slips of the tongue, dreams, reverie, superstitions, and, last but not least, in poetry'.

page 153 Matses: Fleck 2007.

page 156 Effects of language on thought are mundane: Pinker 2007, 135.

7: WHERE THE SUN DOESN'T RISE IN THE EAST

page 157 'In the A.M. four of the Natives': *Captain Cook's Journal during the First Voyage round the World* (Wharton 1893, 392).

page 158 'Mr Gore, who went out this day with his gun': Hawkesworth 1785, 132 (14 July 1770).

page 160 'it is very remarkable that this word': Crawfurd 1850, 188. In 1898, another lexicographer added to the confusion (Phillips 1898), when he recorded other words for the animal: 'kadar', 'ngargelin', and 'wadar'. Dixon et al. (1990, 68) point out that the ethnologist W. E. Roth wrote a letter to the *Australian* in 1898, saying that *gangooroo* was the name of a particular type of kangaroo in Guugu Yimithirr. But this was not noticed by lexicographers.

page 163 Kant's analysis of the primacy of egocentric conception of space: Kant 1768, 378: 'Da wir alles, was außer uns ist, durch die Sinnen nur in so fern kennen, als es in Beziehung auf uns selbst steht, so ist kein Wunder, daß wir von dem Verhältniß dieser Durchschnittsflächen zu unserem Körper den ersten Grund hernehmen, den Begriff der Gegenden im Raume zu erzeugen.' See also Miller and Johnson-Laird 1976, 380–81.

page 164 'we were in the middle of a young diggings township': G. E. Dal-rymple, *Narrative and Reports of the Queensland North East Coast Expedition*, 1873, quoted in Haviland and Haviland 1980, 120. For the history of Guugu Yimithirr, see Haviland 1979b, Haviland and Haviland 1980, Haviland 1985, and Loos 1978.

page 164 'when savages are pitted against civilisation': 'The black police', editorial, *Cooktown Herald and Palmer River Advertiser*, 24 June 1874, p. 5.

page 165 no words for 'in front of' and 'behind': Haviland (1998) argues that Guugu Yimithirr can in some limited circumstances use the noun *thagaal*, 'front,' in relation to space, e.g., in *George nyulu thagaal-bi*, 'George was at the front.' But this seems to be used to describe not spatial position as such but George's leading role.

page 166 Guugu Yimithirr spatial language and orientation: Levinson 2003.

page 167 'two girls, the one has nose to the east': Levinson 2003, 119.

page 169 geographic coordinates in Australian languages: The Djaru language of Kimberley, Western Australia: Tsunoda 1981, 246; Kayardild from Bentinck Island, between the Cape York Peninsula and Arnhem Land: Evans 1995, 218; Arrernte (Western Desert): Wilkins 2006, 52ff.; Warlpiri (Western Desert): Laughren 1978, as quoted in Wilkins 2006, 53; Yankunytjatjara (Western Desert): Goddard 1985, 128. Geographic coordinates elsewhere: Madagascar: Keenan and Ochs 1979, 151; Nepal: Niraula et al. 2004; Bali: Wassmann and Dasen 1998; Hai‖om: Widlok 1997. See also Majid et al. 2004, 111.

page 170 Marquesan: Cablitz 2002.

page 170 Bali: Wassmann and Dasen 1998, 692–93.

page 170 McPhee's *House in Bali*: McPhee 1947, 122ff. In the south of Bali, where McPhee lived, the mountain direction is roughly north, so McPhee follows the usual practise of translating the terms seaward and mountainward as south and north, respectively. It should be noted that the directions of the dance in Bali have religious significance.

page 171 'But white fellows wouldn't understand that': Haviland 1998, 26.

page 172 The orientation skills of the Guugu Yimithirr: Levinson 2003, chs. 4, 6. On orientation skills of other Australian Aborigines, see

Lewis 1976. On Tzeltal, see Brown and Levinson 1993.

page 173 strange sensation that the sun did not rise in the east: Levinson 2003, 128.

page 174 Jack's shark story: Haviland 1993, 14.

page 176 Guugu Yimithirr spatial memory: Levinson 2003, 131.

page 184 The ongoing debate on the 'rotating tables' experiments: See Li and Gleitman 2002; Levinson et al. 2002; Levinson 2003; Majid et al. 2004; Haun et al. 2006; Pinker 2007, 141 ff.; Li et al. (forthcoming). Many varieties of the rotating table experiments were conducted, and in most of them the subjects were not asked to 'complete a picture', as in the set-up demonstrated here, but rather asked to memorise a certain order of objects and then 'make it the same' on a different table. The 'make it the same' instruction has attracted most criticism. Li et al. argue that 'make it the same' is ultimately an ambiguous instruction and that 'in solving ambiguous rotation tasks, when the participant is asked to reproduce the "same" spatial array or path as before, he or she needs to guess the experimenter's intent as to what counts as the "same." To make this inference, people are likely to implicitly consult the way their language community customarily speaks about or responds to inquiries about locations and directions.' This criticism seems to me to be largely justified. However, the 'complete the picture' experiment that I have presented above does not, as far as I can see, suffer from this problem, as it does not rely on the possibly vague and interpretable notion of 'the same'. A further point of criticism by Li et al. that seems largely justified to me is against Levinson's (2003, 153) claim that there is systematic downgrading of egocentric coordinates in the perception of Guugu Yimithirr and Tzeltal speakers. Li et al. did not find any evidence for such downgrading in the experiments they conducted with Tzeltal speakers. What is more, on the face of it, the downgrading claim is reminiscent of the Whorfian fallacy that the lack of a concept in a language necessarily means that speakers are unable to understand this concept. None of the claims made in this chapter rely on downgrading. Rather, they relate to the *additional* level of geographic computation and memory that Guugu Yimithirr and Tzeltal speakers are contin-

ually obliged to do and to the habits of mind that arise in consequence.

page 189 Jaminjung: Schultze-Berndt 2006, 103–4.

page 189 Yukatek: Majid et al. 2004, 111.

page 189 Hai‖om orientation: See Neumann and Widlok 1996 and Widlok 1997.

page 190 Acquisition of geographic coordinates: De León 1994; Wassmann and Dasen 1998; and Brown and Levinson 2000. Some cultural arte-facts may also contribute, of course. In Bali, for instance, houses are always built facing the same direction, the head of family always sleeps on the same side of the house, and children are always put to bed in a particular direction (Wassmann and Dasen 1998, 694).

8: SEX AND SYNTAX

page 196 The significance of the genders in Heine's poem: Vygotsky 1987, 253; Veit 1976; and Walser 1983, 195–96.

page 196 'If I forget thee, O Jerusalem': Heine quotes these lines in a letter to Moses Moser (9 January 1824) written not long after the poems were published: 'Verwelke meine Rechte, wenn ich Deiner vergesse, Jeruscholayim, sind ungefähr die Worte des Psalmisten, und es sind auch noch immer die meinigen' (Heine 1865, 142).

page 198 'I also am a man of importance': Bage 1784, 274.

page 198 Supyire: Carlson 1994.

page 198 Ngan'gityemerri: Reid 1997, 173.

page 200 Manambu: Aikhenvald 1996.

page 202 Underlying regularities in the distribution of genders in Ger-man: Köpcke and Zubin 1984.

page 204 The origin of gender systems: Claudi 1985; Aikhenvald 2000; and Greenberg 1978.

page 206 Loss of the genders in English: Curzon 2003.

page 207 'He that is become hoorse lately': Brunschwig 1561, 14b–15a.

page 207 dialectal uses of feminine nouns: Beattie 1788, 139 Peacock 1877.

page 207 femininity of 'ship': Strangely enough, 'ship' is a relative newcomer on the gender ocean, for in Old English a *scip* was actually neuter, not feminine. So the use of a gendered pronoun here seems to be an actual case of personification, not just an old relic.

page 209 experiment at the Moscow Psychological Institute: Jakobson 1959a, 237; Jakobson 1972, 108.

page 209 German and Spanish comparisons: Konishi 1993.

page 211 French and Spanish comparisons: Sera et al. 2002.

page 212 Italian nonsense words: Ervin 1962, 257.

page 213 Boroditsky and Schmidt's memory experiment: Boroditsky et al. 2003, but detailed results of the experiment based on Boroditsky and Schmidt (unpublished).

9: RUSSIAN BLUES

page 217 Japanese traffic lights: Conlan 2005. The official Japanese standard for green traffic lights shown in figure 7 in the insert is taken from Janoff 1994, and from the website of the Rensselaer Polytechnic Institute's Lighting Research Center (http://www.lrc.rpi.edu/programmes/transportation/LED/LEDTrafficSignalComparison.asp). The official American standard is taken from Institute of Transportation Engineers 2005, 24.

page 220 Kay and Kempton's experiment: Kay and Kempton 1984. More sophisticated experiments of this nature were carried out by Roberson et al. 2000, 2005.

page 222 Russian blues: Winawer et al. 2007.

page 223 the border between *siniy* and *goluboy*: This border (and for English speakers, the border between light and dark blue) was determined after the experiment for each participant separately. Each participant was shown twenty different shades of blue and asked to say whether each one was *siniy* or *goluboy*. English speakers were asked whether each shade was 'light blue' or 'dark blue'.

page 225 left and right visual fields experiments: Gilbert et al. 2006. The results of this experiment inspired a spate of adaptations by different teams in different countries. See Drivonikou et al. 2007; Gilbert et al. 2008 and Roberson et al. 2008. All the subsequent tests corroborated the basic conclusions.

page 226 Broca's area as a seat of language: Broca 1861. For a history, see
          Young 1970, 134–49.
page 229 MRI experiment: Tan et al. 2008.

EPILOGUE: FORGIVE US OUR IGNORANCES

page 234 influence of language on thought can be considered significant
          only if it bears on genuine reasoning: See, e.g., Pinker 2007, 135.

APPENDIX: COLOUR: IN THE EYE OF THE BEHOLDER

page 241 colour sensation in the brain: For further details on the anat-
          omy of colour vision, see Kaiser and Boynton 1996 and Valberg
          2005.
page 247 'with only a little exaggeration': Mollon 1995, 134. On the evolu-
          tion of colour vision, see also Mollon 1999 and Regan et al. 2001.
page 249 memory affects perception of colour: Hansen et al. 2006.

BIBLIOGRAPHY

Adelung, J. C. *Mithridates: Oder allgemeine Sprachenkunde*. 1806–17. Intro. and ed. Johann Severin Vater. Berlin: Vossische Buchhandlung.

Aikhenvald, A. Y. 1996. Physical properties in a gender system: A study of Manambu. *Language and Linguistics in Melanesia* 27:175–87.

———. 2000. *Classifiers*. Oxford: Oxford University Press.

Allen, G. 1878. Development of the sense of colour. *Mind* 3 (9):129–32.

———. 1879. *The colour sense: Its origin and development*. London: Trubner.

Almquist, E. 1883. Studien über den Farbensinn der Tschuktschen. In *Die wissenschaftlichen Ergebnisse der Vega-Expedition*, ed. A. E. von Nordenskiöld, 1:42–49. Leipzig: Brockhaus.

Andree, R. 1878. Ueber den Farbensinn der Naturvölker. *Zeitschrift für Ethnologie* 10:324–34.

Bacon, F. 1861. *The works of Francis Bacon, baron of Verulam, viscount St Alban, and lord high chancellor of England*. Vol. 2. Ed. J. Spedding, R. L. Ellis, and D. D. Heath. Boston: Brown and Taggard.

Bage, R. 1784. *Barham Downs*. Rpt. New York: Garland, 1979.

Bancroft, W. D. 1924. The recognition of blue. *Journal of Physical Chemistry* 28:131–44.

Bastian, A. 1869. Miscellen. *Zeitschrift für Ethnologie und ihre Hülfswissenschaften als Lehre vom Menschen in seinen Beziehungen zur Natur und zur Geschichte* 1:89–90.

Beattie, J. 1788. *The theory of language*. Edinburgh: A. Strahan.

Bebbington, D. W. 2004. *The mind of Gladstone: Religion, Homer, and politics*. Oxford: Oxford University Press.

Berlin, B., and P. Kay. 1969. *Basic colour terms: Their universality and evolution*. Berkeley: University of California Press.

Besterman, T., ed. 1987. *The complete works of Voltaire*. Vol. 33. Geneva: Institut et Musée Voltaire.

Blackie, J. S. 1866. *Homer and the 'Iliad'*. Vol. 4. Edinburgh: Edmonston and Douglas.

Bloomfield, L. 1933. *Language*. London: George Allen and Unwin.

Boas, F. 1910. Psychological problems in anthropology. Lecture delivered at the celebration of the twentieth anniversary of the opening of Clark University, September 1909. *American Journal of Psychology* 21 (3):371–84.

———. 1920. The methods of ethnology. *American Anthropologist*, new series 22 (4):311–21.

———. 1938. Language. In *General Anthropology*, ed. F. Boas, 124–45. Boston: D. C. Heath.

Boman, T. 1960. *Hebrew thought compared with Greek*. London: SCM Press.

Boroditsky, L., L. Schmidt, and W. Phillips. 2003. Sex, syntax, and semantics. In *Language in mind: Advances in the study of language and thought*, ed. D. Gentner and S. Goldin-Meadow, 61–78. London: MIT Press.

Boroditsky, L., and L. Schmidt. Sex, syntax, and semantics. Unpublished ms.

Breva-Claramonte, M. 2001. Data collection and data analysis in Lorenzo Hervás: Laying the ground for modern linguistic typology. In *Historia de la lingüística en España*, ed. E. F. K. Koerner and Hans-Josef Niederehe, 265–80. Amsterdam: John Benjamins.

Broca, P. P. 1861. Perte de la parole, ramollissement chronique et destruction partielle du lobe antérieur gauche du cerveau. *Bulletins de la Société d'Anthropologie de Paris* (Séance du 18 avril 1861) 2:235–38.

Brown, C. H. 2005. Finger and hand. In Haspelmath et al. 2005.

Brown, P., and S. C. Levinson. 1993. 'Uphill' and 'downhill' in Tzeltal. *Journal of Linguistic Anthropology* 3:46–74.

———. 2000. Frames of spatial reference and their acquisition in Tenejapan Tzeltal. In *Culture thought and development*, ed. L. Nucci, G. Saxe, and E. Turiel, 167–97. London: Laurence Erlbaum Associates.

Brunetière, F. 1895. Discours de réception a l'Académie française, 15.2.1894. In *Nouveaux essais sur la littérature contemporaine*. Paris: C. Lévy.

Brunschwig, H. 1561. *The most excellent and perfecte homish apothecarye or homely physick booke for all the grefes and diseases of the bodye. Translated out the Almaine Speche into English by John Hollybush.* Collen: Arnold Birckman.

Cablitz, G. H. 2002. The acquisition of an absolute system: Learning to talk about space in Marquesan (Oceanic, French Polynesia). In *Proceedings of the 31st Stanford Child Language Research Forum: Space in language, location, motion, path, and manner*, 40–49. Stanford: Center for the Study of Language and Information.

Carlson, R. 1994. *A grammar of Supyire*. Berlin: Mouton de Gruyter.

Casson, R. W. 1997. Color shift: Evolution of English colour terms from brightness to hue. In *Color categories in thought and language*, ed. C. L. Hardin and L. Maffi, 224–40. Cambridge: Cambridge University Press.

Charpentier, F. 1683. *De l'excellence de la langue françoise*. Paris: Veuve Bilaine.

Chase, S. 1958. *Some things worth knowing: A generalist's guide to useful knowledge*. New York: Harper.

Christol, A. 2002. Les couleurs de la mer. In *Couleurs et vision dans l'antiquité classique*, ed. L. Villard, 29–44. Mont-Saint-Aignan: Publications de l'Université de Rouen.

Claudi, U. 1985. *Zur Entstehung von Genussystemen*. Hamburg: Helmut Buske.

Clifford, W. K. 1879. *Seeing and thinking*. London: Macmillan.

Colli, G., M. Montinari, M. L. Haase, and W. Müller-Lauter. 2001. *Nietzsche, Werke: Kritische Gesamtausgabe*. Vol. 9.3. Berlin: de Gruyter.

Condillac, E. B. de. 1822 [1746]. *Essai sur l'origine des connoissances humaine: Ouvrage où l'on réduit à un seul principe tout ce qui concerne l'entendement humain*. New ed. Paris: Imprimerie d'Auguste Delalain.

Conklin. H. C. 1955. Hanunóo colour categories. *Southwestern Journal of Anthropology* 11:339–44.

Conlan, F. 2005. Searching for the semantic boundaries of the Japanese colour term 'AO.' PhD dissertation, Faculty of Community Services, Education, and Social Sciences, Edith Cowan University, Western Australia.

Corbett, G. 2000. *Number.* Cambridge: Cambridge University Press.

———. 2005. Number of genders. In Haspelmath et al. 2005.

Corbett, G., and G. Morgan. 1988. Colour terms in Russian: Reflections of typological constraints in a single language. *Journal of Linguistics* 24:31–64.

Crawfurd, J. 1850. On the words introduced into the English from the Malay, Polynesian, and Chinese languages. *Journal of the Indian Archipelago and Eastern Asia* 4:182–90.

Crystal, D. 1995. *The Cambridge encyclopedia of the English language.* Cambridge: Cambridge University Press.

Curzon, A. 2003. *Gender shifts in the history of English.* Cambridge: Cambridge University Press.

Darnell, Regna. 1990. *Edward Sapir: Linguist, anthropologist, humanist.* Berkeley: University of California Press.

Darwin, C. R. 1881. Inheritance. *Nature: A Weekly Illustrated Journal of Science* 24 (21 July).

Darwin, C. R., and A. R. Wallace. 1858. On the tendency of species to form varieties; and on the perpetuation of varieties and species by natural means of selection. *Journal of the Proceedings of the Linnean Society of London, Zoology* 3:61.

De Beer, G. 1958. Further unpublished letters of Charles Darwin. *Annals of Science* 14 (2):88–89.

De León, L. 1994. Exploration in the acquisition of geocentric location by Tzotzil children. *Linguistics* 32 (4–5):857–84.

Delitzsch, Franz. 1878. Der Talmud und die Farben. *Nord und Süd* 5:254–67.

———. 1898. Farben in der Bibel. In *Realencyklopädie für protestantische Theologie und Kirche,* ed. Albert Hauck. 3rd ed. Vol. 5. Leipzig: J. C. Hinrichs.

Dench, A. 1991. Panyjima. In *Handbook of Australian. Languages,* vol. 4, ed. R. M. W. Dixon and B. J. Blake, 125–243. Oxford: Oxford University Press.

Deutscher, G. 2000. *Syntactic change in Akkadian: The evolution of sentential complementation.* Oxford: Oxford University Press.

———. 2005. *The Unfolding of Language.* New York: Metropolitan.

———. 2009. Overall complexity – A wild goose chase? In Sampson et al. 2009, 243–51.

Dixon, R. M. W. 1989. *Searching for aboriginal languages: Memoirs of a field worker.* Chicago: University of Chicago Press.

———. 1997. *The rise and fall of languages.* Cambridge: Cambridge University Press.

———. 2006. Complementation strategies in Dyirbal. In Dixon and Aikhenvald 2006, 263–80.

Dixon, R. M. W., and A. Y. Aikhenvald, eds. 2006. *Complementation: A cross-linguistic typology.* Oxford: Oxford University Press.

Dixon, R. M. W., W. S. Ramson, and M. Thomas. 1990. *Australian Aboriginal words in English: Their origin and meaning.* Oxford: Oxford University Press.

Doering, F. W. 1788. *De colouribus veterum.* Gotha: Reyher.

Donders, F. C. 1884. Noch einmal die Farbensysteme. *Albrecht von Graefes Archiv für Ophthalmologie* 30:15–90.

Drivonikou, G. V., P. Kay, T. Regier, R. B. Ivry, A. L. Gilbert, A. Franklin, and I. R. L. Davies. 2007. Further evidence that Whorfian effects are stronger in the right visual field than the left. *Proceedings of the National Academy of Sciences* 104:1097–102.

Durham, J. I. 2002. *Word biblical commentary: Exodus.* Dallas: Word, Inc.

Eggan, D. 1966. Hopi dreams in cultural perspective. In *Culture and personality: Contemporary readings*, ed. A. Levine, 276. Chicago: Aldine: 1974.

Emerson, R. W. 1844. *Essays.* 2nd series. Boston: James Munroe and Company.

Ervin, S. 1962. The connotations of gender. *Word* 18(3):249–61.

Evans, N. 1995. *A grammar of Kayardild.* Vol. 15 of *Mouton grammar library.* Berlin: Walter de Gruyter.

Everett, D. 2009. Pirahã culture and grammar: A response to some criticisms. *Language* 85:405–42.

Finkelberg, M. 2005. *Greeks and pre-Greeks: Aegean prehistory and Greek heroic tradition.* Cambridge: Cambridge University Press.

Fleck, D. 2006. Complement clause type and complementation strategies in Matses. In Dixon and Aikhenvald 2006, 224–44.

——. 2007. Evidentiality and double tense in Matses. *Language* 83:589–614.

Foley. W. A. 1997. *Anthropological linguistics: An introduction.* Oxford: Blackwell.

Forston, B. W. 2004. *Indo-European language and culture.* Oxford: Blackwell.

Foster, B. R. 1990. Two late old Akkadian documents. *Acta Sumerologica* 12:51–56.

Francis, D. R. 1913. *The Universal Exposition of 1904.* St Louis: Louisiana Purchase Exposition Company.

Franklin, A., M. Pilling, and I. Davies. 2005. The nature of infant colour categorisation: Evidence from eye movements on a target detection task. *Journal of Experimental Child Psychology* 91: 227–48.

Frey, R. G. 1975. Ein Eisenbahnunglück vor 100 Jahren als Anlaß für systematische Untersuchung des Farbensehens. *Klinische Monatsblätter für Augenheilkunde* 167:125–27.

Fromkin, V., R. Rodman, and N. Hyams. 2003. *An introduction to language.* 7th ed. Boston: Thomson/Heinle.

Gatschet, A. S. 1879. Adjectives of colour in Indian languages. *American Naturalist* 13 (8):475–81.

Geiger, Lazarus. 1868. *Ursprung und Entwickelung der menschlichen Sprache und Vernunft.* Vol. 1. Stuttgart: Verlag der Cotta'schen Buchhandlung.

——. 1869. *Der Ursprung der Sprache.* Stuttgart: Verlag der Cotta'schen Buchhandlung.

——. 1872. *Ursprung und Entwickelung der menschlichen Sprache und Vernunft.* Vol. 2. Stuttgart: Verlag der Cotta'schen Buchhandlung.

——. 1878. Ueber den Farbensinn der Urzeit und seine Entwickelung. Gesprochen auf der Versammlung deutscher Naturforscher in Frankfurt a. M., den 24.9.1867. In *Zur Entwickelungsgeschichte der Menschheit,* 2nd ed., 45–60. Stuttgart: Verlag der Cotta'schen Buchhandlung.

Gilbert, A., T. Regier, P. Kay, and R. Ivry. 2006. Whorf hypothesis is supported in the right visual field but not the left. *Proceedings of the National Academy of Sciences* 103 (2):489–94.

——. 2008. Support for lateralization of the Whorf effect beyond the realm of colour discrimination. *Brain and Language* 105:91–98.

Givón, T. 2002. The society of intimates. *Biolinguistics: The Santa Barbara Lectures.* Amsterdam: John Benjamins.

Gladstone, W. E. 1858. *Studies on Homer and the Homeric age.* 3 vols. Oxford: Oxford University Press.

——. 1869. *Juventus mundi: The gods and men of the heroic age.* Rpt., Whitefish, MT: Kessinger Publishing, 2005.

——. 1877. The colour-sense. *Nineteenth Century* (Oct.): 366–88.

Goddard, C. 1985. *A grammar of Yankunytjatjara.* Alice Springs: Institute for Aboriginal Development.

Goethe, J. W. 1810. *Zur Farbenlehere.* Vol. 2. *Materialien zur Geschichte der Farbenlehre.* Tübingen: Cotta'schen Buchhandlung.

Goulden R., P. Nation, and J. Read. 1990. How large can a receptive vocabulary be? *Applied Linguistics* 11(4):341–63.

Graber, V. 1884. *Grundlinien zur Erforschung des Helligkeits- und Farbensinnes der Tiere.* Prague: F. Tempsky und G. Freytag.

Greenberg, J. H. 1978. How does a language acquire gender markers? In *Universals of Human Language,* ed. J. H. Greenberg, C. Ferguson, and E. Moravcsik, 47–82. Stanford: Stanford University Press.

Haddon, A. C. 1910. *History of anthropology.* London: Watts.

Haeckel, Ernst. 1878. Ursprung und Entwickelung der Sinneswerkzeuge. *Kosmos* 2 (4):20–114.

Hansen, T., M. Olkkonen, S. Walter, and K. R. Gegenfurtner. 2006. Memory modulates colour appearance. *Nature Neuroscience* 9:1367–68.

Harvey, W. 1996. Linguistic relativity in French, English, and German philosophy. *Philosophy Today* 40:273–88.

Haspelmath, M., M. S. Dryer, D. Gil, and B. Comrie. 2005. *The world atlas of language structures.* Oxford: Oxford University Press.

Haudricourt, A. G. 1961. Richesse en phonèmes et richesse en locuteurs. *L'Homme* 1 (1):5–10.

Haun, D. B. M., C. Rapold, J. Call, G. Hanzen, and S. C. Levinson. 2006. Cognitive cladistics and cultural override in Hominid spatial cognition. *Proceedings of the National Academy of Sciences* 103 (46):17568–73.

Haviland, J. B. 1979a. Guugu Yimidhirr. *The Handbook of Australian Languages*, ed. R. M. W. Dixon and B. J. Blake, 1:27–182. Amsterdam: John Benjamins.

——. 1979b. How to talk to your brother-in-law in Guugu Yimidhirr. In *Languages and their speakers*, ed. T. Shopen, 160–239. Cambridge: Winthrop.

——. 1985. The life history of a speech community: Guugu Yimidhirr at Hopevale. *Aboriginal History* 9:170–204.

——. 1993. Anchoring, iconicity, and orientation in Guugu Yimithirr pointing gestures. *Journal of Linguistic Anthropology* 31:3–45.

——. 1998. Guugu Yimithirr cardinal directions. *Ethos* 26:25–47.

Haviland, J. B., and L. K. Haviland. 1980. 'How much food will there be in heaven?' Lutherans and Aborigines around Cooktown before 1900. *Aboriginal History* 4:119–49.

Hawkesworth, J. 1785. *An account of the voyages undertaken by the order of His present Majesty, for making discoveries in the Southern Hemisphere*. 3rd ed. Vol. 4. London: Strahan and Cadell.

Hay, J., and L. Bauer. 2007. Phoneme inventory size and population size. *Language* 83 (2):388–400.

Heider, E. R. 1972. Universals in colour naming and colour memory. *Journal of Experimental Psychology* 93 (1):10–20.

Heine, H. 1865. *Heinrich Heine's Sämmtliche Werke: Rechtmässige Original-Ausgabe*. Vol. 19: *Briefe*. Hamburg: Hoffman und Campe.

Herder, J. G. 1812 [1784–91]. *Ideen zur Philosophie der Geschichte der Menschheit*. Leipzig: J. F. Hartknoch.

Hertwig, O. 1907. *Die Entwickelung der Biologie im neunzehnten Jahrhundert. Zweite erweiterte Auflage mit einem Zusatz über den gegenwärtigen Stand des Darwinismus*. Jena: Gustav Fischer.

Hilgert, M. 2002. *Akkadisch in der Ur III-Zeit*. Münster: Rhema.

Hjelmslev, L. 1943. *Omkring Sprogteoriens Grundlæggelse*. Copenhagen: Bianco Lunos.

Hochegger, R. 1884. *Die geschichtliche Entwickelung des Farbensinnes*. Innsbruck: Wagner'sche Universitäts-Buchhandlung.

Hockett, C. 1958. *A course in modern linguistics*. New York: Macmillan.

Holmgren, F. 1878. *Die Farbenblindheit in ihren Beziehungen zu den Eisenbahnen und der Marine*. Leipzig: F. C. W. Vogel.

Humboldt, W. 1820. Über das vergleichende Sprachstudium in Beziehung auf die verschiedenen Epochen der Sprachentwicklung. In Leitzmann 1905, 1–34.

———. 1821a. Versuch einer Analyse der mexikanischen Sprache. In Leitzmann 1905, 233–84.

———. 1821b. Über das Entstehen der grammatischen Formen und ihren Einfluß auf die Ideenentwicklung. In Leitzmann 1905, 285–313.

———. 1827. Ueber die Verschiedenheiten des menschlichen Sprachbaues. In *Wilhelm von Humboldt: Werke in fünf Bänden*. Vol. 3. Darmstadt, 1963.

Institute of Transportation Engineers, 2005. Vehicle traffic control signal heads – Light emitting diode (LED) circular signal supplement. Washington, D.C.

Jacobs, K. W., and F. E. Hustmyer. 1974. Effects of four psychological primary colours on GSR, heart rate, and respiration rate. *Perceptual and Motor Skills* 38:763–66.

Jakobson, R. O. 1959a. On linguistic aspects of translation. In *On translation*, ed. R. A. Brower, 232–39. Cambridge: Harvard University Press.

———. 1959b. Boas' view of grammatical meaning. In *The anthropology of Franz Boas: Essays on the centennial of his birth*, ed. W. Goldschmidt, 139–45. Memoirs of the American Anthropological Association 89, Menasha, WI.

———. 1972. Language and culture. Lecture delivered in Tokyo on 27 July 1967. In *Roman Jakobson. Selected Writings*, ed. S. Rudy, 7:101–12. Berlin: Mouton, 1985.

Janoff, M. S. 1994. Traffic signal visibility: A synthesis of human factors and visual science literature with recommendations for required research.' *Journal of the Illuminating Engineering Society* 23 (1):76–89.

Jespersen, O. 1955. *Growth and structure of the English language*. 9th ed. Garden City: Doubleday.

Jooken, L. 2000. Descriptions of American Indian word forms in colonial missionary grammars. In *The language encounter in the Americas, 1492–1800*, ed. E. G. Gray and N. Fiering, 293–309. New York: Berghahn.

Kaiser, P. K., and R. M. Boynton. 1996. *Human colour vision*. 2nd ed. Washington: Optical Society of America.

Kant, I. 1768. Von dem ersten Grunde des Unterschiedes der Gegenden im Raume. *Vorkritische Schriften II. 1757–1777*. Das Bonner Kant-Korpus (http://korpora.org/kant/).

Kay, P., and W. Kempton. 1984. What is the Sapir-Whorf hypothesis? *American Anthropologist* 86:65–79.

Kay, P., and L. Maffi. 1999. Color appearance and the emergence and evolution of basic colour lexicons. *American Anthropologist* 101: 743–60.

Kay, P., and T. Regier. 2006a. Color naming universals: The case of Berinmo. *Cognition* 102 (2):289–98.

———. 2006b. Language, thought, and colour: Recent developments. *Trends in Cognitive Sciences* 10:51–54.

Keenan, E. L., and E. Ochs. 1979. Becoming a competent speaker of Malagasy. In *Languages and their speakers,* ed. T. Shopen, 113–58. Cambridge: Winthrop.

Keller, J. 1883. *Lazarus Geiger und die Kritik der Vernunft*. Wertheim am Main: E. Bechstein.

Koerner, E. F. K. 2000. Towards a 'full pedigree' of the 'Sapir-Whorf hypothesis': From Locke to Lucy. In *Explorations in Linguistic Relativity*, ed. M. Pütz and M. H. Verspoor, 1–23. Amsterdam: John Benjamins.

Komarovaa, N., K. Jameson, and L. Narensc. 2007. Evolutionary models of colour categorisation based on discrimination. *Journal of Mathematical Psychology* 51 (6):359–82.

Konishi, T. 1993. The semantics of grammatical gender: A cross-cultural study. *Journal of Psycholinguistic Research* 22:519–34.

Köpcke, K., and D. Zubin. 1984. Sechs Prinzipien für die Genuszuweisung im Deutschen: Ein Beitrag zur natürlichen Klassifikation. *Linguistische Berichte* 93:26–50.

Krause, E. 1877. Die Geschichtliche Entwickelung des Farbensinnes. *Kosmos* 1:264–75.

Kroeber, A. 1915. The Eighteen Professions. *American Anthropologist* 17:283–89.

Kuschel, R., and R. Monberg. 1974. 'We don't talk much about colour here': A study of colour semantics on Bellona Island. *Man* 9:213–42.

Lamarck, J.-B. P. A. 1809. *Philosophie zoologique, ou Exposition des consi-dérations relatives à l'histoire naturelle des animaux.* Vol. 1. Rpt. Brussels: Impression Anastaltique, 1970.

Lambert, W. G. 1960. *Babylonian Wisdom Literature.* Oxford: Oxford University Press.

Latacz, J. 2004. *Troy and Homer: Towards the solution of an old mystery.* Oxford: Oxford University Press.

Laughren, M. 1978. Directional terminology in Warlpiri. *Working Papers in Language and Linguistics* 8:1–16.

Lazar-Meyn, H. A. 2004. Color naming: 'Grue' in the Celtic languages of the British Isles. *Psychological Science* 15 (4):288.

Le Laboureur, L. 1669. *Avantages de la langue françoise sur la langue latine.* Paris: Guillaume de Luyne.

Leitzmann, A. 1905. *Wilhelm von Humboldts Gesammelte Schriften. Herausgegeben von der Königlich Preussischen Akademie der Wissenschaften.* Vol. 4. Berlin: B. Behr's Verlag.

Levinson, S. C. 2000. Yélî Dnye and the theory of basic colour terms. *Journal of Linguistic Anthropology* 10:3–55.

———. 2003. *Space in language and cognition: Explorations in cognitive diversity.* Cambridge: Cambridge University Press.

Levinson, S. C., S. Kita, D. B. M. Haun, and B. H. Rasch. 2002. Returning the tables: Language affects spatial reasoning. *Cognition* 84:155–88.

Levinson, S. C., and D. P. Wilkins, eds. 2006. *Grammars of space.* Cambridge: Cambridge University Press.

Lévi-Strauss, C. 1968. *Structural anthropology.* London: Allen Lane.

Lewis, D. 1976. Observations on route findings and spatial orientation among the aboriginal peoples of the Western Desert Region of Central Australia. *Oceania* 46:249–79.

Li, P., and L. Gleitman. 2002. Turning the tables: Language and spatial reasoning. *Cognition* 83:265–94.

Li, P., L. Abarbanell, A. Papafragou, and L. Gleitman (forthcoming). Spatial reasoning without spatial words in Tenejapan Mayans. Unpublished ms.

Lindsey, D. T., and A. M. Brown. 2002. Color naming and the phototoxic effects of sunlight on the eye. *Psychological Science* 13 (6):506–12.

Lizot, J. 1971. Remarques sur le vocabulaire de parenté Yanõmami. *L'Homme* 11:25–38.

Locke, J. 1849 [1690]. *An essay concerning human understanding.* 30th ed. London: William Tegg.

Loos, N. A. 1978. The pragmatic racism of the frontier. In *Race Relations in North Queensland*, ed. H. Reynolds. Townsville: James Cook University.

Lupyan, G., and R. Dale. 2010. Language structure is partly determined by social structure. PLoS ONE 5(1):e8559.

Lyons, J. 1999. Vocabulary of colour with particular reference to ancient Greek and classical Latin. In *The language of colour in the Mediterranean*, ed. A. Borg, 38–75. Stockholm: Almqvist and Wiksell.

Maclaury, R. E. 1997. *Color and cognition in Mesoamerica: Constructing categories as vantages.* Austin: University of Texas Press.

Maddieson, I. 1984. *Patterns of sounds.* Cambridge: Cambridge University Press.

——. 2005. Vowel quality inventories. In Haspelmath et al. 2005.

Magnus, H. 1877a. *Die Entwickelung des Farbensinnes.* Jena: Hermann Dufft.

——. 1877b. *Die geschichtliche Entwickelung des Farbensinnes.* Leipzig: Veit.

——. 1877c. Zur Entwickelung des Farbensinnes. *Kosmos* 1:423–32.

——. 1880. *Untersuchungen über den Farbensinn der Naturvölker.* Jena: Gustav Fischer.

——. 1881. *Farben und Schöpfung. Acht Vorlesungen über die Beziehungen der Farben zum Menschen und zur Natur.* Breslau: Kern's Verlag.

——. 1883. *Ueber ethnologische Untersuchungen des Farbensinnes.* Berlin: Carl Habel.

Majid, A., M. Bowerman, S. Kita, D. B. M. Haun, and S. Levinson. 2004. Can language restructure cognition? The case for space. *Trends in Cognitive Sciences* 8:108–14.

Maxwell-Stuart, P. G. 1981. *Studies in Greek colour terminology.* Vol. 1. Leiden: Brill.

Mayr, E. 1991. *One long argument: Charles Darwin and the genesis of modern evolutionary thought.* London: Penguin.

McPhee, C. 1947. *A house in Bali.* London: V. Gollancz.

McWhorter, J. 2001. The world's simplest grammars are creole grammars. *Linguistic Typology* 5:125–66.

Michaelis, J. D. 1760. *Beantwortung der Frage: Von dem Einfluß der Meinungen in die Sprache und der Sprache in die Meinungen, welche den von der Königlische Academie der Wissenschaften für das Jahr 1759 gesetzten Preis erhalten hat.* Berlin.

Migne, J. P. 1845. *Sancti Eusebii Hieronymi Stridonensis Presbyteri opera omnia. Patrologiae cursus completus. Series prima.* Vol. 23. Paris: Vrayet.

Miller, G., and P. Johnson-Laird. 1976. *Language and perception.* Cambridge: Cambridge University Press.

Mollon, J. D. 1995. Seeing colour. *Colour: Art and science,* ed. T. Lamb and J. Bourriau. Darwin College Lectures. Cambridge: Cambridge University Press.

———. 1999. Color vision: Opsins and options. *Proceedings of the National Academy of Sciences* 96:4743–45.

Morley, J. 1903. *The life of William Ewart Gladstone.* Vol. 3. London: Macmillan.

Morpurgo Davies, A. 1998. *Nineteenth-century linguistics.* Vol. 4 of *History of Linguistics.* Ed. Giulio Lepschy. London: Longman.

Müller, M. 1861. *Lectures on the science of language.* London : Longmans, Green.

———. 1873. Lectures on Mr Darwin's philosophy of language. *Frazer's Magazine* 7 and 8. Rpt. in R. Harris, *The origin of language,* 147–233. Bristol: Thoemmes, 1996.

Myers, J. L. 1958. *Homer and his critics.* Ed. Dorothea Gray. London: Routledge.

Neumann, S., and T. Widlok. 1996. Rethinking some universals of spatial language using controlled comparison. In *The construal of space in language and thought,* ed. R. Dirven and M. Pütz, 345–69. Berlin: Mouton de Gruyter.

Nevins, A., D. Pesetsky, and C. Rodrigues. 2009. Pirahã exceptionality: A reassessment. *Language* 85:355–404.

Newcomer, P., and J. Faris. 1971. Review of Berlin and Kay 1969. *International Journal of American Linguistics* 37 (4):270–75.

Nichols, J. 2009. Linguistic complexity: A comprehensive definition and survey. In Sampson et al. 2009, 110–25.

Nietzsche, F. 1881. *Morgenröthe, Gedanken über die moralischen Vorurt-heile*. In *Friedrich Nietzsche: Morgenröte, Idyllen aus Messina, Die fröhliche Wissenschaft*, ed. G. Colli and M. Montinari. Berlin: Walter de Gruyter, 2005.

Niraula, S., R. C. Mishra, and P. R. Dasen. 2004. Linguistic relativity and spatial concept development in Nepal. *Psychology and Developing Societies* 16 (2):99–124.

Ogden, C. K., and I. A. Richards. 1923. *The meaning of meaning: A study in the influence of language upon thought*. London: Trubner.

Olsén, J. E. 2004. *Liksom ett par nya ögon: Frithiof Holmgren och synsinnets problematik*. Malmö: Lubbert Das.

Orsucci, A. 1996. *Orient-Okzident: Nietzsches Versuch einer Loslösung vom europäischen Weltbild*. Berlin: Walter de Gruyter.

Özgen, E. 2004. Language, learning, and colour perception. *Current Directions in Psychological Science* 13 (3):95–98.

Parkinson, R. B. 1996. Khakheperreseneb and traditional belles lettres. In *Studies in Honor of William Kelly Simpson*, ed. P. Manuelian, 647–54. Boston: Museum of Fine Arts.

Peacock, E. 1877. *A glossary of words used in the wapentakes of Manley and Corringham, Lincolnshire*. English Dialect Society.

Perkins, R. D. 1992. *Deixis grammar and culture*. Amsterdam: John Benjamins.

Peschier, E. 1871. *Lazarus Geiger: Sein Leben und Denken*. Frankfurt am Main: F. B. Auffarth.

Phillips, R. 1898. Vocabulary of Australian Aborigines in the neighbourhood of Cooktown, North Queensland. *Journal of the Anthropological Institute of Great Britain and Ireland* 27:144–47.

Piattelli-Palmarini, M., ed. 1983. *Language and learning: The debate between Jean Piaget and Noam Chomsky*. London: Routledge.

Pinker, S. 1994. *The Language Instinct*. New York: Penguin.

———. 2007. *The stuff of thought: Language as a window into human nature*. London: Allen Lane.

Pitchford, N., and K. Mullen. 2002. Is the acquisition of basic colour terms in young children constrained? *Perception* 31:1349–70.

Ray, V. F. 1952. Techniques and problems in the study of human colour perception. *Southwestern Journal of Anthropology* 8 (3):251–59.

———. 1953. Human colour perception and behavioural response. *New York Academy of Sciences* 2 (16):98–104.

Regan, B. C, C. Julliot, B. Simmen, F. Viénot, P. Charles-Dominique, and J. D. Mollon. 2001. Fruits, foliage, and the evolution of primate colour vision. *Philosophical Transactions of the Royal Society, London. B: Biological Sciences* 356:229–83.

Regier, T., and P. Kay. 2004. Color naming and sunlight: Commentary on Lindsey and Brown (2002). *Psychological Science* 15:289–90.

Regier, T., P. Kay, and R. S. Cook. 2005. Focal colours are universal after all. *Proceedings of the National Academy of Sciences* 102:8386–91.

Regier, T., P. Kay, and N. Khetarpal. 2007. Color naming reflects optimal partitions of colour space. *Proceedings of the National Academy of Sciences* 104 (4):1436–41.

Reid, N. 1997. Class and classifier in Ngan'gityemerri. In *Nominal classification in aboriginal Australia*, ed. M. Harvey and N. Reid, 165–228. Amsterdam: John Benjamins.

Rivarol, A. de. 1784. *De l'universalité de la langue française: Discours qui a remporté le prix a l'Académie de Berlin.* Paris: Bailly.

Rivers, W. H. R. 1900. Vision. In *Text-book of physiology*, ed. E. A. Schäfer, 2:1026–148. Edinburgh: Young J. Pentland.

———. 1901a. Vision. In *Reports of the Cambridge Anthropological Expedition to the Torres Straits.* Ed. A. C. Haddon. Vol. 2: *Physiology and Psychology.* Cambridge: Cambridge University Press.

———. 1901b. Primitive colour vision. *Popular Science Monthly* 59:44–58.

Roberson, D., I. Davies, and J. Davidoff. 2000. Color categories are not universal: Replications and new evidence from a stone-age culture. *Journal of Experimental Psychology: General* 129 (3):369–98.

Roberson, D., J. Davidoff, I. Davies, and L. R. Shapiro. 2005. Color categories: Evidence for the cultural relativity hypothesis. *Cognitive Psychology* 50:378–411.

———. 2006. Colour categories and category acquisition in Himba and English. In *Progress in colour studies*, ed. N. Pitchford and C. Bingham, 159–72. Amsterdam: John Benjamins.

Roberson, D., H. Pak, and J. R. Hanley. 2008. Categorical perception of colour in the left and right visual field is verbally mediated: Evidence from Korean. *Cognition* 107:752–62.

Rosenthal, L. A. 1884. *Lazarus Geiger: Seine Lehre vom Ursprunge der Sprache und Vernunft und sein Leben*. Stuttgart: I. Scheible.

Rothfels, N. 2002. *Savages and beasts: The birth of the modern zoo*. Baltimore: Johns Hopkins University Press.

Russell, B. 1924. Logical atomism. Rpt. in *Bertrand Russell: Logic and knowledge. Essays, 1901–1950*, ed. R. C. Marsh, 321–44. London: Routledge, 2004.

———. 1983. *Cambridge essays, 1888–99*. Ed. K. Blackwell et al. London: Allen and Unwin.

Sahlins, M. 1976. Colors and cultures. *Semiotica* 16:1–22.

Sampson, G. 2005. *The 'language instinct' debate*. London: Continuum.

———. 2009. A linguistic axiom challenged. In Sampson et al. 2009.

Sampson, G., D. Gil, and P. Trudgill, eds. 2009. *Language complexity as an evolving variable*. Oxford: Oxford University Press.

Sapir, E. 1921. *Language: An introduction to the study of speech*. New York: Harcourt, Brace and Company.

———. 1924. The grammarian and his language. *American Mercury* 1: 149–55. Rpt. in *Selected writings of Edward Sapir in language, culture, and personality*, ed. D. G. Mandelbaum. Berkeley: University of California Press, 1963.

———. 1931. Conceptual categories in primitive languages. Paper presented at the meeting of the National Academy of Sciences, New Haven, CT, Nov. 1931. Abstracted in *Science* 74:578.

Schleicher, A. 1860. *Die deutsche Sprache*. Stuttgart: J. G. Cotta.

Schultze-Berndt, E. 2006. Sketch of a Jaminjung grammar of space. In Levinson and Wilkins 2006, 103–4.

Sera, M. D., C. Elieff, J. Forbes, M. C. Burch, W. Rodriguez, and D. P. Dubois. 2002. When language affects cognition and when it does not: An analysis of grammatical gender and classification. *Journal of Experimental Psychology: General* 131:377–97.

Shaw, G. B. 1921. *Back to Methuselah*. London: Constable.

Sinnemäki, K. 2009. Complexity in core argument marking and population size. In Sampson et al. 2009.

Skard, S. 1946. The use of colour in literature. A survey of research. *Proceedings of the American Philosophical Society* 90:163–249.

Slobodín, R. 1978. *W. H. R. Rivers*. New York: Columbia University Press.

Steiner, G. 1975. *After Babel: Aspects of language and translation*. Oxford: Oxford University Press.

Swadesh, M. 1939. Edward Sapir. *Language* 15:132–35.

Tan, L. H., A. H. D. Chan, P. Kay, P. L. Khong, L. K. C. Yip, and K. K Luke. 2008. Language affects patterns of brain activation associated with perceptual decision. *Proceedings of the National Academy of Sciences* 105 (10):4004–09.

Tennyson, H. T. 1897. *Alfred Lord Tennyson: A memoir, by his son*. Vol. 1. London: Macmillan.

Titchener, E. B. 1916. On ethnological tests of sensation and perception with special reference to tests of colour vision and tactile discrimination described in the reports of the Cambridge anthropological expedition to Torres Straits. *Proceedings of the American Philosophical Society* 55:204–36.

Trudgill, P. 1992. Dialect typology and social structure. In *Language contact: Theoretical and empirical studies*, ed. E. H. Jahr, 195–211. Berlin: Mouton.

Tsunoda, T. 1981. *The Djaru language of Kimberley, Western Australia*. Canberra: Research School of Pacific Studies.

Turner, R. S. 1994. *In the eye's mind: Vision and the Helmholtz-Hering Controversy*. Princeton: Princeton University Press.

Tylor, E. B. 1871. *Primitive culture: Researches into the development of mythology, philosophy, religion, art, and custom*. London: J. Murray.

Valberg, A. 2005. *Light, vision, colour*. Hoboken: Wiley.

Valdez, P., and A. Mehrabian. 1994. Effects of colour on emotions. *Journal of Experimental Psychology: General* 123: 394–409.

Vaugelas, F. de C. 1738. *Remarques de M. de Vaugelas sur la langue françoise, avec des notes de Messieurs Patru & T. Corneille*. Paris: Didot.

Veit, P. F. 1976. Fichtenbaum und Palme. *Germanic Review* 51:13–27.

Virchow, R. 1878. Die zur Zeit in Berlin anwesenden Nubier. *Verhandlungen der Berliner Gesellschaft für Anthropologie, Ethnologie, und Urgeschichte* 333–55.

——. 1879. Über die im letzten Monat in Berlin ausgestellten Nubier, namentlich den Dinka. *Verhandlungen der Berliner Gesellschaft für Anthropologie, Ethnologie, und Urgeschichte* 388–95.

Vygotsky, L. S. 1987. *Thinking and speech: Collected works of L. S. Vygotsky.* Vol. 1. New York: Plenum Press.

Wallace, A. R. 1858. On the tendency of varieties to depart indefinitely from the original type. In C. R. Darwin and A. R. Wallace, On the tendency of species to form varieties; and on the perpetuation of varieties and species by natural means of selection. *Journal of the Proceedings of the Linnean Society of London, Zoology* 3:46–50.

———. 1877. The colours of animals and plants. *Macmillan's Magazine* 36: 384–408, 464–71.

———. 1878. *Tropical nature and other essays.* London: Macmillan.

Walser, M. 1983. Heines Tränen. *Liebeserklärungen*, 195–96. Frankfurt am Main: Suhrkamp, 1983.

Wassmann, J., and P. R. Dasen. 1998. Balinese spatial orientation: Some empirical evidence of moderate linguistic relativity. *Journal of the Royal Anthropological Institute* 4 (4):689–711.

Waxman, S. R., and A. Senghas. 1992. Relations among word meanings in early lexical development. *Developmental Psychology* 28:862–73.

Weismann, A. 1892. Über die Hypothese einer Vererbung von Verletzungen. *Aufsätze über Vererbung und verwandte biologische Fragen.* Jena: G. Fischer.

Wemyss Reid, T. 1899. *The life of William Ewart Gladstone.* London: Cassell.

Wharton, W. J. L., ed. 1893. *Captain Cook's journal during his first voyage round the world made in H.M. Bark 'Endeavour,' 1768–71: A literal transcription of the original mss.: with notes and introduction.* Rpt. Forgotten Books, 2008.

Whiting, R. M. 1987. *Old Babylonian letters from Tell Asmar.* Chicago: University of Chicago.

Whitney, W. D. 1875. *The life and growth of language.* New York: Appleton.

Whittle, P. 1997. W. H. R. Rivers: A founding father worth remembering. Talk given to the Zangwill Club of the Department of Experimental Psychology, Cambridge University, 6 Dec. 1997 (http://www.human-nature.com/science-as-culture/whittle.html).

Whorf, B. 1956. *Language, thought, and reality: Selected writings of Benjamin Lee Whorf.* Ed. J. B. Carroll. Cambridge: MIT Press.

Widlok, T. 1997. Orientation in the wild: The shared cognition of Hai‖om bushpeople. *Journal of the Royal Anthropological Institute* 3 (22):317–32.

Wilkins, D. P. 2006. Towards an Arrernte grammar of space. In Levinson and Wilkins 2006.

Wilson, G. 1855. *Researches on colour-blindness, with a supplement on the danger attending the present system of railway and marine coloured-signals.* Edinburgh: Sutherland and Knox.

Wilson, G. D. 1966. Arousal properties of red versus green. *Perceptual and Motor Skills* 23: 942–49.

Winawer, J., N. Witthoft, M. C. Frank, L. Wu, A. R. Wade, and L. Boroditsky. 2007. Russian blues reveal effects of language on colour discrimination. *Proceedings of the National Academy of Sciences* 104 (19):7780–85.

Wittgenstein, L. 1922. *Tractatus logico-philosophicus*. Intro. Bertrand Russell. London: Kegan Paul.

Woodworth, R. S. 1910a. Racial differences in mental traits. Address of the vice president and chairman of Section H – Anthropology and Psychology – of the American Association for the Advancement of Science, Boston, 1909. *Science* 31:171–86.

– – –. 1910b. The puzzle of colour vocabularies. *Psychological Bulletin* 7:325–34.

Young, R. M. 1970. *Mind, brain, and adaptation in the nineteenth century: Cerebral localization and its biological context from Gall to Ferrier.* Oxford: Oxford University Press.

ACKNOWLEDGMENTS

I am extremely grateful to those friends who gave generously of their time to read earlier drafts of the entire book, and whose insights and suggestions saved me from copious blunders and inspired many improvements: Jennie Barbour, Michal Deutscher, Andreas Dorschel, Avrahamit Edan, Stephen Fry, Bert Kouwenberg, Peter Matthews, Ferdinand von Mengden, Anna Morpurgo Davies, Reviel Netz, Uri Rom, Jan Hendrik Schmidt, Michael Steen, and Balázs Szendröi.

The manuscript benefited enormously from the professional scrutiny of my agent, Caroline Dawnay, and my editors, Drummond Moir, Jonathan Beck, and above all Sara Bershtel, whose incisive insertions and excisions were invaluable for navigating out of numerous cul-de-sacs and wrong turnings. I am grateful to all of them, as well as to my copy editor, Roslyn Schloss, Grigory Tovbis at Metropolitan, and Laurie Ip Fung Chun at William Heinemann.

I would also like to thank all those who provided helpful information or corrections, especially Sasha Aikhenvald, Eleanor Coghill, Bob Dixon, David Fleck, Luca Grillo, Kristina Henschke, Yaron Matras, Robert Meekings, John Mollon, Jan Erik Olsén, Jan Schnupp, Eva Schultze-Berndt, Kriszta Szendröi, Thomas Widlok, Gábor Zemplén.

Most of all, I am grateful to Janie Steen, whose help cannot be quantified, and without whom the book would never have happened.

G. D., March 2010

ILLUSTRATION CREDITS

Colour plates

1. Holmgren colour-blindness test: courtesy of The College of Optometrists, London
2. Rainbow over Trees © Pekka Parviainen / Science Photo Library
3. Field of poppies © Andrzej Tokarski / Alamy
4, 5. Colour systems: Martin Lubikowski
6. Berlin and Kay set: Hale Color Consultants, courtesy of Nick Hale
7. Japanese traffic light hues: see note for p. 217 on p. 272
8. Russian blues: Winawer et al. 2007 (adapted by Martin Lubikowski)
9. Circle of squares: Gilbert et al. 2006 (adapted by Martin Lubikowski)
10. Colours in Chinese: Tan et al. 2008 (adapted by Martin Lubikowski)
11. The visible spectrum © Universal Images Group Limited / Alamy
12. Sensitivity cones: Martin Lubikowski

Integrated pictures

p. 47, Train crash in Lagerlunda: Swedish Railway Museum

p. 65, W. H. R. Rivers: Museum of Archaeology and Anthropology, Cambridge

p. 138, Edward Sapir: Florence Hendershot

p. 151, Franz Boas: National Anthropological Archives, Smithsonian Institution

p. 151, Roman Jakobson: Peter Cunningham

p. 159, George Stubbs's 'Kongouroo': New Zealand Electronic Text Centre

p. 167, Levinson 2004 (adapted by Martin Lubikowski)

pp. 177–185: Martin Lubikowski

p. 227, Cognitive Science Lab, UC Riverside (adapted by Martin Lubikowski)

INDEX

(page numbers in italic face denote illustrations)